Heathen Traditions of the PENNSYLVANIA DUTCH

About the Authors

© Krista Lynn Photography

Robert L. Schreiwer is a cofounder of the Urglaawe tradition within Heathenry. He is a trained Braucher within the Oley Freindschaft guild and the founder of the Blobarrick Freindschaft of Braucherei and Hexerei. He also founded In-Reach Heathen Prison Services and Philadelphia Pagan Pride Day. He served as the Steersman (president and CEO) of The Troth from 2016 to 2022 and continues to serve The Troth as clergy and in advisory roles. He was a member of the team that authored Declaration 127. He is a senior manager of Heathens Against Hate and one of the managers of Philadelphia's Parade of Spirits. He is a special education teacher by day and an instructor of the Pennsylvania Dutch language at night.

© Krista Lynn Photography

Michelle A. Jones is a Hex, an Urglaawe Ziewerin, and secretary of die Urglaawisch Sippschaft vum Distelfink. She has served on the boards of both Philadelphia Pagan Pride Day and South Jersey Pagan Pride Day. Michelle is a founding member of the Primitive Grove Circle eclectic coven based in South Jersey. She graduated from the Homestead Herbalism course at Farm at Coventry (now The Still Room at Pitch Pines). While there, her teacher and mentor emphasized the Deitsch herbal tradition.

© Krista Lynn Photography

Stacey Lynne Stewart is a Ziewerin within Distelfink Sippschaft and a Braucherin who has a passion for herbalism, runes, and inclusive Heathenry. She is involved with several local Pagan Pride Day events, active with Heathens Against Hate, and is a past member of the High Rede of The Troth. Stacey started exploring Paganism at sixteen years old and spent over twenty years with Blue Star Wicca before she was drawn to Urglaawe. As an artist, she is actively creating Urglaawe art with an eye on traditional Pennsylvania Dutch styles and a foot firmly in the future.

Heathen Traditions of the PENNSYLVANIA DUTCH

An Urglaawe Primer

ROBERT L. SCHREIWER
MICHELLE A. JONES
STACEY LYNNE STEWART

LLEWELLYN
WOODBURY, MINNESOTA

First Edition
First Printing, 2026

Cover design by Kevin R. Brown
Interior illustrations by Athena Dugan
Runes provided by the authors

Library of Congress Cataloging-in-Publication Data (Pending)
ISBN: 978-0-7387-7733-7

Llewellyn Publications
A Division of Llewellyn Worldwide Ltd.
2143 Wooddale Drive
Woodbury, MN 55125-2989
www.llewellyn.com

Printed in the United States of America

GPSR Representation:
UPI-2M PLUS d.o.o., Medulićeva 20, 10000 Zagreb, Croatia,
matt.parsons@upi2mbooks.hr

Other Books by These Authors

A Dictionary of Urglaawe Terminology (Schreiwer, coauthor)

The First Book of Urglaawe Myths (Schreiwer)

Llewellyn's Complete Book of North American Folk Magic (Schreiwer, contributor)

The Diviner (Stewart)

Magical Mandalas Moons and More (Stewart)

Magical Mandalas the Herbalist (Stewart)

For Dan Riegel, Sarah Lyter, Cherie Perez, and all the other seekers who have gone to the Mill just as their journeys were beginning. May the knowledge you sought here be revealed to you in realms beyond this place.

For our brother, Larry Goble, Jr., who contributed so much to our community and to our lives but who went to the Mill before seeing this work come to fruition. You are remembered! We will meet again.

CONTENTS

DISCLAIMER

The material in this book is not intended as a substitute for trained medical or psychological advice. Readers are advised to consult their personal healthcare professionals regarding treatment. The publisher and the authors assume no liability for any injuries caused to the reader that may result from the reader's use of the content contained herein and recommend common sense when contemplating the practices described in the work.

INTRODUCTION

The *Deitsche*, also commonly known as the *Pennsylvania Dutch* or *Pennsylvania Germans*, have a long history of beliefs that some would see as superstitions. However, among us, these notions are what we've been raised with or heard about growing up in the *Deitscherei*. You might consider them folklore or a set of collective habits found among our people.

Collective superstitions and collective habits aren't the only things that identify a culture. Other things that contribute are the arts, traditions, beliefs, achievements, and lifeways as well as the time and specific place. Most notably, the Plain sects (i.e., Amish, Mennonites, and Brethren) of the *Deitsche* are excellent demonstrations of this definition, having remained isolated from the general population. Many men wear broadfall pants with suspenders; many women wear bonnets and aprons. Many use horse-drawn transportation. It is easy to see the distinct cultural ways among the Plain segments of the *Deitsche*. Even among the Fancy folk, who make up the vast majority of the *Deitsche*, there are still many expressions of the culture. While their clothing and transportation are the same as those of mainstream America, they are still *Deitsche*, and many of the old ways are as strong among the Fancy as they are among the Plain.

What *Deitsch* house is without the annual pork and sauerkraut feast on New Year's Day? Where else will you find shoofly pie, pot pie (the stew), scrapple, and chow chow? These are common, treasured cultural markers that are found in the early Pennsylvania Dutch settlements in Pennsylvania,

Maryland, and upstate New York. From those locations, the people, language, and culture spread throughout the United States, Canada, and the rest of the Americas.

As far as arts, we have Fraktur and hex signs that are unique to our culture. You've likely seen some form of each on barns and other buildings dotting the countryside from Maryland through Ontario, Canada. Have you ever driven through the areas mentioned above during the Christian season of Easter and seen eggs hanging from the limbs of trees? That's an old *Deitsch* tradition that is rooted in ancient Germanic Heathen practices. It is but one example of many living traditions that carry information and insights from the beliefs and practices of our remote forebears. Old ways die hard. While most *Deitsche* identify as Christian, many of those old ways of relating to existence around us still thrive within the culture. Old chants turn up as counting-out rhymes. Stories of the old gods and goddesses become fairy tales. Along with other entities known well to our ancestors, they were dismissed in the modern day as superstitions. Magic lives on within the practices of *Braucherei* and *Hexerei*. This is where *Urglaawe* begins.

Urglaawe is a modern iteration of the ancient Germanic religion as viewed through the lens of the living Pennsylvania Dutch culture. The adherents of *Urglaawe* cherish these old folk practices and perspectives. *Urglaawer* embrace the old Germanic deities and seek to create bonds with other lost Germanic deities whose relationships with us were cut by the autocracy of the Christian religion. Although *Urglaawe* emanates from the *Deitsch* culture, one need not be *Deitsch* to adhere to the *Urglaawe* faith. Anyone who is called by our deities or to our practice can call themselves an *Urglaawer*. There are *Urglaawer* on the East and West Coasts of the US and even in Canada.

Folk Practice and Magic

The *Deitsche* people have a long history of belief in folk healing, known as *Braucherei*. And, yes, we hold a storied belief in witchcraft, known as *Hexerei*. We will discuss the distinction between the two later, as that subject deserves its own forum. For now, please understand that *Braucherei* and *Hexerei* are heirloom traditions within the *Deitsch* culture. *Braucherei* was a cultural institution prior to the rise of modern allopathic medicine. *Braucherei* utilizes multiple modalities to meet the health needs of the individual and of the community. Among these many modalities are energy work, or *die Meggeheilkunscht* in *Deitsch*, sympathetic magic, or *der Mitleidzauber*, and herbalism, or *die Blanzeheilkunscht*.

Of these three modalities, sympathetic magic is probably the least familiar to most people, but it is also the most commonly used modality of all. It is also called *imitative* or *corresponding magic* in English, which reflects how the practice draws a functional, analogous relationship between the purpose of the spells and an ordinary object. Something is done to that object, and the results of the action taken on the object will also affect the original purpose. For example, as is the case with magical and healing practices in many cultures, *Braucherei* and *Hexerei* practitioners frequently use dolls, usually made of wood with moving joints, to represent the human form.

If a client had suffered an injury, such as a sprained ankle, the practitioner would utter chants that create a correspondence between the client's ankle and the ankle of the poppet. Then, the practitioner could use wire to reinforce the ligaments on the poppet, with the intention being that the ligaments on the ankle will also strengthen. This is a very simple example. Some sympathetic actions are complex, involving tasks such as walking in counterclockwise circles around objects in order to undo or to minimize the effects of time on something.

Although many cultures and religions around the world have similar concepts or even describe sympathetic magical actions in their scripture, it is this modality that is most often described as superstitious, backward, and even sinful. These stigmatizing descriptions increase in their intensity when the practitioner identifies with *Hexerei* rather than *Braucherei*—a trend that only emerged in the twentieth century. The similarities and differences between *Braucherei* and *Hexerei* will be discussed later, but before the rise of anti-German sentiment in the United States prior to World War I, *Braucherei* and *Hexerei* were not viewed in moral terms, such as good and evil or positive vs. negative acts. Fortunately, while many of the *Deitsch* folkways are today considered quaint or somewhat backward, most do not suffer from legal harassment as *Braucherei* did in the 1920s and 1930s or from denouncement from church pulpits as *Hexerei* experienced once World War I began.

Some of these beliefs were brought to the colonies with our ancestors; others developed as we cultivated and acclimated to our new land. Some of these are still followed; others are from a bygone time. In no way is this list exhaustive, and some of the behaviors may seem unenlightened (and even downright humorous).

Some examples include folklore related to brooms and good luck: One was never to take an old broom into a new house, or one could expect bad luck to follow. Additionally, the new broom was to be carried across the meadow to avert evil consequences. Also, to have luck in married life, a married couple should step over a broom on entering their house.

Another set of examples of old folkways that were brought from Europe and continued or were adjusted to the new land related to forecasting the weather based on the behavior of animals. Groundhog Day (February 2) is an American observance, but its origins are in badger lore in the German lands. When the settlers arrived, they discovered there were no badgers in the new lands, and the burrow structures and the behaviors of groundhogs were sufficient to meet the old lore. However, the similarities between badgers and groundhogs ends with them both being burrowing mammals. Thus, the *Deitsch* traditions reflect some of the nature of the groundhog, such as being concerned with when planting can begin because the herbivorous groundhogs want to sample the crops! Groundhog Day as an observance will be discussed later in this book.

In addition to the groundhog, many other animals have been used in forecasting the weather. They include the beaver, bear, bull, cat, cattle, chipmunk, deer, dog, donkey, fox, goat, horse, mole, mouse, rabbit, sheep, squirrel, and wolf. And the *Deitsche* use birds of all sorts as well as trees, shrubs, grasses, clouds, fog, frost, the moon, the sun, and stars.

Woolly bear caterpillars foretell the severity of winter by their coloring. If the ends are black, the beginning and end of winter will be harsh. Likewise, if their middle is black, the middle of winter will be bad.

Over the years, we *Deitsche* have kept what works and discarded what doesn't. We still look for the woolly bears every autumn!

Who Are the Deitsche, Exactly?

Often, one sees the *Deitsche* people portrayed as caricatures in stereotypes of the *Deitsch* culture, such as an Amish person hanging a hex sign on a barn, which does not happen because such signs are not in keeping with their church's *Ordnung*, or rules. Sometimes, the *Deitsche* are relegated to bygone eras in history books, describing a culture that *was* rather than *is*. Perhaps the most frequent interaction that people have with the *Deitsch* culture is in the context of the tourist attraction: farm festivals, hex sign tours, quilts, quaint humor, and the inverted word order of the *Deitsch*-influenced English dialect called *Dutchified English* or *Pennsylvania Dutch English*. It's possible that any attention that advances the understanding of our people and our culture is worthy, but we want to ensure that beyond the misinformation and kitschy souvenirs, more folks understand that there is a rich history and heritage that should be explored.

The *Deitsche* arrived as economic and religious refugees and lived within the Pennsylvania colony starting in the seventeenth century and, in most ways, assimilated into that society publicly while maintaining their way of life privately. The *Deitsche* are an American subgroup that developed within the American identity. We didn't come from any single one of the currently existing European countries. Instead, most of our ancestors hail from regions now within present-day Germany, Switzerland, France, the Netherlands, Luxembourg, Austria, and even Transylvania in modern-day Romania. The *Deitsche* became their own subset of colonial Americans, and our language evolved as its own dialect, mixing German and English. We have established ourselves across the United States, with the largest populations still in southeast Pennsylvania where our ancestors originally settled.

Deitsch, Dutch, Pennsylvania Dutch, Pennsylvania German, or German?

This is always a complicated topic. Different generations have called it different things. *Dutch* is very common, particularly among the elderly. *Pennsylvania Dutch* is common among the WWII generation. *Pennsylvania German* is common among those born in the 1950s and 1960s. *Deitsch* is increasingly common among us now. Why?

Here's what you need to know: Despite common claims to the contrary, *Dutch* is not a bastardization of *Deutsch* or *Deitsch*. It is a cognate of both of those words but not a replacement for either. Instead, the word *Dutch* once had a much wider meaning in English, referring not only to Holland or the Netherlands but to a wide swath of German-speaking lands. This is the primary reason for the term *Dutch* being used to describe our ethnicity and language.

Throughout the colonial era, the settlers were referred to most frequently as *Palatines*, referencing the area of Germany they emigrated from. This was in spite of the fact that there were also significant numbers of settlers from Alsace-, Switzerland-, Silesia-, and Swabian-speaking lands, many of whom had never set foot in the Palatinate. Sometime in the mid-twentieth century, there was an increasing recognition that the terms *Dutch* and *Pennsylvania Dutch* were complicated. Many people were listing "Dutch" on the census, for example, but actually meant "Pennsylvania Dutch." For the purpose of this book, we encourage the use of *Deitsch* for the culture and language but *Deitsche* for the people.

The word *Deitscherei* refers to the noncontiguous areas in which the Pennsylvania Dutch settled in large numbers. This designation includes virtually all of eastern and central Pennsylvania, large sections of western Pennsylvania, portions of southern New Jersey (particularly the earlier West Jersey colony), much of northern Delaware, sections of upstate New York, most of Ohio and Indiana, southern Wisconsin, central Maryland to the north and west of Baltimore, the Shenandoah Valley of Virginia southward into North Carolina, and the area around Kitchener in Ontario. There are other regions that one could consider to be the *Deitscherei* today, but these are the principal areas whence much of our lore comes.

Heathenry and *Urglaawe*

The customary understanding of what a Heathen is describes people who do not practice Christianity, Judaism, or Islam. There are, however, more nuances and modern interpretations that have made what was an often-disparaging remark into a descriptor of what religion one follows. Modern Heathen religions, such as Ásatrú, Anglo-Saxon Heathenry, and Firne Sitte, among others, are based in the Old Norse, Anglo-Saxon, and old continental Germanic cultures respectively. *Urglaawe* bears many similarities to these religions. In the cases of most other Heathen denominations, though, the focus was originally on trying to reconstruct the Heathen religions and other cultural mores based on texts, such as the *Poetic Edda*, the *Prose Edda*, church documents, and the records of historians. Historic curation, linguistics, anthropology, and other disciplines have also provided information about likely practices of the early Heathen Germanic peoples, and they also provide fertile ground for more theories and philosophical developments within each modern Heathen denomination.

In contrast, *Urglaawe* began by focusing less on reconstruction and more on reviving the Heathen elements that were still present in some form within the *Deitsch* culture. As the Norse and Anglo-Saxon Heathen groups began to develop their philosophies as modern religions in the modern time, *Urglaawe* began to work on reconstructing systems that were broken within our folklore, such as the runes used by some *Hexerei* practitioners. The first source for the establishment of *Urglaawe* were the beliefs and practices that took root in the Americas. The second source was the body of knowledge from continental Germanic regions, and the third was the broader Germanic sources, particularly Norse and Anglo-Saxon lore.

Just as the living *Deitsch* culture continues to bear many of the old ways, we seek to blend modern theory and practice with pieces of Heathenry that survived in prayers and stories passed down from our folk magic practices of *Braucherei* and *Hexerei*. *Braucherei* and *Hexerei* came with the settlers from the German-speaking lands, and they each took root and became institutions of the *Deitsch* culture in the forms of folk healing and magic.

Folk Magic in *Urglaawe*

There has been much confusion between and among the folk magic traditions of *Powwow*, *Braucherei*, and *Hexerei*, and the religious belief system of *Urglaawe*. They are distinct practices. The folk magic traditions help to influence our knowledge and implementation of the religious practice. However, one can practice *Urglaawe* without practicing the folk magic. Likewise, one can practice any (or all) of the folk magic traditions without being an *Urglaawer*. Let's look at some basics.

Braucherei and *Hexerei* are healing traditions and folk magic that have been passed on through generations. Traditionally, a practitioner was known as a *Braucher* (masculine) or *Braucherin* (feminine). *Urglaawe* practitioners recognize the breadth of gender and gender identity, so one may also be known as a *Braucheres* (nonbinary, neutral genders). *Hexerei* practitioners are typically called a *Hex* (all genders).

These traditions, by definition, are practiced within the context of any belief system except the lack of one. One will find Christian *Powwows* or *Braucher/in/es*. One will also find syncretic practitioners; this is where we find some overlap between Christian belief and the "old ways." And then there are practitioners who work within the *Urglaawe* context. Additionally, one can find practitioners in other spiritual systems, including Wicca and Gnosticism. In all cases, the path to learning the magical art is through an apprenticeship with a practitioner who has had the power passed. Historically, training has been cross gender—male training female, female training male—so as to ensure a balance in practitioners. It is a long-term process and can take years. It involves delving into much more esoteric topics than the religious systems in which it is practiced.

As practices have evolved through the generations, many Christian practitioners have come to refer to themselves as *Powwows*. In that context, one could also refer to the practitioner as a *Braucher/in/es*. While *Braucherei* is considered by many Christians to be a faith healing practice, *Hexerei*, in stark contrast, is considered outright witchcraft in the traditional understanding, and one would typically not find a Christian *Hex*—at least not one who openly admits it.

In our *Urglaawe* tradition, we embrace both *Braucherei* and *Hexerei* on equal footing and do not use the term *Powwow*. Additionally, we recognize that gender is nonbinary, and the tradition of passing from female to male and male to female is expanded within the context of our tradition. We still strive to ensure that no one gender identity monopolizes the practice and accept apprentices accordingly.

We have come to define *Braucherei* as the outward and expansive expression of the art, generally working for other people and the greater good of the community. We identify *Hexerei* as a more inward and immersive working either to foster our own evolution or to take preemptive protective measures. Both utilize herbalism, energy work, and sympathetic magic, to name a few modalities, and both include deeper esoteric and occult studies.

Urglaawe is therefore not *Braucherei* or *Hexerei*. It is a stand-alone religious tradition. The magical practices are separate from the religion yet inform and are informed by it. One does not automatically become a *Braucher/in/es* or *Hex* by adhering to the *Urglaawe* tradition or vice versa. Each requires its own individual commitment and devotion to learning. While this book may refer to *Braucherei* or *Hexerei* at times because many of the *Urglaawe* concepts are gleaned from the folk magic practices (because they were a vehicle by which the pre-Christian concepts survived), it is not intended to inform on the folk magic practices. Training in *Braucherei* and *Hexerei* is a lifelong journey and is done within a mentor-apprentice relationship.

About Your Authors

Robert L. Schreiwer has been active in efforts to promote the Pennsylvania Dutch culture and language since the mid-1980s. For many years, he straddled the line between the Plain (Mennonite and Brethren) and Fancy (Lutheran, Reformed, nonreligious, or folk religious elements) segments of the culture, gradually becoming more disillusioned by the tenets of Christianity while continuing to admire the community cohesiveness of the Plain sects. In 2007, he founded *der Urglaawe*, which is called simply *Urglaawe* in English, as a modern iteration of the ancient Germanic religion through the lens of the living Pennsylvania Dutch culture.

In 2008, he entered *Braucherei* instruction through the Oley Freindschaft, or guild, and the Three Sisters Center for the Healing Arts. He began the Folklore Research Project, which followed on the heels of the work of earlier guild members who interviewed and recorded lore from practitioners of *Braucherei* across the United States and Canada. In 2010, he expanded this project to include *Hexerei* practitioners. The power was passed to him in 2011, thus allowing him to take on apprentices of his own and to expand the lore and practice of *Braucherei*. Since then, he has studied and learned the practices of *Braucherei* and *Hexerei* from many regions throughout the areas in which the Pennsylvania Dutch settled, and in 2016, he founded the Guild of Urglaawe Practitioners of Braucherei and Hexerei as a sub-guild within the Oley Freindschaft.

Michelle A. Jones was born and raised in the city of Reading, Berks County, Pennsylvania, in the heart of the Pennsylvania Dutch country. Her grandparents spoke *Deitsch* but only around her when the subject was intended to be kept secret from her. Sadly, the language was never passed on to her, but she is making efforts to correct that in recent times. Michelle grew up in the UCC Church, also known as the German Reformed Church, a denomination endemic to the PA Dutch culture. All the while, she was researching and studying more esoteric subjects on her own. She found herself drawn further into those subjects as time progressed and, eventually, left the Christian faith altogether around 2000. Michelle came to *Urglaawe* in 2012 and quickly found a place of community within it. She is a Godswoman, or *Ziewerin*, of the faith and served as secretary of her kindred, die Urglaawisch Sippschaft vum Distelfink. She has served on the boards of both Philadelphia Pagan Pride Day and South Jersey Pagan Pride Day. Michelle is a practicing *Hex* and had the power passed to her from her mentor, Robert L. Schreiwer, in 2016. She is a member of the Blobarrick Freindschaft guild.

Michelle is also a founding member of the Primitive Grove Circle eclectic coven based in southern New Jersey. She graduated from the Farm at Coventry's (now The Still Room at Pitch Pines) Homestead Herbalism course, where her teacher and mentor emphasized the *Deitsch* herbal tradition. Michelle uses that knowledge to lead the occasional herbal hobbyist workshops from her private residence in southern New Jersey just inside the boundary of the Pine Barrens, where she tends to her gardens and bees and handcrafts herbal goodies. In her spare time, Michelle looks to her *Deitsch* heritage for inspiration and wisdom in all matters, learns about and incorporates real, traditional foods into her lifestyle, works on her historical home's renovations and maintenance, hangs out with her Rottweiler, and spends time with the oak that sits prominently in the yard.

Stacey Lynne Stewart picked up her first book on witchcraft and a tarot deck while working in a bookstore in 1985. She began reading tarot for friends, and in the early 1990s, she found herself working at a metaphysical store as a professional tarot reader. She studied herbs and eventually became an herbalist. Crystals and essential oils were another interest she studied with earnest. She eventually became a third-degree high priestess in a Wiccan tradition, but she always felt the pull of the Norse deities and drifted toward a generally Heathen practice. When she began doing some genealogy on her lost paternal history, she found her history solidly rooted in the *Deitsch* culture. She is a member of the Blobarrick Freindschaft guild.

When she found *Urglaawe*, Stacey was inspired not just spiritually but artistically. As an artist and fiber worker, she was given so much inspiration by the myths and practices of *Urglaawe*, and she truly thrived. It provided her the opportunity to create tangible forms of many *Urglaawe* concepts and deities. She threw herself into creating hex signs devoted to each deity, different styles of art of the myths, and wood-burned statuary of the *Urglaawe* deities. Stacey eventually became a Godsperson in *Urglaawe* and a *Braucherin*. She sees little division between mundane and magical and strives to create art for others to experience the deities in their own way.

What to Expect in This Book

This book lays out the foundation for a functional understanding of the *Urglaawe* religion and related cultural practices. It sets out a year-long reference on a multitude of topics for practicing *Urglaawer*. You will find our interpretation of our cosmology and descriptions of our worldview and of our deities. There are chapters on celebrations, deities, and rites of passage, with folklore sprinkled throughout. The section on our celebrations will show anyone how they can celebrate, either solitary or with others, and the chapter on rites of passage will help one create their path should they wish to become an *Urglaawer*. There is also a pronunciation guide and glossary in the back. We reiterate that anyone can practice *Urglaawe*; you do not need to be *Deitsch* to be called by our deities.

It can be challenging to know where to start when taking on learning something new, especially with something as all-encompassing as a spiritual identity. You can read this book in order as intended, or you can certainly jump into the next holiday coming up and start there, or you can choose a deity a day to read about to get you started. This book is meant to show you what our practice looks like when we gather together, but be creative in using it to build your own practice.

We have certain standards as to what *Urglaawe* is, but those standards do not supersede one's sovereignty of self. This is a religion of orthopraxy, or right action, not orthodoxy, or right thought. Our practice welcomes meaningful modification that increases our connection to the land, to our communities, and to the gods and goddesses. *Urglaawe* is a religion of conscience, not of compulsion.

1

URGLAAWE COSMOGONY AND WORLDVIEW

In this chapter, we will explore the concepts of the *Urglaawe* worldview and how we see the realms of the universe and the positions of the many entities in it. We also cover our understanding of the soul and our core values. There is a lot of information in this chapter about the core of what *Urglaawe* is. *Urglaawe* is a relatively new organization of ancient things. Our first sources come from within our own culture: proverbs, folktales, legends, superstitions, family stories, counting-out rhymes, and historical descriptions. Many of these concepts are found in our healing and magical practices of *Braucherei* and *Hexerei*. Our second set of sources are continental Germanic lore, such as Jacob Grimm's *Teutonic Mythology*, historical texts, and the beliefs and superstitions from the Germanic people of mainland Europe. The third set of sources are the Anglo-Saxon and Scandinavian lore, which are most often used comparatively in the development of *Urglaawe* theories and philosophies.

The information below is the result of many years of research and experiential living. Those who grew up in a *Deitsch* household often did not realize that our upbringing was different from that of many of our classmates or other peers. We heard stories about beings such as the Eternal Hunter, or Ewicher Yeeger, while not realizing that such tales were expressions of our unique culture and were not part of the wider American folkloric landscape. Our *Braucherei* training introduced us to the world tree, or *es Lewesbaam.* And the Urglaawe Folklore Research Project brought together the many strands of seemingly disconnected pieces of lore, giving rise to our understanding of what the cosmos consists of and our place within existence.

The World Tree

Our cosmogony begins with a world tree, or what we call *es Lewesbaam.* The best physical depiction of the *Urglaawe* world tree would be a sculpture because it has a definite three-dimensional feel. The tree is described as having five worlds, or realms, on the trunk, and within the branches are four distinct regions, for a total of nine locations. In the center of the trunk is the realm called the heartwood, or *es Hatzholz.* This is the universe that we can see with our eyes and with our scientific tools. Within the *Hatzholz* is a place called *es Mannheem*, or home of humans. This is not just earth in *Deitsch* traditional lore; it also includes the sun, moon, and the planets that were visible to the naked eye. While there is no set definition of where *Mannheem* ends, the space age of the 1950s led some *Hexerei* practitioners to conclude that *Mannheem* extends as far as humanity can reach without encountering another life-form.

On the trunk of the tree outside of the *Hatzholz* are branches that form two distinct arcs around the trunk. These are the regions of the eastern leaves, or *die Oschtbledder*, and the western leaves, or *die Weschtbledder*. These regions separate the other two branched regions, the northern leaves, or *die Naddbledder*, at the top of the tree, and the southern leaves, or *die Suddbledder*, closer to the bottom of the tree. The *Naddbledder* branches stem from the trunk near the two uppermost realms: *die Hohegegend*, or high region, at the top, and the sky or heaven region, or *die Himmelgegend*, which is on the tree trunk between *Hohegegend* and *Hatzholz.* Further down the trunk, below *Hatzholz* at the base of the tree, is a realm called the under region, or *die Unnergegend.* The deepest realm, the dark region, or *die Dunkelgegend*, is in the roots of the tree. These roots spread far and wide, spiraling in many directions and touching the multiverses of other world trees.

DUNKELGEGEND

LEWESBAAM

Each of the nine locations on the tree is home to various beings. Some are distinctly named in the oral traditions of *Braucherei* and *Hexerei*. Some of the locations serve purposes in *Braucherei* and *Hexerei* work. We have good descriptions of some of the locations; others are considered inhospitable for the consciousness to journey to, and some of the oral tradition has some drastic warnings about what might happen if one were to enter some areas, particularly the *Suddbledder*. Here are descriptions of the nine locations.

Hohegegend: The Realm of Divinity

This is the home of the deities, or *die Ziewe*. Older Germanic beliefs recognized two distinct tribes of deity: the *Wane* and the *Ase*, each originating in opposite ends of the *Hohegegend*. In the distant past, a war took place between the two, resulting in a stalemate. *Hexerei* oral tradition states that the two tribes recognized the futility of their conflicts and that the strife between them had shaken the world tree and brought instability to its heartwood. They began to live and work together to the point that many *Urglaawer* see no separation or differentiation between the tribes.

Himmelgegend: The Realm of Elves and Beings of Higher Consciousness

This is the home realm of the elves, or *Elwe*, but other beings are said to dwell here as well, particularly the spirits of some humans and some dwarves, or *Zwarich*, who have achieved a higher state of consciousness and take on the role of *die Idise*. The *Idise* are typically identified as matriarchal spirits, perhaps in large part due to the grammatical gender of the singular form, *Idis*, being feminine. Oral tradition and even general folktales of fairy godparents reveal that gender and sex are not defining factors for *Idise*. It is the advancement of the consciousness and the spirit that leads to one becoming an *Idis*. *Idise* serve as guides, advisors, and protectors of subsequent generations. According to *Braucherei* oral lore, most *Idise* will reenter the cycle of life, death, and rebirth on occasion to serve as leaders or as prodigies who will assist the advancement of humanity in general. *Braucherei* oral lore also reports that there was a belief among some *Deitsche* that all humans would be born once under each of the twelve fixed moon signs on our lunar zodiac, or *Muunraad*, which we will discuss later. Once they have finished the twelfth life, they will go on to become an *Idis*. There is a thirteenth moon sign that appears only in some years, and anyone who was born under that sign—hare, or *Haas*—in any of the first twelve lives will become an *Idis* but return for a thirteenth life as a teacher, leader, or prophet. This belief is an outlier that likely serves as a metaphor both for the partial-soul-rebirth concept within *Urglaawe* and for the purpose in an *Idis* returning in human form.

Naddbledder: The Place of Ice

Naddbledder is the highest of the branch regions of the world tree. It is considered to be the location of the icy rime that met with fire to create the multidimensional universe that is our tree. It is the home of the frost giants, or *Reifries*, who are a race of antagonists to the deities and to humans. The *Reifries* seek to claim the realms on the tree that their ice helped to form; thus, they are seen as destabilizing forces to the advancement of all other beings. Metaphorically, they use ice to bring stagnation to existence, which could lead to an evolutionary dead end across all realms. They interrupt the advancement of all beings' consciousnesses by removing spirits from the cycle of life, death, and rebirth. In stories about their actions, they will take the spirits of young, tender plants or bring about death by exposure to the cold in humans and dwarves. The spirits they capture are taken to a section at the uppermost tip of the *Naddbledder* colloquially called the *Cellar of the Frozen*, or *der Verfroreskeller*, thus resulting in these prisoners being known as the *Frozen*, or *die Verfrore*. Because they are preserved in that location by their stagnancy, it is believed that they can be retrieved by skillful journeyers and placed back onto their evolutionary trajectories. It is said that it takes a *Reifries* twelve to fourteen days to travel from the *Naddbledder* to *Mannheem*. The best known *Reifries* are three who make this journey using different routes in the months of May, or *Wonnet*, and November, or *Newweling*. These giants' names are Dreizehdax, Vatzehvedder, and Fuffzehfux.[1]

Suddbledder: The Place of Fire

This realm is the lowest of the branch regions of the world tree. It is the location of the primal fire that provided sparks to meet with the ice from the top

1. Jesse Tobin, "Walpurgis Nacht," *Hollerbeier Haven: Newsletter for Herbal and Healing Arts* 1, no. 6 (2007): 6.

of the tree to form the multidimensional universe in which we reside. This is the home of the fire giants, or *Feierries*. The *Feierries* are, in many distinct ways, the opposites of the *Reifries*. Their actions are also antagonistic toward deities and humans. They want to claim the whole of the tree for themselves. Like the *Reifries*, they remove spirits and souls from the cosmic cycles of life, death, and rebirth, but their weapons are not ice and stagnation; they are fire and consumption. The *Suddbledder* has a remote location on one of its branches as far from the trunk of the tree as possible. This place is colloquially referred to as the *Ashbin of the Incinerated*, or *die Verbrennteskischt*. The souls and spirits that the *Feierries* seize are called the *Incinerated*, or *die Verbrennte*, and, unlike those taken by the *Reifries*, the Incinerated cannot be retrieved.

Oschtbledder: The Place of Magic

The *Oschtbledder* is the world on our tree that contains the home or estate of the goddess Weisskeppichi Fraa, or the White-Haired Woman. She is the very personification of life-force energy, or *die Megge*, so it follows that *Megge* begins its circuit in the *Oschtbledder* and then wends its way throughout the entire *Lewesbaam*. It is eventually drawn back to the *Oschtbledder*, where Weisskeppichi cleanses it (some say absorbs or disintegrates it, but cleansing it is the most common report) and sends it back out again. This realm is located close to *Mannheem* on the tree, so it is often visited by those who engage in journeywork. This realm is noted for its orangish glow and for a distinct—and somewhat unpleasant at first whiff—smell in the atmosphere. The smell is said to come from the volume of *Megge* itself. *Oschtbledder* is also where *Braucherei* oral tradition places the beginning of magic as a conscious practice. The origin of this tradition appears to be in the role *Megge* plays in the realization of applied intent. This realm is also believed to be the original home of the beings called *Kowwolds*, which are household spirits or goblins, many of which are believed to have moved into *Mannheem* with the development of cobalt mines.

Weschtbledder: The Place of Spiritual Journeys

The *Weschtbledder* is the realm located the closest to *Mannheem*. A cosmic wind often brushes these branches against the tree at the *Hatzholz*, thereby making this the easiest realm for spiritual journeyers to visit. This is the most dynamic realm on the tree, so much so that parsing out what all is happening there is often accomplished only by using familiar frames of reference, such as seeing what appear to be large shopping venues, temples, and identifiable neighborhoods. This realm is about motion and connection. It is the primary journeying point for many practitioners of *Braucherei* and *Hexerei*, and it is also the easiest point from which to fulfill many of the *Hexich*, which is the native *Deitsch* word for functions similar to the shamanic practices of the Evenki and related tribes of Siberia, endeavors that a practitioner may be called upon to do. As is the case with the *Oschtbledder*, this realm has a distinct smell. It is not at all unpleasant at first whiff, but, over time, it can become tedious. Many spiritual journeyers report a mountainous landscape in this realm as well as lighter gravity.

Hatzholz: The Heartwood

Hatzholz is the heartwood of the world tree. Contained within this realm is *Mannheem*, the home of humanity and the physical plane and known universe. Additionally, the *Hatzholz* represents places and times that can be utilized for journeywork. There are three pools that originate in the *Hatzholz* and flow into the *Dunkelgegend*: *Schprudlendi*, *Gwellendi*, and *Fliessendi*. *Schprudlendi* is the brimming stream, *Gwellendi* is the bubbling brook, and *Fliessendi* is the flowing river. These pools can physically be found at *Hexenkopf*, which is located in Pennsylvania in *Mannheem*. Folklore states that the roots of all elder trees or bushes originate here in the *Hatzholz* and extend to the *Dunkelgegend* via the pools.

Unnergegend: The Realm of Spirits

Unnergegend is the home of the dwarves, or *die Zwarich*. It is a dark world with a gritty feel to its environment. Unlike the dynamism of the *Weschtbledder*, motion in this realm is more sluggish. *Braucherei* oral tradition describes its residents as being suspicious and even confrontational to spiritual journeyers. This realm is also home to the goddess Berchta, who, along with her sister, Holle, plays a pivotal role in the continuity of the cycle of life, death, and rebirth. Her home itself is a rather modest cottage, frequently described as being sepia in color, like an old photograph. Near the cottage is a large, sepia-colored hall, which provides a haven for newly constructed souls who are awaiting birth or rebirth.

Dunkelgegend: Where It All Ends and Begins

Dunkelgegend is the realm of destruction and transformation and is the domain of the goddess Holle. This is also the location of the Well of *Wurt*, which is where the wells of the known planes end up and where our actions transform into reactions and consequences. Also found here are Holle's home, *es Heisli*, the apple woods, or *der Ebbelwald*, and *die Miehl*, which is Holle's Mill, in which the great grindstone, Soul Breaker, or *der Seelbreecher*, crushes the soul constructs of the deceased so that the individual parts can be released to serve their next purpose.

Also in this realm is an area called the flax meadow, or *die Bollwies*, from which Holle brought the first flax to the people in *Mannheem*. Another landmark is a large field called *es Weiwerfeld*, which means field of wives or field of women, where ancient servants of Holle, who used to bear sickles on their feet, continue to work with Holle today.

There are also some creepy characters in this realm. When the soul of a deceased person arrives in *Dunkelgegend*, it arrives in a forest that eventually opens up into Holle's apple woods. While in the forest, some are approached by a being known as the Woodchopper, or *der Holzhacker*. No one actually knows what the woodchopper's true nature is because he is a shapeshifter who can sense one's desires and make himself appear to be exactly what one wants. He then attempts to lead the soul into the forest, never to be seen again. Another similar character, perhaps of the same race, appears after the soul has been crushed by *Seelbreecher* and a new construct has been built. New souls travel from *Dunkelgegend* to *Unnergegend*, and, along the way, some are accosted by a being known as the Milkmaid, or *die Melkern*. Her true nature is also unknown, but she can also change her appearance and her behavior to meet the naive new soul's understanding of someone in need of help. Using the soul's compassion as a tool, she attempts to convince the soul to help her carry her milk buckets to her barn. What happens to those who go with her is unknown, but it is believed that they never become incarnate again.

Mysteries of the Lewesbaam

Although *Dunkelgegend* is located in the roots of the world tree, the cosmology does not end there. There are many references in *Braucherei* oral tradition to the roots of the world tree in the *Dunkelgegend* connecting to the roots of other world trees in a forest of world trees. This also means that some beings might have the ability to travel from one world tree to another. The world tree is also a living entity, and *Hexerei* oral tradition states that old branches can die off and new shoots can grow. While the imagery is likely the product of the human mind's capacity to make sense of things that are not easily understood or explained, the framework of the multidimensional universe as a tree with identifiable locations can help one to grasp the enormity and wonder of existence. Our tree is but one tree among many that connect to one another at the roots to form the multiverse.

Wurt and Urleeg

One of the more challenging aspects of any form of polytheism is the explanation of how all that has been made manifest came to be. What caused the primal ice and primal fire to interact? Who set the cosmic cycles into motion? Was the force behind the creation of these cycles conscious? Nonconscious? Unconscious? Proto-conscious? Those are among the questions that relate to *Wurt*, the *Deitsch* term for the force of *Wyrd*, a concept seen most clearly in Anglo-Saxon Heathenry. *Wurt* compares roughly to fate or destiny. However, the future is not set, and while it is possible to predict likely outcomes based on the present, one may alter their *Wurt* through actions and deeds. All living things, including the deities, are subject to *Wurt*. One's *Urleeg*, or the results of the actions of one's life, are recorded and transmitted into the next life as the hand you are dealt at birth. The function of *Wurt* is a complex discussion in its own right.

The working theory is that *Wurt* is the Maker (*der Macher*), and whether consciously or unconsciously, *der Macher* created the environment in which the remainder of existence can come into being and move through the cycle.

Der Macher did not make everything. This is not an omnipotent being. No, it created the stage and, perhaps, the first performers, who then used their own creativity to set the ensuing generations into motion. *Der Macher* holds things to its cycles, though. There is a theory that these cycles are like the training wheels on a bicycle; we will eventually outgrow the need for them. While we have them, though, they balance and counterbalance our actions so as to direct us closer and closer to the concept of the perfected human.

Wurt and the Wurthexe

Wurt is known in other Heathen traditions as *Wyrd*, and it is ultimately from whence the English word "weird" comes. The *Wurthexe* are also known in other cultures. To the Norse, they are the Norns. In *Macbeth*, William Shakespeare makes reference to the three Weird Sisters, who are often equated with the Fates of Greek mythology. While the roles of the Weird Sisters and the Fates are similar, the comparison is not fully accurate because predestination is not a significant factor in Germanic lore as opposed to in Greek lore.

The Norns in Norse mythology are seen as weaving the fabric of *Wurt* for all living beings in creation. One represents the past, one the present, and one the most likely future. The three Norns are known in Scandinavian lore as Urðr, Verðandi, and Skuld, but there are also other Norns from the elves and from the dwarves.[2] The *Urglaawe* concept of the *Wurthexe* is best understood through these three Norse Norns. While the goddess Freid spins the thread, the strands are woven by the other *Wurthexe* according to one's *Urleeg*, or actions in this lifetime. Drawing on information from *Hexerei*'s oral traditions, *Urglaawe* philosophy is that linear time is a human measurement. Since time is nonlinear, one who is adept enough could technically move among the realms in any time context and could even exist at the same time and in the same place, just "out of phase" with the physical plane.

The *Wurthexe* process and manage the fabric of life for each human. Because we are in the physical world and therefore subject to linear time, one's actions in the past create the choices in the present, and those choices open up possibilities for a future that is undetermined. The materials used for the fabric of life are spun by the goddess Freid, but two other goddesses, Holle and Berchta, are seen as playing complementary roles in managing the cosmic cycles. Holle generally governs the expansion phases and Berchta

2. Rudolf Simek, *Dictionary of Northern Mythology*, trans. Angela Hall (Boydell & Brewer, Ltd., 2007), 236–37.

the contraction phases. Due to the roles that the *Wurthexe* and these three goddesses play in the dynamism of our multidimensional universe, there is a common belief that they are not subject to the effects of *Wurt* in the same way that humans experience the effects of the past setting the reality of the present and laying out possible futures. This does not automatically mean that they are impervious to *Wurt*, though. Most *Urglaawer* do not view *Wurt* as a godhead due to it being a proto-conscious force, but it is still viewed as the supreme force that provides or denies the space in which things can take form, including its own managers. *Wurt* is believed to be the creator of the earliest deities and many other beings, but then those creations began to make creations of their own.

Wurt as a Cosmic Spider Web

As noted, the goddess Freid spins the fiber that Holle and Berchta and the other *Wurthexe* use to create the web of *Wurt*. The *Wurthexe*, taking this fiber, create the patterns and pathways of the web. And, because this necessarily means that Freid is not actually on the web because she supplies the fiber for it, she would be outside (literally) of its effects or, at a minimum, not affected like we are. The *Wurthexe* are on the web and therefore can be affected by it. All deities and other entities in addition to us humans are also on the web and subject to it.

So, while the web is spun and there are strands that are predetermined, the entities on the web can choose which strand to travel when they come to any particular junction of fibers. This means they can progress straight ahead, go back from whence they came, make a turn onto a totally new strand, or choose to remain at rest.

If you think of how a fly landing on a web alerts the spider due to vibrations on the strands, it is much the same for entities on the web of *Wurt*. All of our actions are ultimately felt by any other entity on the same web and maybe other connected webs. And, ultimately, this vibration creates a sort of consciousness of the web itself. So that even if a particular entity on the far end of the web hasn't moved, they will sense the movement of the web when an unseen entity moves on the opposite far end. To the first entity, the web itself moved.

Now, consider the spiderweb in nature once again. Most are two dimensional, such as the web built between a windowsill and frame or a web built between two fence posts. But you can certainly find three-dimensional webs out there too. This is how *Urleeg* can be explained. The strand that connects one 2D web to another is that pathway between realms. As one entity stands on the web directly above the strand connecting the two, that entity's movement creates vibrations across both 2D webs. That movement, to the second entity, now generates a response, and when the second entity ultimately makes their next move, it will then create a movement on the 2D web where they reside. Therefore, the actions of an entity on a different plane (e.g., realm, generation) can affect the actions and decisions of an entity on their own plane. The deities and "others" have knowledge of these cross strands and can therefore travel among the webs more easily, whereas we humans are really only aware of our generational strands. But with practice and guidance from those deities we work with, we can locate the others.

Creation Myths

Among the Germanic tribes, it appears that only the Norse have an intact creation myth from ancient Heathen times. It is lamentable that there is no Germanic creation myth in the form of a primary source from the ancient Heathen era. Even the Norse lore was written down after the conversion to Christianity. However, the Eddas were likely heirlooms passed down in an oral tradition akin to the oral lore of *Braucherei* and *Hexerei*. Outside of the Norse lore, little information about the creation myths of the Germanic peoples has survived into the present day. Bits and pieces of information made it into *Braucherei*'s and *Hexerei*'s oral traditions, and they refer to primal ice and fire interacting and giving rise to the *Lewesbaam*, or world tree, but there is no coherent ancient Germanic myth about the creation of existence present within *Deitsch* lore.

However, syncretic-era creation stories and fragments have been recorded by other Germanic tribes. (The syncretic era occurred after the introduction of Christianity to an area, but before the new faith demanded the destruction of pagan altars and faiths.) German historian and folklorist Jacob Grimm provides an example of a syncretic myth that turns up in the oral traditions of *Hexerei*.[3] The notable differences are that the syncretic interpretation ascribes the creation to the Christian deity whereas the *Hexerei* interpretations indicate multiple deities participating in the creation process, with the goddess Weisskeppichi setting *Megge*, or life-force energy, and the god Wudan providing the breath of life.

There are theories that suggest that the existence of the universe—and of the *multiverse*—is the result of ongoing cycles of expansion and contraction referred to as *cosmic days* and *nights*.

Urglaawe Cosmic Cycles

Urglaawer understandings of the cosmic cycles do vary, but the general belief is that the multiverse itself experiences a cosmic day, during which existence expands from a singular point, followed by a cosmic night, during which existence contracts to a singular point. What set this motion into action and what keeps it going is a topic of debate. Many *Urglaawer* see the force of *Wurt* as being what drives the cosmic cycles.

Urglaawe Creation Myth for Humans

The created beings also became creators, whether by reproducing with their own kind or with other beings, or by fashioning new beings. *Hexerei* oral tradition provides information about the order of creation, but an intact Germanic creation myth about the creation of the first human does not exist in *Deitsch* lore. Some myths do exist in older, syncretic texts that include both Christian and older Heathen elements. One in particular describes how the first human was created from materials of the natural world. This syncretic myth, which is described in volume 2 of Grimm's *Teutonic Mythology*, appears as part of a twelfth-century poem on the four Gospels.[4] In contrast to the Genesis myth of Jehovah creating man from dust, eight materials are each used once in the construction of the first human. In our own lore, there is a ninth element, the breath of life, which is also in the Genesis account.

3. Jacob Grimm, *Teutonic Mythology*, vols. 2 and 4 ed., trans. by James Steven Stallybrass (Dover Publications, 1966), 566–69.

4. Grimm, *Teutonic Mythology*, vol. 2, 566–69.

When asked during interviews about their own concepts of the creation of humans from a Heathen perspective, *Hexerei* practitioners and some syncretic *Braucherei* practitioners described the involvement of several deities in the creation of the first human. Which deity added what to the human form was not consistent throughout the interviews, but the breath of life was attributed to the god Wudan, and a tenth factor, *die Megge*, or life-force energy, was attributed to the goddess known as Weisskeppichi Fraa, or the White-Haired Woman, who is more commonly referred to as Weisskeppichi in *Urglaawe*. Wudan and Weisskeppichi are the only deities whose names have been set into the *Urglaawe* myth of the creation of the first human. Other deities' names were provided in the context of one item, such as the goddess Erda providing the loam for the flesh, or the goddess Sunna providing the gleam of the eyes, but there was not enough of a consensus among those interviewed to include their names in the *Urglaawe* myth.

From loam is created flesh.
From dew is created sweat.
From stone is created bone.
From worts (herbs) are created veins.
From grass is created hair.
From the sea is created blood.
From the clouds are created the mood and mind.
From the sun are created the eyes.
From Weisskeppichi Fraa the *Megge* flows.
Wudan gives the breath of life.[5]

At the moment that *Wurt* began the expansion into this cosmic day, two oppositional objects were created. One was a primal heat or fire and the other a primal cold or ice. The energy and the motion of the expansion brought portions of the two into one another's proximity. The sparks from the fire met with the crystals from the ice in different proportions throughout the growing expanse, creating additional materials that would combine to fill the

5. Grimm, *Teutonic Mythology*, vol. 2, 567; "What Distinguishes Urglaawe From Other Heathen Paths?" *Urglaawe, BlogSpot*, July 19, 2013, https://urglaawe.blogspot.com/2013/07/what-distinguishes-urglaawe.html.

expanse. The expansion and dynamism of creation continued without conscious supervision or guidance.

Wurt, as *der Macher*, or the Maker, was the force behind the expansion, but it did not have a plan for what was to come. The expansion continued, and the combinations of the elements and building blocks continued, eventually giving rise to *es Lewesbaam*, or the world tree. Upon this tree formed nine distinct realms and the connections among them. These realms are the multidimensional universe in which we live.

Our *Lewesbaam* took shape within the confines of *Wurt*. As *Wurt* was the creator, attributes of it became part of the expansion, and the first protoconscious beings, the giants, or *die Ries*, appeared as pure and primal forces. Each realm began its own evolutionary trajectory. In the center of the trunk of the tree, a universe arose in which the physical realm began to take shape. This realm was unique, and *Wurt* became aware of its creation.

The *Ries* had reproduced and taken on identities as tribes. Those who were born of fire became known as fire giants, or *die Feierries*. Those born of ice were called frost giants, or *die Reifries*. As new building blocks came into existence, other tribes of *Ries* came into being, but the two oldest and oppositional forces held the most power, and they began to compete with one another to control the expanse.

As their battle approached the physical universe in the heartwood of the tree, the sleeping *Wurt* brought into being a new entity who could protect this special realm from being destroyed. This being would have the capability to learn and to evolve as the expansion of the tree continued. This being took in nourishment from the cosmos and, in turn, applied his will to the protection of this realm. Thus, the deity known as the Sky Father, Ziu, came into being.

Wurt continued the expansion. The awareness of the heartwood realm, *es Hatzholz*, and the creation of the first god led *Wurt* to dream of how to maintain the order. *Wurt* created from itself the ability to manage itself in the form of the *Wurthexe*. These entities set the constructs of time and space throughout the *Lewesbaam*, and they discovered that the physical realm in the *Hatzholz* was bound by limitations of movement within time and space. *Wurt* appeared to move in one direction from that which had already taken place into what was forming, and there was no ability for objects constructed of physical material to move backward on that trajectory.

Over time, more deities came into being, first from *Wurt* and then from interaction and reproduction with some of the *Ries* tribes and with one another. Sun and stars, forest, fowl, and different entities emerged into all the worlds of the *Lewesbaam*. The plants and herbs, animals and minerals all interacted and built relationships with each other, yet the frost and fire giants still battled each other over access to the *Hatzholz*.

The deities sought to create order, so they pushed the primal fire into the lowest branches and the primal ice into the highest. The deities set their home in the uppermost realm, *Hohegegend*, on the trunk of the tree. They discovered *die Elwe*, or the elves, in the next realm down the trunk of the tree, *Himmelgegend*. The deities found many types of beings throughout the tree. However, none appeared to be suitably equipped to maintain order in the *Hatzholz*.

The deities decided to create beings who could meet that role. The deities gathered together and created the race of beings known as *die Zwarich*, or the dwarves. The *Zwarich* were formless spirits by design, but the deities gave them the power to change shape in order to meet the needs of the moment. They were given intelligence and magical skills. As the cosmic expansion continued and the *Zwarich* began to reproduce, the deities discovered that the ability to change shape was not sufficient to meet the needs of the physical realm; the *Zwarich* were not able to maintain a physical form long enough to maintain order in the *Hatzholz*. The *Zwarich* did not adapt well to the changing nature of the physical realm. The deities gave the *Zwarich* the second-lowest realm on the tree, *die Unnergegend*.

The deities then decided that they should construct new beings who could keep a permanent presence in the *Hatzholz*. Within the *Hatzholz* was a location in which the goddess Erda had mated with Ziu and given birth to the god Tuisko. The deities decided that this world, *Mannheem*, would be the home of the new physical creatures. This world, which was created by Erda as a cradle for Tuisko, was ever evolving, so the deities decided that the new beings would have to grow and to evolve within the context of this world.

Their forms would be constructed from the environment of the world. They would learn and advance over time, with the goal being that they would be at the same level of conscious evolution at the end of the cosmic day as the deities were at the beginning of it. So, from loam was created flesh, from dew was created sweat, from stone was created bone, from worts were created veins and arteries, from grass was created hair, from the sea was created blood, from the clouds were created the mood and mind, from the sun were created eyes.[6] Weisskeppichi drew upon the energy of the cosmos, concentrated into a life force, or *Megge*, and imbued the physical form of the new creation with the power to process, to obtain, and to share this energy. Wudan took up the new creation and blew into it the breath of life. Humanity became.

The *Reifries* and the *Feierries* continue to covet control over *es Hatzholz*. The locations of their home realms on the world tree keep a full-on assault at bay, but humans need to continue to evolve, including consciously, within the context of this physical realm. If *Mannheem* is destroyed, then the whole of the tree will perish up and down the trunk from the center. There are many who believe that the advancement of human consciousness is being slowed by religious institutions that insist on thought control and submission and that suppress the use of the mind and exploration of the whole of existence.

Soul Construction and Partial Soul Rebirth

When we die, our souls join Holle on the Wild Hunt, and when we are dropped off at her Mill at the end, our souls, or *die Seele*, are then broken back down into the following twelve parts. Two parts, *der Folyer* and *der Leich* stand alone, and a container called *der Geischt* consists of the remaining ten parts.

Der Folyer, die Folyern

This is the Fetch, also called the *Guardian Spirit* or the *Journeyer*. This being is a separate, individual entity that becomes part of the human soul construct at formation. It serves as a guide throughout the human's life. There is a belief among some *Braucherei* practitioners that this being has an opposite

6. Grimm, *Teutonic Mythology*, 567; "What Distinguishes Urglaawe From Other Heathen Paths?"

sex to that of the human in whose soul it is encapsulated. For example, a male fetch, *der Folyer*, would be within the soul construct of a human female, and a female fetch, *die Folyern*, would be part of a male human's soul construct. However, *Hexerei* lore reflects a less binary understanding of these beings, which is reflected in *Urglaawe* belief. The gender or sex of the human is not dependent on the identity of the *Folyer* or *Folyern*.

The Fetch can separate from the rest of the soul for journeywork. At death, the Fetch may attach itself to other souls. There is a belief across both traditions that a *Folyer* might abandon the soul of a living human if that person engages in substantial destructive or harmful behavior. A human who has been abandoned by the *Folyer* is said to be bereft of morals and is very likely to experience misfortune and tragedy.

Die Leich

This refers to the space in which the soul permeates the physical body. While the entire soul construct may extend further than the skin on our bodies, *die Leich* is what exists inside that boundary.

Der Geischt

Der Geischt is a combination of ten separate parts of the soul. These are the nonphysical portions of the self.

es Gemiet: This is the complete self, including one's shadows and temperament.

die Gewut: This is the center of one's desires, passions, and aspirations. It is what motivates us to action.

es Glick: This is where one collects and calls upon their own personal power and builds up their stores of luck.

der Hoch: This part of the soul processes and analyzes the experiences of the entirety of being a human.

die Megge: The energy that is in all life, what some might call *universal energy*. This energy is what is called upon for healing in *Braucherei*.

der Meind or der Sinn*:* This part of the soul is where your memories are stored, both the ones you make during your own lifetime and your ancestral memories from generation to generation.

der Ochdem: The literal breath of life given to humanity by Wudan at the time of our creation.

der Seelhaut: The part most often recognized as a "ghost," this is the soul skin, which is an ethereal mold of the physical body.

es Urleeg: The most primal layer of the soul, this is where our actions from our lifetime are recorded, the reverberations of which follow us into our next incarnation.

der Wille: Literally translates to "our will." The capacity to make things happen.

Partial Soul Rebirth

Most *Urglaawer* believe in some form of reincarnation, the predominant form being partial soul rebirth. In partial soul rebirth, parts of the soul may be reborn into a future full soul construct. Our actions in each lifetime shape our soul construct and give us the chance for advancement to higher consciousness. When a soul construct passes from this reality into the next, the *Folyer* or *Folyern* will attach itself to a new soul construct. The soul parts and even our physical body parts don't decompose at the same rate. Although there is a chance for all soul parts to be reborn, the most likely to do so are the *Hoch*, *Urleeg*, and *Glick*. Even an entire soul construct may make the journey intact to be reborn.

Doom of the Gods

The Doom of the Gods, also called *die Ziewedemmerung* or *die Gedderdemmerung*, as viewed in *Urglaawe*, is similar to the Ásatrú concept of Ragnaök, or the end of the world. In both concepts, chaos is released into the *Lewesbaam* and destroys all but a few things, paving the way for a new tree to be created. The defining difference that *Urglaawe* has from the Ásatrú model of the afterlife is that we do not have souls in the halls of the gods preparing each day for the eventual battle. We believe that our purpose is to advance our consciousness so as to be closer to the level of the gods as they are now when we are rebuilding after the Doom of the Gods.

Worldview

Urglaawe's worldview is not a prescribed set of rules set forth. Again, we are not an orthodoxy practicing right belief; we are an orthopractic religion. When we come together, we practice ritual in the same way, we call the deities by the same names, and we follow the same set of social guidelines. Within the orthopraxy concepts, some guidelines and expectations do exist, including the importance of adhering to oaths and the upholding of certain core values in our interactions with people of all backgrounds.

Der Fruchsfriede

Der Fruchsfriede is an *Urglaawe* concept relating to *Frith* in the Norse and Anglo-Saxon traditions. *Fruchsfriede* is what shapes the nature of our social interactions, both individual and as groups. It is the foundation of our social customs and the laws of our communities and nations. It is seen in our manners and etiquette, laws and protocols, actions and mores. It combines all of those things to create a state of peace and standard for social conduct.

All beings on earth deserve *Fruchsfriede*. We share the earth and the resources on it, so caring for others, including animals and plants, is in all our best interests. We share the tightest bond of *Fruchsfriede* with our inner circles, ourselves, our family, and the other people we share our daily lives with. Then, the circle of *Fruchsfriede* extends outward to include the spiritual groups we gather with or the neighborhood we live in. These circles grow larger, moving further away from ourselves to include our extended family, our city or state, our nations, and then all of humanity. All-encompassing, Fruchsfriede would also stretch to include the deities and wights.

While all are deserving of *Fruchsfriede*, a person's choices may put them in a position of having broken the *Fruchsfriede* extended to them, and therefore they will feel some kind of consequence, be it from the laws of the land or the treatment they receive from their peers. We have an expectation of some level of peace and order, security and structure, and opportunity for occasional joy. If one disrupts those general expectations, the circles of *Fruchsfriede* will feel the effects.

Another concept found in *Urglaawe* is a bit more complicated to describe. *Gemietlichkeet* has no direct English translation, but one of the more prominent feelings it invokes is that of a sense of belonging—not just that we belong, but we feel it so much that it brings a sense of coziness and happiness along with it. Finding and providing *Gemietlichkeet* is a major aspiration for personal and community goals. While we can wrap ourselves in soft comfy blankets and drink warm cups of tea, it's because of the people around us, and sharing special moments with them, that brings us that fulfilled feeling of *Gemietlichkeet.*

Society as a whole has been moving away from deep connections, not only with the earth that sustains us but within our communities as well. Many of us are too busy at our jobs, dealing with politics, worrying about money, and any other number of distractions that fill our time to focus on our own spirituality. From another angle, rugged individualism has been presented and upheld as the ideal, and we tend to push ourselves too far too often. We avoid asking for help to our own detriment. Communities are built for a reason! These missing connections have become the social giants of our era, and we are working to defeat those giants and restore those essential connections in ways that uplift everyone.

Eighteen Core Values

Es Bedenk is a general term for an ethical value. *Urglaawe* has eighteen such values that we practice as the core of our beliefs. While one can focus on a single core value, in *Urglaawe*, we recognize the importance of understanding that there is an interplay among all of the core values. For example, without applying wisdom to courage, one could find themselves in a perilous situation. *Urglaawe*'s philosophies on compassion are derived from ethics originated from the myths and stories of Holle. Compassion is a core value, but now we purposely avoid calling core values *virtues* because the execution is actually more important than simply sensing them. It's also important to remember that any value can quickly morph into a vice. As you read through them, consider meditating on each core value. Think about how the other values play into the implementation of it. We tend to use the twelve nights of *Yuul*, our winter solstice holiday, as the most common time to focus on these core values. *Yuul* is a natural time of introspection, but you can apply them and meditate on them at any time during the year.

Compassion: *Es Mitleid*

Es Mitleid is a feeling of deep sympathy and sorrow for another who is stricken by misfortune, accompanied by a strong desire to alleviate the suffering. Community is built by people helping each other, and it makes the entire world a better place. However, acting upon compassion requires judiciousness; there is a fine line between helping someone out of a predicament and enabling someone to prolong a destructive pattern. The focus of *Mitleid* is to show appropriate compassion for others who may be in situations that are detrimental to themselves but that they did not directly create. Or, if they did create them, they are working to change their habits. Allowing one to continue being irresponsible is detrimental to the community. However, not allowing someone to redeem their wrongdoings and find a way back into *Fruchsfriede* with the community is equally detrimental.

Courage: *Der Mut*

The modern world gives us conflicting messages about courage. At the same time, we are encouraged to break the rules and innovate, and we are continually coached on the importance of fitting in with the crowd and being popular. Courage, like introspection and wisdom, complements and supports the application of all the other core values. In combination, these three core values help to make all our endeavors more successful.

Curiosity: *Die Neigierheit*

Life is full of mysteries and opportunities to learn more about ourselves and the universe. In the Information Age, knowledge is power. The desire to better understand our existence helps improve not only our own condition, but also contributes to the advancement of human consciousness. Curiosity is a driving force in the continuous development of humankind, and it complements the core value of spirituality. Our innate curiosity can help us identify opportunities for personal growth. We can ask ourselves what we wish we knew more about, then identify what is needed to acquire that knowledge. In addition to the personal acquisition of knowledge guided by curiosity, we can also seek to satiate the curiosity of others by teaching what we know and by contributing to the community's knowledge base.

Discipline: *Die Addning*

Discipline is the key to successfully achieving most things in life. Exercising moderation and self-control helps us to focus on our priorities. Living life with intention requires carefully choosing where to expend our time and energy. It also demands that we show respect for ourselves as well as for others. How much could you change if you applied discipline to your life, even to just one problem you are facing? Are there other areas in your life that need more discipline? Can your discipline be an example for others who are struggling with their own challenges? Discipline taken to the extreme can also be self-destructive because you miss out on the gifts of spontaneity.

Generosity: *Der Edelmut*

Generosity is closely related to hospitality and the concept of "a gift for a gift." Not only are generous acts a sign of our love for other beings, but they also help to build and strengthen our community through reciprocal acts. Consider generosity carefully when the recipient does not have the ability to provide a return gift of equal value. Doing so before the giving of a gift can avoid having the imbalance become a problem during or after the gift exchange. There is a need for self-awareness when dealing with generosity, as giving too much can leave you wanting. This isn't limited to material items. Giving too much of yourself or your time can leave you in poor, diminished health. We must always remember to be generous to ourselves as well as others, or we may end up in a state where we are of no use to either.

Honor: *Die Ehr*

It is important to consider the role of honor in our actions. Are your actions reflective of your words? Does your community know you by your deeds or your empty boasts? Recognize that you have a choice to provide a good example and help minimize the loneliness and disconnection that our modern society creates.

Hospitality: *Die Uffwaarting*

Die Uffwaarting is arguably one of the most important values of all Heathens. Inviting others into your home and being a good host are the hallmarks of hospitality. The act of sharing your personal space with others, breaking bread with them, and attending to their needs during their visit generates goodwill between you and your guests. It also serves your kindred and the community by providing a safe and positive environment for those whose personal circumstances limit their opportunities to experience that connection and support.

Industriousness: *Die Schaffichhheit*

Die Schaffichhheit shows when one regularly works to make positive contributions to the community. These contributions can be as narrowly focused as improving or maintaining your own state of being or as broad as community service. The goal is to be an active participant in life rather than an observer. This subject is often hard to reconcile when we think of our neurodivergent or physically challenged friends and members. Often, we are told to "do our best," but who gets to judge what our own best is? This is a perfect example of how personal these core values are and how we should examine them in relation to each other as well as individually.

Interdependence: *Die Gschwisichabhhenkichkeet*

While it is virtuous to be as self-reliant as possible, and indeed it was one of our original core values, it tends to ignore the fact that humans are social creatures who need the skills and products of others in order to survive. Rugged individualism is an interesting concept, but how many people really live a life completely by their own hand? In an ideal world, interdependence would be the result of voluntary participation in communities, which would ensure that everyone is taken care of. Working together with others is important to the success of certain endeavors and the community.

This is one of the most admirable aspects of conservative Mennonite communities. Many Plain sectarian communities continue old Germanic community lifestyles but with the leaders of those Plain groups setting the rules. Unfortunately, most Heathen communities are not yet established with the resources to engage in that type of self-management, but it is an aspiration for the future.

Introspection: *Der Selbschtreiguck*

Der Selbschtreiguck is the task of examining and paying attention to your own ideas, thoughts, and feelings. In doing so, we endeavor to know ourselves in our totality. Many people consider introspection to be taking inventory of our weaknesses and faults and finding ways to better ourselves. While this is important, it is equally important to recognize our positive qualities and strengths and give ourselves the appropriate praise for them. It is often through this process that we set our self-improvement goals.

Kinship: *Die Verwandschaft*

We all need to belong to a community, and kinship helps to create the safe and trusting environment we crave. Our kin provide us with valuable feedback on how we are functioning in the world. They can help us identify our blind spots as well as our unrealized potential. Do you graciously accept both compliments and constructive feedback? Do you give the same in return?

Perseverance: *Die Ausdauer*

Effort is the key to accomplishment. Even if you fail to obtain your goal, if you put in your best effort to achieve that goal, then you will have succeeded in learning what your limits are. Continuing to work in the face of difficulty is honorable and often needed in our modern instant-gratification culture. But we must proceed with caution. Perseverance is a double-edged sword that requires the application of wisdom to allow us to discern when we have taken matters too far beyond our good intentions. Your perseverance can be seen as a reflection of your *troth* (fidelity or trustworthiness) and truth. If you work with strong perseverance, it is more likely that your community will have compassion for you and support you in your failed effort because you have demonstrated industriousness and self-reliance. Perseverance ties into many of the core values.

Self-Improvement: *Die Selbschtverbesserung*

The biggest pitfall in undertaking self-improvement is selecting too many things to change at once. Before deciding to make any changes or take any oaths, you must first consider what you can reasonably change. Lofty goals can inspire us, but failing to reach them can be devastating. It can be helpful to write down all your thoughts and then whittle down the list using the following questions: Is this achievable in my current situation? If not, what needs to change? Can I break this item down into smaller steps and revise my goal to focus on achieving the first step in this process? It is recommended that you seek feedback on your proposed resolutions from trusted friends or kin. They can also provide support as you work to accomplish them.

Spirituality: *Die Geischtlichkeet*

Die Geischtlichkeet is the connection we find when we nurture a relationship with our own higher self, our own inner spirit, and the spirits of animals, minerals, plants, and the majority of all living things. It is about the energetic symbiotic relationship between all living things and an acknowledgment and respect for this relationship. This connection is not limited to living things, as the soul exists beyond the physical body, thus our connection with the ancestors.

Stewardship: *Die Verwalting*

Die Verwalting is tied to the *Urglaawe* concept of *Zusaagpflicht*, which is the understanding that a symbiotic relationship between humans, animals, minerals, plants, and the majority of all living things exists to ensure continuance of life and betterment of the world. All of Heathenry, including *Urglaawe*, still constitutes only a small segment of society. However, small rocks can create a big wake by making a splash. The most effective way of making change is to lead by example.

Troth/Loyalty: *Die Treie*

In *Urglaawe*, the act of making an oath, pledge, or devotion is regarded as a very serious matter and is usually done as part of a spoken blessing ritual, or *Sege*, and includes an indebtedness, or *Schuld*, for not fulfilling the terms. When becoming a member of a kindred or freehold, an oath is taken by the new and existing members as a pledge to support each individual and the community at large in their lives and continued growth. These public declarations allow us to support one another in our efforts and to also hold one another accountable. Dependability and loyalty to our faith and values are of the utmost importance. This concept includes diligence in our work and in our duties. We also must ensure that we are engaging in activities and projects for the right reasons. Partaking in endeavors for the wrong purposes corrupts the work and results in the potential for unexpected consequences.

Truth: *Die Waahrheit*

We must deal with reality no matter how hard it can be. This applies when facing our own challenges and when interacting with others. Basing our decisions and actions on truth creates a positive and supportive environment for all human beings. What can you do to ensure that your actions reflect *troth* and truth? Are you always honest with yourself and others? Being honest with others can be easy; often, being honest with ourselves is much more difficult.

Wisdom: *Die Weisheit*

Wisdom is the lens through which we survey our inner landscape and is the key to making good decisions about what actions to take. Just as glasses help us to see correctly, wisdom aids us in evaluating what we perceive within and around us. Discernment is an important aspect of wisdom, using it for keen insight and good judgment. Wisdom also plays an important role in supporting the successful application of all other core values. Wisdom is especially powerful when applied to spirituality. When we encounter things beyond our physical manifestation, we must use our wisdom to put these experiences into perspective.

Die Zusaagpflicht: The Sacred Duty

Finally, we have one more concept to share with you that permeates every part of *Urglaawe*: *die Zusaagpflicht*. Best described as "sacred promise" or "sacred duty," *Zusaagpflicht* is the unspoken moral and ethical commitment between all beings on earth. This includes humans, animals, plants, minerals, and beings in the spirit realm. The knowledge that we are interconnected to one another and all entities of this world and beyond is the driving force behind living deliberately.

While there is no way to know when these thoughts or concepts began, they certainly reflect the Heathen worldview and, as a part of the living *Deitsch* culture, evolved into this iteration. The core value of stewardship really comes into play with the idea of *Zusaagpflicht*. This isn't a one-way relationship of caretaker and charge, but one of partnership. By caring for plants in a deliberate way, both cultivated and wild, they offer us healing properties. By hunting carefully or responsibly raising cows, pigs, or other meat animals, we are able to be nourished. Each domain—human, plant, animal, mineral—has their own role in the cycles of life and over thousands of years has developed an interwoven pattern of partnerships with each other. The evolution into a commitment to each other became the unwritten spiritual social contract we call the *Zusaagpflicht*.

Our modern lives have caused us to lose our connection not only to the seasons, but to the plant and animal kingdoms as well. Even if we are lucky enough to live near farmland, most of our own food probably doesn't come from it. We have supermarkets where we find processed foods shipped from states away and out-of-season fruits and vegetables from other countries. Everything is marketed to fast and easy, not deliberate and intentional. We understand that there are times when one needs to choose fast and easy. A good understanding of *Zusaagpflicht* will help one honor the living things that went toward that fast-and-easy food choice while honoring yourself by making it.

If we put ourselves at the top of the food chain, we need to have all the more respect for the living beings below. Being at the top does not mean we are free to partake in reckless overhunting or the misuse of farmland. It doesn't condone overfishing of the oceans or over-drilling for minerals or oils. What it means is we have more of a responsibility for all of those things because we are the ones who have the ability to change.

It is unrealistic to think that one can make it through life without having an impact on the world around us, even causing harm to some extent or another. One does not have to make restrictive dietary decisions or give up everything that makes one's life easier to honor those beings that give us food or the minerals that become the energy that fuels our car. But there are better choices we can make that will not only benefit the earth, but everyone and everything on it. We have been watching humanity's choices negatively affect the environment for decades. Even with some large strides that have been made to reverse the environmental damage already caused, we are currently making more decisions that may significantly alter our ability to recover.

We want to stress that the expectation is not one of absolutes. You should do what you can, how you can, when you can. One person isn't going to change our precarious environmental situation by recycling perfectly. The things that will change that situation are things that are far bigger than the individual. What understanding the concept of *Zusaagpflicht* will do is bring *Urglaawe* from being a religion to being a way of life.

Structure of Urglaawe

A *Sippschaft* is an *Urglaawe* kindred that has oaths for the members. A *Freibesitz*, or freehold, is a group of *Urglaawer* who are not oathed to each other. Leaders of the group are called Godspeople, or *der Ziewer* (male), *die Ziewerin* (female), or *es Ziewermensch* (nonbinary). *Die Ziewer* (plural) will generally lead the rituals and may request other participants offer readings or take on other parts of the ritual. One may become a Godsperson based on consensus or election by their local *Sippschaft* or *Freibesitz*.

As mentioned earlier, *Urglaawe* is a religion of orthopraxy. When we are gathered together, we all engage in the same way of conducting ritual. However, an *Urglaawer* may practice alone or with others in a family or small group. In these contexts, the *Urglaawe* religion allows for flexibility and adaptation in how people worship. We do ask, though, that elements of one's personal practice that deviate from *Urglaawe* standard practice not be identified as being *Urglaawe* in nature.

We gave you a lot of information in this chapter. You explored the world tree, or *Lewesbaam*, and learned what entities reside where. You read about the soul construct and partial soul rebirth. We also shared our core values and our animistic concept of *Zusaagpflicht*, or "sacred duty." You do not have to try to absorb all of it at once. Perhaps journal about one core value at a time or write about the different realms of the *Lewesbaam*. However you prefer to process the information given, take your time and develop your own opinions and worldview.

2

DEITIES

In *Urglaawe*, there are two accepted groups of deities. The first of these is the *Ase* (plural term), *der As* (singular masculine), and *die Asin* (singular feminine). The *Ase* are the tribe of deities known in Scandinavian lore as the *Aesir*. The *Ase* are considered to be deities of consciousness and higher thought. Among the most familiar of the *Ase* are Ziu, Wudan, Freid, Dunner, Siwwa, die Eppeldraagerin (Idunn), Volla, Zisa, and many others.

The second group of deities are *die Wane* (plural term), *der Wan* (singular masculine), and *die Wanin* (singular feminine). This is the tribe of deities known to the Scandinavians as the *Vanir*. These deities are generally associated with the rhythms and cycles of nature. Among the most well-known of the *Wane*, we find Holle, Berchta, Fro, Frouwa, Tuisko, and Ewicher Yeeger.

Our orthopraxy is to observe the *Wane* at *Hoietfescht* in late July or early August at the first harvest and the *Ase* on *Erntfescht*, the high harvest on the autumn equinox. In the following descriptions and associations, you will find the related feast days and holidays that we talk about in more detail in the chapter that covers our observances. It is important to note that not all deities are associated with a specific observance and might be hailed or honored as part of a group of deities who are connected by tribe or attributes in response to particular circumstances.

In this chapter, we will share the various deities from the *Urglaawe* pantheon and list their associations, including any feast days, special celebrations, associated runes, and more.

The Apple Bearer

Apples play a central role in many Germanic tales, including that of Fraa Holle. They are an object used for safety, the passing of tests, and even for danger and death, depending on how they are being wielded. In the *Poetic* and *Prose Eddas*, the apple goddess is known as Idunn. She is known in our lore by the name Eppeldraagerin, and we honor her as the apple harvest comes in. She, along with the goddess Siwwa, are among the primary deities honored at the autumnal equinox observance of *Erntfescht*.

Her associations

Holiday: *Erntfescht*

Colors: Red and yellow

Animals: Pollinators

Plants: Apple trees, apple blossoms, and apples

Tool: None specified

Rune: No specific rune

Berchta

Berchta is the goddess Holle's sister, and she resides in *Unnergegend* during the light half of the year. She oversees the dark half of the year in the *Hatzholz*. As part of her role of overseeing the dark half of the year, she brings in the souls that missed the Wild Hunt.

Her holiday is observed on December 31. She is concerned with orderliness of the mind and mental health. As is the case with many Teutonic goddesses, she is known for spinning, and as such is associated with linen and flax. In the Christian era, her honor has been tainted by the church, though the horrid masks that appear as depictions of the Wild Hunt in parts of Germany and Switzerland carry both a fear and a respect for the powerful goddess.

Her associations

Holidays: *Yuul* (generally), sundown December 20–December 31; *Berchtaslaaf* (specifically), sundown December 31

Colors: Gray, white, and silver

Animals: Barn owl, snow owl, geese, and beavers

Plants: Blue cornflower and birch

Tools: Goose prod or stick

Rune: *Baerke*

Dunner

Dunner is the god of regular folks and one can sense him in the crashing thunder, bright lightning, and heavy rains. Thursday is named for him in both *Deitsch* and English. Dunner is compassionate and supportive when called upon for strength, courage, and even fertility. He hears the calls of those who are trying their best yet still struggling.

He is seen as the protector of work and production animals, particularly goats and cattle. In the early *Deitscherei*, in the spring, cattle were put out to pasture for the first time on a Thursday, and cattle were only put out on Tuesdays and Thursdays.[7] Wedding days were also most commonly scheduled for Tuesdays and Thursdays.[8]

Dunner is associated with the color red. Wedding attire of the *Deitsch* was often the color red. In fact, any red garment could carry the power and protection of Dunner. Therefore, Deitsch folklore—and Braucherei practice—is to recommend the wearing of red flannel underwear as a guard against rheumatism.[9]

Dunner trains the spiritually activated scarecrows, or *Butzemenner*, in May for the annual battle with the frost giants, or *die Reifries*. His role in training the *Butzemenner* army is key in their success through the growing season and the reason that most *Butzemenner* are constructed and activated before May 12.

7. Edwin Miller Fogel, *Beliefs and Superstitions of the Pennsylvania Germans* (Center for Pennsylvania German Studies, 1995), 9.
8. Fogel, *Beliefs and Superstitions*, 8.
9. Fogel, *Beliefs and Superstitions*, 8.

His associations

Holiday: *Erntfescht*

Colors: Red, burgundy, and copper

Animals: Goats, bears, foxes, robins, redstarts, cattle, and stag beetles

Plants: Sedums, hens and chickens, houseleeks, and oaks and acorns

Tools: Hammer (similar to a sledgehammer or carpenter's hammer, not Mjölnir); *Ruckschtee*, which is a stone that protects against lightning strikes

Rune: *Dunner*

Erda

Erda is a goddess of the earth and soil. Generally associated with the wild areas, such as fields and forests, she also has a hand in domestic gardens. Soil itself is a living ecosystem (a far cry from the dirt under your nails). It provides an anchor for plant roots while being ever changing at the same time. The fact that soil is something that connects many places in the world, even if they don't look connected on the surface, lends credence to her being known as a connector of spaces between. In *Deitsch*, the American lotus is known as *Wassermann*. Literally translated, it means "water man." The full name of the plant is *Wasserharrsgschenk*, or "water lord's gift." The gift is said to be given to the "earth lady," who is also known in *Hexerei* lore as Erda. She is also the mother of Dunner.

No iron tools may be used when working with her, and iron tools may never be used when cutting blue or white vervain, as it is sacred to her. Devotees of Erda may seek out tools that do not contain iron so that they can use them for all of their gardening and other soil working.

Her associations

Holiday: *Hoietfescht*

Colors: Brown, orange, gold, and green

Animals: Pigs, earthworms, birds, squirrels, and chipmunks (anything that could propagate plants or aerate soil)

Plants: Blue and white vervain, strawberries, and American lotus

Tool: Trowel, never iron

Rune: No specific rune

Freid

Freid is the hearth goddess—and yet so much more! She spins the very material from which the *Wurthexe* weave our *Wurt*, and this, to us, places her so high in the cosmic scheme that she is essentially a goddess of time, energy, and matter as well as a goddess of the home. As a spinner, the distaff and spindle are tools associated with and used to honor her. She rules the institutions of marriage and motherhood and is concerned with affairs of the home and garden.

As the matron of the hearth, she is also seen in the beauty of the entire realm of feminine creative energies, regardless of whether that be expressed through art, food, poetry, or nurturing relationships. Tied to matriarchal spirits, Freid is the wife of Wudan and sister of Volla and Voll. She is a constant reminder of the fact that without a safe place to lay our head at night, there can be no growth or true success; the home and hearth are key to human life.

Fettekuche, yeast and potato doughnuts, are made and eaten in her honor at the *Entschtanning* celebration to symbolize the baby bump aspect of the growing season just begun. Another aspect of *Entschtanning* is the ceremonial cleansing of the hearth. As part of the cleaning, the fire was allowed to go out in the hearth. A new fire was to be started with birch, one of her sacred trees, symbolizing fresh starts, renewal, and birth.

Her associations

Holiday: *Entschtanning*, February 2–14

Colors: Sky blue and white

Animals: Cats, storks, herons, and beavers

Plants: Poplar and birch

Tools: Spindles, distaff, and keys

Rune: No specific rune

Fro

Fro, of the *Wane*, is the deity of increasing bounty and the upholder of the social order of *Fruchsfriede*. He is Frouwa's twin brother and the son of Erda. Fro is, perhaps, best known in the context of the *Yuul* observance. After the scarcity of the prescribed meal of *Berchtaslaaf*, the god Fro gleefully and enthusiastically picks up where Berchta left off on Twelfth Day, or *Zwelfder Daag* (sunrise January 1 to sunset January 1) of *Yuul*, with his feast. Traditionally, among the *Deitsch*, this meal consists of pork and sauerkraut, although there are many common side dishes accompanying the meal. Interestingly, pigs and boars are sacred to Fro, and each strand of cabbage eaten on New Year's Day represents a bit of currency.

His associations

Holidays: *Frofescht* (Feast of Fro), *Zwelfder Daag* (Twelfth Day of *Yuul*, running from sunrise to sunset on January 1), also honored among the *Wane* at *Hoietfescht*

Colors: Pine or mossy green

Animals: Pigs and boars

Plant: Cabbage

Tool: None specified

Rune: *Engel*

Frouwa

Frouwa, or the Lady, is widely known among the Germanic peoples. The Netherlands Dutch know her by the honorific of *Vrouw*. In English, she is called Freya, and in Norse, she is called Freyja. Each culture perceives her a little bit differently, but there are also some common elements throughout her lore. What is discussed below is the lore from the *Urglaawe* perspective, which, due to the ins and outs of the forced conversion to Christianity, brings some unique perspectives to the understanding of one of the most vibrant and readily accessible deities in the Germanic pantheon.

She is a goddess of the *Wane*, though her understood lineage from Norse lore does not fully match ours. She is the matron of all cats. She is associated with love, lust, beauty, sex, fecundity, sowing, and reaping the bounty of the land. She is also shrewd and wise, and—oral tradition has indicated—has a business acumen like no other.

Attributes of Frouwa were spun into an acceptable Christian context that became attached to St. Gertrude, and the lore of St. Gertrude was applied to the date of her death, March 17. It is interesting that St. Gertrude's Day observances were retained by the overwhelmingly Protestant and Anabaptist Pennsylvania Dutch, not so much as a religious icon but as a cultural indicator and tradition.

Urglaawer generally accept that the retention of this lore is relevant to our worship of Frouwa, again calling to the Lady of the *Wane*. Although it is virtually certain that the church did not intend to keep parts of the story of Frouwa alive, we *Urglaawe* still tip the hat to St. Gertrude for serving as the vehicle that has provided us with a method to rebuild the severed relationship with Frouwa.

Because St. Gertrude of Nivelles was created through an appropriation and grafting process of many traits of Frouwa, one could argue that a syncretic honoring of Frouwa has (wittingly or unwittingly) been going on since the seventh century. We *Urglaawer* will watch to ensure that our use of the ritual, absent its Christian overlay, evolves to meet Frouwa's needs.

Her associations

Holidays: *Der Grumbieredaag*, March 17; also usually placed on the altar among the *Wane* at *Hoietfescht*

Color: Emerald green

Animals: Beetles, butterflies, boars, and cats

Plants: Spring onions, potatoes, lily of the valley, and meadowsweet

Tool: None specified

Rune: No specific rune

Holle

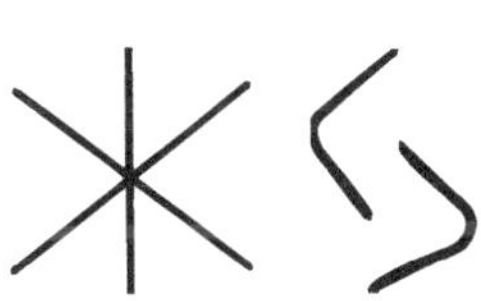

Holle is the matron of *Urglaawe*, and in *Braucherei*, she is believed to have been the motivation that pushed our ancestors to sail across the ocean. Martin Luther, the Reformation leader and founder of the

Lutheran Church, identified her as the personification of reason, which was not meant as a compliment:

"Reason is the greatest enemy that faith has: it never comes to the aid of spiritual things, but—more frequently than not—struggles against the Divine Word, treating with contempt all that emanates from God."[10] From Luther's perspective, Holle's standing as a wise woman with supernatural wisdom and powers makes her a prime target for denouncing reason as an enemy of faith. Holle was associated with witch trials during Luther's lifetime, and he associated her with human knowledge and with Heathen books.[11] The wisdom for which Luther eschews Holle is among the very reasons that Holle is held in high esteem among *Urglaawer*.

The activities of Holle mark some of the major *Urglaawe* holidays. The dark half of the year starts at sunset on October 30, or 31. Gehling on the *Urglaawe* calendar, with *Allelieweziel*. This is when she leaves on the Wild Hunt. The Wild Hunt runs from *Allelieweziel* to *Hexenacht* on April 30, when the light half of the year, or *Brechthelft*, begins. In Germanic lore, when it snows, it is said Holle is shaking out her bedspreads.

The *Blobarrick*, or the Blue Mountain Ridge that runs from central Pennsylvania to the Delaware Water Gap by New Jersey, is sacred to Ewicher Yeeger. This meets the mountain pillar known as *Hexenkopf*, sacred to Holle, which is north of the Delaware Water Gap. This is the thought behind him being considered her consort. It could also be tied to both deities' connection to death and the processing of souls. She is the mother of the Nine Winds: *die Neine Winde*.

Her associations

Holidays: *Hexenacht* (sundown April 30), *Allelieweziel* (sundown October 30)

Colors: Blue (from pale blue to cobalt to navy) and white

Animals: Geese, bees, hounds, ladybugs, and swans

10. Martin Luther, *The Table Talk, or Familiar Discourse of Martin Luther*, trans. William Hazlitt (David Bogue, Fleet Street: 1848), 164.
11. Edgar A List, "Frau Holda as the Personification of Reason." *Philological Quarterly* 32 (1953): 446–48.

Plants: Elder and mugwort

Tool: Sickle

Runes: *Haagel* and *Yaahr*

Holler, Ewicher Yeeger

Depending on which aspect of this deity you are working with, he is known to us as Ewicher Yeeger or as Holler. He is Death personified, a god of consequences, and a god of second chances. As Holler, he represents the bounties specifically from water (fishing) and from responsible hunting. He is also associated with archery, skiing, or moving on snow by any conveyance. As Ewicher Yeeger, he is known for killing plants and taking their spirits at the end of *Allelieweziel*, or the last harvest, so that the *Reifries* cannot remove them from the cycle of life, death, and rebirth. The benevolent aspect of his work is seen in the tale of how he rescued early settlers from starvation in the *Blobarrick* in northeastern Pennsylvania.

His associations

Holidays: *Ewicher Yeeger Sege* (November 11); also honored among the *Wane* at *Hoietfescht*

Color: Orange

Animals: Rabbits, hares, deer, trout, turkey buzzards, and *Blokgeil* (plague horses)

Plants: Hay or straw for offerings

Tools: Bow and arrow, staff

Rune: No specific rune

Nehalennia

Nehalennia's lore is best known from the Netherlands, though inscriptions make it clear that Roman, Celtic, and Germanic people all honored her. She is associated with agricultural bounty and water. All indicators point to her being viewed as a goddess to appeal to for safe passage over water, specifically the North Sea between the Netherlands and England. Since the *Deitsche* left Europe primarily from ports in the Netherlands on ships bound first for

England, it is highly appropriate for *Urglaawer* to honor Nehalennia and to give thanks to her for the safe journeys rendered to the Americas.

Her associations

Holiday: *Hoietfescht*

Color: None specified

Animal: None specified

Plants: Aquatic plants

Tool: None specified

Rune: No specific rune

Die Oschdre

These are the sisters Helling, Nacht, and Oschdra, who introduced color and cardinal directions to the *Hatzholz*. Very little about the Oschdre sisters in the way of ancient lore has survived to reach us, although *Deitsch* oral lore provides some additional insights. The Oschdre are counted among the *Wane*.

Nacht is the personification of night, darkness, and black. Her black, when added to the colors of her sisters, gives us many shades. Darkness provides our eyes, our bodies, and our minds with time to relax, to rejuvenate, and to dream.

Helling represents daylight and white—bright and beaming, sometimes even blinding. Her white, when added to the colors of her sisters, gives us many tints. Her time provides us the ability to explore, investigate, and make our dreams realities.

Oschdra is the goddess of the dawn, lady of gray yet also of all color, whom, along with her sisters, we honor at *Oschdresege*, or the spring equinox ritual, as the bringers of color and joy back to a winter-weary world.

Their associations

Holiday: *Oschdresege* (spring equinox ritual observance)

Colors: All of them

Animals: Hares and distelfinks

Plant: Hyacinth

Tool: Paintbrush

Rune: No specific rune

Saaga

Saaga is the keeper of stories of all sorts and across all media. She serves as an inspiration for all forms of art: music, poetry, drawing, prose, sculpture, song, dance—any type of creative aspirations. Although she is of unknown ancestry, she is counted among the *Ase* by many *Urglaawer*.

Her associations

Holidays: All holidays, but she is specifically honored at *Summeraafang* to signify ongoing enlightenment

Colors: Yellow and blue

Animals: Songbirds

Plants: Sage and St. John's wort

Tools: Special pen and personal journal

Rune: No specific rune

Siwwa

In *Urglaawe* practice, Siwwa is a goddess of the *Ase* who is prominently honored at *Erntfescht*, the second harvest observance. A relationship between the grain goddess and the storm god, Dunner, is quite clear; thus, Siwwa is seen as the consort of Dunner.

Her associations

Holiday: Prominently honored at *Erntfescht*

Colors: Gold and beige

Animals: Those traditionally used in agriculture: horses, mules, and donkeys

Plants: All cultivated grains, especially wheat

Tool: None specified

Rune: *Engel*

Sunna and Muun

Sunna is the personification of the sun. She is directly mentioned in the Merseburg charms, and her sister is thought to be *Mariyeschtann*, which is the Morning Star (Venus).[12] Muun is the personification of the moon and represents all of its powers. He is the star-crossed lover of Sunna.

When the lovers were separated in the sky by the trickster god, Schadde, it had the unexpected effect of bringing stability to the waters of earth. For this reason, they were asked by Ziu to stay in their new positions in the sky. They remain separated but come together to consummate their love during solar eclipses. Their children, the dandelions, are a representation of both of their celestial parents.

Her associations

Holiday: *Summeraafang*

Colors: Yellow, orange, and gold

Animal: Eagles

Plants: Dandelions and sunflowers

Tool: None specified

Rune: *Sunne*

His associations

Holidays: New and full moons, high and low tides

Color: Silver

Animal: Whippoorwills

Plant: Moonflowers

Tool: None specified

Rune: No specific rune

12. D. L. Ashliman, trans., "Merseburg Incantations," updated April 23, 2021, https://sites.pitt.edu/~dash/merseburg.html.

Die Waahra

Waahra is a goddess who oversees the taking of oaths. She is invoked at any ritual or occasion when an oath is to be heard, including weddings, new member inductions, the assumption of an office, and more. Because breaking an oath is considered to be one of the most damaging acts any Heathen can engage in, one would do well to hold those oaths so as not to earn her displeasure.

Her associations

Holidays: Weddings and anytime oaths are taken

Color: None specified

Animal: None specified

Plant: None specified

Tool: Oath ring

Rune: *Gewwe*

Weisskeppichi Fraa

She is known as the White-Haired Lady and is the personification of life-force energy, or *Megge*. She is believed to have a home in the *Oschtbledder*. This goddess is known to us through *Braucherei* lore, which states that Weisskeppichi Fraa projects that very life-force energy into all of us, and this *Megge* is the very "spirit" that we all share.

While theories have been postulated that link her to Gullveig of Norse lore, Weisskeppichi Fraa is, most likely, a White Lady whose name may have been lost to time. She is a complex figure. She is thought to exist periodically in this realm through incarnations that go as far back as the prophetess Velcda and include historical figures, such as Hildegard von Bingen, Meister Eckhart, and most recently as *Deitsch* folk legend Maria Jung, "Mountain Mary," or die Baricke Mariche. The belief is that she incarnates when needed to ensure that *Braucherei* and the healing practices of energy work that she rules over do not become extinct or irrelevant. Weisskeppichi Fraa is known to be the paramount of healing—physically, mentally, and spiritually. She is a central figure within *Braucherei*, and *Braucherei* is a central part of the

Deitsch identity. *Urglaawer* honor her as our primary goddess of healing and as the source of *Megge*.

Her associations

Holiday: Mountain Mary's Death, November 16 (observed on the closest Sunday)

Colors: White and iridescent

Animal: Golden owl

Plants: She is pervasive throughout all of nature

Tools: Quartz or selenite crystals

Runes: *Daag*, *Reit*

Wudan

Wudan, known in Norse as Odin, can be a little shifty, but he assists with spiritual quandaries, facing oneself, and questions of internal struggle. He is looked to for wisdom, especially in circumstances where out-of-the-box thinking and cunning thinking are necessary, and matters involving travel or wandering. As Wudan helps us with our dilemmas and mental challenges, it is appropriate that in *Urglaawisch* lore he is said to have passed along the runes to us. He accompanies Holle on the Wild Hunt but remains in the *Hatzholz* during the dark half of the year. His home is in *Hohegegend*.

Urglaawer identify him with the *Deitsch* character of der Belsnickel and certain aspects of Santa Claus. While there have been concerted efforts to link Santa Claus to St. Nicholas, Wudan's aspect of wish-granter can easily be seen in our modern-day version of the poem "The Night Before Christmas" that so many love.

In der Belsnickel we see the familiar guise of Wudan as a poor wanderer or a seeker of wisdom. As der Belsnickel, a man would dress in animal pelts and knock on doors asking riddles. Sometimes the riddles would be simple, but sometimes they would be harder and more esoteric. If answered correctly, the Belsnickel would gift a chestnut. An incorrect answer would have Belsnickel offering the chestnut but also swinging a switch at the person's hand while they tried to take it! In *Deitsch* culture, there are some clues that indicate that chestnuts are sacred to Wudan, which strengthens link between der Belsnickel and Wudan.

His associations

Holidays: *Yuul* (December 21); Erntfescht

Colors: Purple and blue

Animals: Crows, ravens, magpies, horses, and wolves

Plants: Hickory and willow (in the form of switches), horse chestnuts, dried fruits, and nuts

Tools: Rune sets and switches

Rune: *Winsch*

Zisa

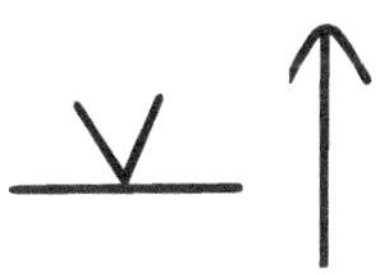

Zisa finds her way to *Urglaawe* through her connection with what is now the city of Augsburg. She is credited as protecting the city from the Roman invasion after the Suevi settled there, mixing with the Alemanni and other tribes.[13] The people of these tribes that knew her would become some of the biggest contributors to what would become the *Deitsch* nation. Since the symbol of Augsburg was a pine cone, this became her symbol as well.

She found herself being superimposed upon the Virgin Mary with the added moniker of "Undoer of Knots." As indicated by Christian art and statuary, it is believed she has the ability to remove obstacles or even to undo *Urleeg* if one's cause is honorable. Both Christian Catholics and *Urglaawer* alike believe that she is the remover of obstacles and undoer of knots. *Urglaawer*, however, also believe she can create obstacles if they are needed for one's growth or right action. This is yet another way that our deities strive to help us maintain balance and order along our path of advancement.

Zisa is thought to be personified by the South Star, Vega. The North Star has long had a strong association with Ziu or with other skyfather gods. What had long puzzled many *Brauchers* and *Hexes*, though, were references to the

13. Nigel Pennick, "The Goddess Zisa," in *Tyr: Myth, Culture, Tradition*, vol. 1, eds. Joshua Buckley, Collin Cleary, and Michael Moynihan (Ultra, 2002), 107–10.

South Star in the form of a consort of the North Star in charms or verse. How did landlocked people in the middle latitudes of the Northern Hemisphere come to know the South Star? The nomenclature is somewhat deceiving, as Vega is not seen in the Southern Hemisphere, nor has it ever been. What is intriguing, however, is that Vega was actually at one point the North Star.

Her associations

Holiday: *Zisasege*, which is the Feast of Zisa, September 28

Color: Red

Animal: Female cardinal

Plants: Pine cones and evergreens

Tools: Knots, red string, or yarn

Runes: *Kerze*, *Tuisko*

Ziu

Ziu is thought to be personified by the North Star. His home is in *Hohegegend*. He is concerned with justice, right-mindedness, and right action, which ties in with his ruling over the *Ding*, which was the annual gathering of many Germanic tribes to reconcile quarrels, pass judgment, and assess taxes. Less shifty than Wudan, Ziu is often clear-cut, direct, and will assist us if our intentions are well thought out and based in actual fact, not dreams or false hopes. Tuesday is Ziu's day, and the *Deitsch* name for Tuesday, *Dinschdaag*, contains a truncated form of "Ding."

His associations

Holiday: *Dingsege*

Color: Crimson red

Animals: Foxes and male cardinals

Plants: Wormwood and aconite (Please note that wormwood can be toxic if misused, and aconite is highly toxic and should not be ingested in any way.)

Tools: Gloves and spears

Rune: *Tuisko*

Peripheral Entities

These are deities that are present in some of our myths and folk stories that have been passed down from generation to generation. They are integral to the stories in which they appear but tend to be secondary figures to the more well-known deities with whom they interact.

Schadde

Schadde is the primary trickster figure within the *Urglaawe* pantheon. He knows the weaknesses and desires of others, including the deities, and exploits them for his own benefit or amusement. In the process, though, he often brings about resolutions to greater problems. Schadde is best known for his role in the myth of "Schadde un Schlumm."

Schlumm

The god associated with sleep, dreams, altered states, and visions. He is the brother to Holler (Ewicher Yeeger). He communicates through riddles and uses darts to induce slumber.

Es Elbedritsch

Elbedritsch literally translates to "elf-twitch" and means "snipe." *Elbedritsches* are known to play pranks on unsuspecting humans.

Buckliches Mannli

"The Buckled Man" is a creepy figure who will take over the empty *Butzemenner*, or spiritually activated scarecrow, shells that aren't burned prior to *Allelieweziel.* He lurks along perimeters of one's property and is likely the origin of pucks or the bogeyman.

Gedreier Eckhart

He is a folk hero who runs before the Wild Hunt to warn humans of the coming party so they can avoid being swept up in the Hunt. Holle allows him immortality of sorts to be of service to her for this purpose.

Rips or Riewezaahl

He is the main deity observed during *Ziegdaag*,

Dwarves, Elves, Kowwolds (Kobolds), Reifries, Feierfries, Wasserfries, etc.

These are the other entities that can be met either on the *Lewesbaam* or during challenging times. The *Fries* are giants—the fire, ice, and water giants that are present-day challenges we face in the world, either personal or global. The most well-known of these beings is King Frost, whom we rail against at the Ewicher Yeeger observance.

Nine Winds, die Neine Winde

Die Neine Winde are the children of Holle. Their names are derived from earlier generations' understandings of the winds and how each wind relates to the *Deitscherei*:

North: Gibbel, whose name means "top" or "summit."

South: Bodde, whose name means "bottom."

East: Schteig, whose name means "rise."

West: Setz, whose name means "set."

Northeast: Schnall, whose name means "buckle," which relates to the collision of cold air masses from Canada with warmer air masses over the Atlantic Ocean. The masses "buckle" together, often bringing powerful nor'easter storms to Pennsylvania.

Southeast: Warrem, whose name means "warm."

Northwest: Kalt, whose name means "cold."

Southwest: Riffel, whose name means "ripple," which likely refers to the prevailing westerlies, which blow from the southwest to the northeast due to the Coriolis effect: The winds are moving at a rate faster than the land and water on the earth's surface below. The winds are also moving in a direction in opposition to the waves of the Atlantic Ocean, which can bring about rippling of the water.

Whirlwind: Wärwel, whose name means "whirl," as in a whirlwind or tornado.

Lesser-Known Deities

These are deities that are known in our lore but do not have their own feast days or holidays.

Alcis

The Alcis are brother gods of the Ase who protect brothers during wartime.

Der Luul

Luul protects young greens that hold on through winter. He represents the newness of time, including infancy of the year and plants. He is considered to be like a doula to the yearly cycle of nature. He is known as a keeper of secrets, always holding his tongue.

Voll and Volla

They are twins of the *Ase* and siblings of Freid. They are considered the god and goddess of abundance.

Wurthexe

The *Wurthexe* manage destiny by spinning the fiber produced by Freid; at least one *Braucherin* has referred to their location as a "spinning shop." They are thought to reside in *Himmelgegend*.

In this chapter, you met many of the *Urglaawe* deities and learned their myths, their associations, and their feast days, if they have any. This is a good place to start when building your practice. Perhaps find the deities that speak the most to you and do research to learn more about them. You could also say small greetings or words of gratitude to them upon waking or at bedtime.

3

NINE SACRED HERBS

The nine sacred herbs, or *Neine Heiliche Gegreider*, are plants that are considered sacred within *Urglaawe* practice due to their magical, medicinal, and spiritual properties. They came to us from the folk healing tradition of *Braucherei*. Of the nine sacred herbs, three are from the garden, three from the field, and three from the wood. These are powerful healing herbs and can be used equally from medical, sympathetic, and spiritual perspectives. They are traditionally gathered after May 15. Here is a brief list with more information to follow. This chapter is intended for informational purposes only. Readers should consult with medical professionals prior to using any herbal remedy or supplement.

From the Garden

- *Deitscher Tee* (thyme), *Thymus pulegioides*
- *Edann* (horehound), *Marrubium vulgare*
- *Salwetee* (sage), *Salvia* spp.

From the Field

- *Fimffingergraut* (cinquefoil), *Potentilla* spp.
- *Grundelreewe* (ground ivy), *Glechoma hederacea*
- *Katzegraut* (catnip), *Nepeta cataria*

From the Wood

- *Bruschttee* (wintergreen), *Gaultheria procumbens* and *Gehlwassergergraut* (Pipsissewa), *Chimaphila umbellata*
- *Hollebeer* (black elderberry), *Sambucus nigra*
- *Hundsholz* (dogwood), *Cornus* spp.

The Unofficial Tenth Sacred Herb: Aldi Fraa

Before sharing details on those nine herbs, we must first introduce you to one of the most overarching herbs within *Urglaawe: Aldi Fraa*, more commonly known as mugwort (*Artemisia vulgaris*).

Aldi Fraa (mugwort), Artemisia vulgaris

In *Urglaawe*, *Aldi Fraa*, "Old Lady," is the preferred cleansing herb. *Aldi Fraa* is used as a bug repellent and to promote dreaming.[14] *Urglaawer* especially use it as a dreaming herb during the harvest holidays. Since we cannot burn elder because it is sacred to Holle, mugwort can be used as a "stand in" for those times elder is needed. According to *Deitscher* Christopher Sauer, *Aldi Fraa* "is one of the key herbs in [*Deitsch*] folk medicine."[15]

Aldi Fraa is a perennial that can grow anywhere from two to five feet tall. It is most often identified by the underside of the dark green leaves, which appear silver. The flower heads are yellow or reddish looking and appear at the end of the growing season. *Aldi Fraa* is invasive in nature; the plant will die off in winter but return in spring.

14. Susan Hess, "Mugwort," in *Hollerbeier Haven: Newsletter for the Herbal and Healing Arts* 1, no. 3 (2007): 11.

15. William Woys Weaver, *Sauer's Herbal Cures: America's First Book of Botanic Healing* (Routledge, 2001), 218.

Taste: Bitter

Energy: Hot and dry

Parts used: Entire plant

Harvest or gathering time: Late summer just before flowering

Properties: Antiseptic, diaphoretic, emmenagogue, laxative

Traditional Medicinal Uses

Excellent for female complaints related to premenstrual symptoms and suppressed menstruation. Useful in reducing inflammation. Used to eliminate worms. A digestive herb that can help improve appetite, increase bile flow, as well as aid in the absorption of nutrients. May help bring on menstruation.

Cautions and Contraindications

Do not use during pregnancy. It is important to make sure you properly identify this plant, as related plants in the genus *artemisia* can be toxic, especially so with oils or tinctures.

History, Folklore, Magic, and Other Interesting Tidbits

Also called *mater herbarum* ("mother of herbs"), mugwort has been a part of well-rounded herbal knowledge for thousands of years. It has been widely used from Asia to Europe, where it even made the trip across the ocean to the "New World." Directly associated with Holle, the herb is said to aid in childbirth when tied to the left thigh and then immediately removed after the child is born.

It is a premier hex-breaking herb. Encourages vivid dreaming and aids in dream recall. To encourage dreaming and dream recall, place the herb in a sachet and place under pillow. It is a major healing, smoke cleansing, journeying, and spiritual herb in *Braucherei* and *Hexerei.*

To fully cover all the interesting information on this herb would encompass a workshop unto itself.

From the Garden

These three herbs would be planted in the garden closer to home for easier harvesting.

Deitscher Tee (Thyme), Thymus pulegioides

Deitscher Tee is a perennial herb growing to roughly 8 inches with ovate leaves and tiny pink-to-purple flowers. It has woody stems and a taproot. *Deitscher Tee* is native to temperate parts of Europe.

Taste: Savory

Energy: Cool and moist

Parts used: Leaves and sprigs

Harvest or gathering time: Summer

Properties: Antiseptic, antioxidant, deodorant, disinfectant, expectorant, tonic

Traditional Medicinal Uses

Used for gastrointestinal issues. Helpful for colds, coughs, and bronchitis. Can be used as a gargle for sore throats. Ingested as a tea, syrup, or a culinary herb and used topically as a foot bath.

Cautions and Contraindications

None known.

History, Folklore, Magic, and Other Interesting Tidbits

In *Deitsch* culture, it's called *Deitscher Tee*, or *Deitsch Tea*. It's thought to increase one's courage aromatically, and placing the plant near a door or window will combat fear. Spiritually, this plant is used to purify and as a strong ally in all workings.

Edann (White Horehound), Marrubium vulgare

Native to Europe, Africa, and Asia, *Edann* is naturalized to North and South America. It's a square-stemmed perennial that grows to roughly 20 inches with toothed, downy leaves and double-lipped white flowers.

Taste: Bitter

Energy: Cool and neutral

Parts used: Leaves

Harvest or gathering time: Spring before flowering

Properties: Bitter tonic, diaphoretic, expectorant

Traditional Medicinal Uses

Used mainly for upper respiratory tract complaints. Can be beneficial to lung function and can be used in a variety of lung problems. Good for treating bronchitis with a non-productive cough and dry sticky mucus. Generally good herb for treating wheezing, bronchitis, bronchiectasis, bronchial asthma, and whooping cough. Increases the appetite and supports the function of the stomach. Most commonly used as a tea or in tincture form.

Cautions and Contraindications

None known but consult a physician prior to use if pregnant.

History, Folklore, Magic, and Other Interesting Tidbits

Known as white horehound, it should not be confused with black horehound, *Ballota nigra*, which has different indications and properties. This is the herb used in the ubiquitous horehound candy and cough drops. Most frequently taken as a syrup made with honey or sugar in ancient times.

Salwetee (Sage), Salvia spp.

Salwetee is an evergreen plant that grows up to 32 inches with square stems and hairy, gray-green or purple leaves. Native to the Mediterranean, it is now cultivated all around the world, thriving in sunny conditions. *Salwetee* can be grown from seed, and the plants are replaced after 3 to 4 years.

Taste: Pungent and bitter

Energy: Warm and dry

Parts Used: Leaves

Harvest or gathering time: Before flowering

Properties: Astringent, antibacterial, antifungal, antiviral, antiseptic, antioxidant, anti-galactogogue, carminative, estrogenic, expectorant

Traditional Medicinal Uses

Used equally well in cooking and medicine. Ideal for treating sore throats, especially with inflamed tissue and painful swallowing. Works well with colds, flu, or skin conditions with excess secretions. Will cause a good sweat when used as a hot tea but will stop sweating if used as a cool tea. Can stimulate memory. Its astringent properties aid in drying up milk production during weaning. May be helpful for irregular and light menstruation and as a remedy during menopause. Most commonly used in tea and tincture form and is a common culinary herb.

Cautions and Contraindications

Not recommended for pregnant women except in culinary preparations. Avoid direct contact of undiluted essential oil of sage, especially on sensitive skin, mucous membranes, and in the eyes. Contains thujone, which can be toxic in excessive quantities.

History, Folklore, Magic, and Other Interesting Tidbits

The Latin name *Salvia* comes from *salvare*, which means "to cure." In some traditional folk medicine, it was thought that eating a few leaves of sage with salt in the morning before breakfast would protect a person from any contagious diseases and miasma (tainted air) that they would encounter during the day.

From the Field

These three herbs would be gathered from nearby fields for their magic and healing properties.

Fimffingergraut (Cinquefoil), Potentilla spp.

Fimffingergraut is a perennial herb with palmate leaves that have small yellow flowers and dry, inedible fruits. You can find cinquefoil in most of the cooler locations of the northern continents.

Taste: Sweet

Energy: Dry

Parts used: Leaves

Harvest or gathering time: Summer

Properties: Astringent, antiseptic, tonic

Traditional Medicinal Uses

Used as a mouthwash for both bad breath and sore throat. Treats diarrhea. Helpful topically to soothe wounds and irritated skin. Most commonly taken as a tea.

Cautions and Contraindications

None known.

History, Folklore, Magic, and Other Interesting Tidbits

Known as the "helping hand," it is used in both mundane and spiritual applications. It has been used in canning and creating tinctures. In the *Deitsch* folk magic tradition of *Braucherei*, it is carried to prevent forgetfulness. It should not be collected prior to sunrise on May 15. *Fimffingergraut* can also be used to cleanse ceremonial tools.

Grundelreewe (Ground Ivy), Glechoma hederacea

Grundelreewe is native to Europe and western Asia, and it is now naturalized to North America. The plant thrives on the outskirts of woods and along paths. It is a creeping perennial growing to up to 20 inches in height with long, rooting runners that can reach up to seven feet, notched kidney-shaped leaves, and purple-blue flowers.

Taste: Bitter

Energy: Cold and dry

Parts used: Aerial parts

Harvest or gathering time: When in flower

Properties: Anti-inflammatory, antioxidant, antiviral, bitter tonic, expectorant, diuretic, cholagogue

Traditional Medicinal Uses

Used as a tonic, diuretic, and a decongestant. Treats many ailments involving mucus membranes in the ear, nose, throat, and digestive system. Useful in dissolving phlegm. Valuable treatment for gastritis and acid reflux. Helps to counter diarrhea. Stimulates the gallbladder and bile secretion. Cleansing, healing, and promoting urine. Most commonly taken as a tea or in tincture form.

Cautions and Contraindications

None known for humans, but large quantities are toxic to horses.

History, Folklore, Magic, and Other Interesting Tidbits

Known also as *alehoof*, *creeping Charlie*, and *gill-over-the-ground.*

Katzegraut (Catnip), Nepeta cataria

Native to Europe and Asia and naturalized to North America, *Katzegraut* is well-loved by our favorite felines. The plant is a perennial herb growing to 3 feet with heart-shaped, gray-green leaves with spiked flower clusters that are white to purple in color.

Taste: Pungent

Energy: Warm and neutral

Parts used: Aerial parts

Harvest or gathering time: When plant is just flowering

Properties: Anti-spasmodic, carminative, mild anodyne, mild diaphoretic, mild sedative

Traditional Medicinal Uses

Settles the stomach. It stimulates sweating and is therefore useful to reduce fever. Good for treating colds and the flu due to its gentle nature and pleasant taste. It is antiflatulent and settles indigestion and colic. Also useful to treat headaches due to digestion problems. Most commonly used as a tea or in a tincture.

Cautions and Contraindications

None known but consult a physician prior to use if pregnant.

History, Folklore, Magic, and Other Interesting Tidbits

Folklore knowledge of catnip says that it is powerful at repelling mosquitoes. Although known for its excitatory effect on cats, not all cats are enamored with the herb.

From the Wood

While gathered from the wood, often a *Hollebeer*, or elder, would be planted in the garden as well due to its many uses.

Bruschttee (Wintergreen), Gaultheria procumbens and Gehlwassergraut (Pipsissewa),Chimaphila umbellata

Native to North America, Europe, and Asia, *Bruschttee* grows in woodland and shady locations. It is a low-lying evergreen shrub, growing to between 6 and 8 inches. The *Chimaphila* variety has shiny, wedge-shaped leaves and small, flat-topped clusters of white flowers tinged with red, while the *Gaultheria* variety has leathery oval leaves with white or pink bell-shaped flowers and red fruit.

Taste: Bitter, sweet

Energy: Cool and dry

Parts used: *Chimaphila* variety: leaves; *Gaultheria* variety: leaves, fruit, essential oil

Harvest or gathering time: Summer

Properties: Anti-inflammatory, astringent, diuretic, tonic, vulnerary

Traditional Medicinal Uses

Heals wounds and sores. Treats urinary tract problems. Can be used in the treatments of gonorrhea and kidney stones. Also, by way of stimulating urinary flow, it can be beneficial in the treatment of rheumatism and gout. The essential oil can be used as a liniment or ointment for relief of inflamed, swollen, or sore muscles, ligaments, and joints. Leaves may be applied externally to rheumatic joints or muscles and to blisters and sores. Most commonly used as a tea. The berries can be used as a flavoring agent.

Cautions and Contraindications

Avoid long-term use. People with aspirin sensitivity should not use wintergreen internally. Children under the age of twelve should avoid using oil of wintergreen both internally and externally.

History, Folklore, Magic, and Other Interesting Tidbits

The name *wintergreen* has been used loosely to refer to several varieties of plants. Pipsissewa (*Chimaphila umbellata*) is one of the varieties often chosen. However, in the countryside, not much distinction was made, and the plants were used interchangeably. While not used medicinally, in *Deitsch* culture, the berries were used extensively as a flavoring agent, most commonly in the ice cream flavor teaberry. Historically, wintergreen leaves have been used as a substitute for tea, such as during the Revolutionary War.

Hollebeer (Black Elder), Sambucus nigra

Elder is a deciduous tree growing to 20 feet, with oval leaves, cream flowers, and blue-black berries. *Sambucus nigra* is native to Europe, and *Sambucus nigra* ssp. *canadensis* is the native American version. It is found in most temperate regions and is often cultivated. It is propagated from cuttings in the spring. Either species of elder is a staple in most *Urglaawe* gardens because it is sacred to the goddess Holle.

Taste: Flowers—sweet, berries—sweet/sour

Energy: Cool and dry

Parts used: Flowers and berries

Harvest or gathering time: Flowers when in full bloom (June and July); berries when ripe and dark purple, almost black (not red)

Properties: Flowers—diaphoretic, diuretic, anti-viral; berries—nutritive, anti-viral (more than the flowers), immunostimulant

Traditional Medicinal Uses

Flowers break fevers. They can also be used in facial preparations. Flowers are thought to remove freckles.

Berries are useful in treating cold and flu at the first signs as an anti-viral. Berries are rich in vitamin C and have been used in treating rheumatism and certain eruptive skin diseases, i.e., measles and chicken pox. They are mildly laxative and therefore can help with diarrhea. Ingested as a tea or elixir. The leaves are not to be ingested at all.

Cautions and Contraindications

Berries must be cooked before using. Fresh berries contain cyanide compounds in the seeds. Be sure to use only black berries, as some of the red varieties of the berries are poisonous to humans.

History, Folklore, Magic, and Other Interesting Tidbits

This herb has more folklore tied to it than most. Known as "the medicine chest of the country people." It is considered sacred to the ancient spiritual traditions of the Celtic, Germanic, and Norse peoples. Its branches were believed to house a tree spirit—an elder mother, or in Germanic lore: Fraa Holle, or Mother Holle. Thought to be a "threshold" tree, many cultures believed it could be a portal to other realms. Even today, within *Deitsch* lore, bad luck is said to befall anyone who burns elder wood.

Hundsholz (Dogwood), Cornus spp.

Hundsholz is a deciduous tree or shrub growing 10 to 30 feet tall. It has simple, untoothed leaves with curving veins, and its flowers are white (but sometimes pink) with four parts that develop in clusters. Fruit forms as drupes containing one to two seeds in bright pink to red. Indigenous to North America, the plant can be found from Ontario and Maine to Florida and Texas and Kansas in the west.

Taste: Sweet

Energy: Cool and dry

Parts used: Leaves, fruit, and bark

Harvest or gathering time: Summer

Properties: Antimicrobial, astringent, hepatic, emetic, stimulant

Traditional Medicinal Uses

Stimulates appetite. Useful for hemorrhoids and diarrhea. Reduces eczema. Good for the liver. Most commonly used as a decoction of the bark.

Cautions and Contraindications

None known but always be certain to identify species for which the berries are edible prior to consuming.

History, Folklore, Magic, and Other Interesting Tidbits

Known in *Deitsch* as *Hundsholz*. Shavings or cuttings can be used as protection amulets. The flowers are thought to break hexes. In the folk magic practice of *Braucherei*, there are *Verbots* (restrictions, literally "forbids") on using any part of the tree for decorative purposes or making offerings of it to ancestors (although offerings to deity are acceptable). One should leave the tree as intact as possible so it is available for medicinal purposes.

Talking to Plants: A Tradition

Es Blanzegschwetz means "to talk to plants" and is a common practice among many *Braucherei* practitioners. *Blanzegschwetz* practice comes from herbal lore, both medicinal and occult, and it helps deepen the connection and communication between the plants and practitioners. *Blanzegschwetz* is an element incorporated into general gardening practices such as weeding, selection of plant locations, companion planting, etc. There are rules, such as one should never harvest the largest, the smallest, or the first seen of any plant or herb. And never, ever should the originator plant, or *Grossmammi*, be uprooted.

It is common and encouraged to leave offerings in return for harvests taken. *Urglaawer* tend to keep beans on their person when it may be likely they could find themselves in a position to disturb the ground and need to leave an offering. It is both a practical folkway and an esoteric tradition.

Here is a simple plant spirit working for you to begin to develop a relationship with plants. It is useful as you begin this work. You will be touching a plant, so make sure whatever plant you eventually choose is clearly identifiable and is not poisonous.

Directions

First, go to a safe space to sit near or among plants. Walk around your property or a local park until you feel beckoned to a plant. Sit in front of that plant.

Let the descriptions and explanations flow to you in the manner of a child. Forget scientific labels. Use simple descriptors. Focus first on the color. What shade of green is it? Next, notice the shape of the leaves. How are they arranged along the stem? What is the shape of the stem? Its color? What is the color of the leaves? What is the texture of the leaves?

Now, touch the leaf and really feel it with your fingers. Let that sensation of touch fill you. Allow that sensation to be the only thing that you are experiencing.

Bend closer to the plant so that the leaf is near your nose. Let it brush against your skin, and sense how that feels.

Now breathe. Take in a long, slow breath as if you were taking in the subtle, deep scent of someone you love. Let that smell be all that exists in your awareness.

Time to write down your experience.

4

TOOLS OF THE URGLAAWER

There are no required tools for an *Urglaawer* beyond their own desire and intent to honor the deities. While the following are useful for personal practice and nice for group practice, nothing elaborate or expensive is ever needed. A personal working altar can be as simple as a windowsill with a deity picture and candle or as elaborate as a flower-filled table with embroidered cloths and statuary. Neither is better than the other. We are including this list as examples of what you might see on an *Urglaawe* altar if you are ever able to attend an event. There are *Urglaawe* groups across the country and internationally.

Group *Urglaawe* altars are usually very well decorated. The first act of any ceremony is for those present to place a wide array of flower and herb offerings on the altar for the deities of the day. A variety of statuary, steins, candles, a ceremonial bowl, and other offerings or decorations may be present on any *Urglaawer* altar. Although this is what we do in our group, your own needs, financial ability, or personal preference may have you doing something different. That is fine! We completely understand and welcome variety.

Kindred altar

Der Aldaar (Altar)

An *altar* is a temporary location to place items for ritual use. It is meant to be portable or removable. It is prepared each time it is used, unlike a shrine, which is set to a purpose and meant to represent that purpose all of the time. Your altar, therefore, can be a portable folding table, the top of a picnic table, a large rock near a creek, or a fallen tree in the woods. Always pack out what you pack in. Be mindful of any offering left behind. If it isn't organic, don't do it.

Personal altars are decorated as the practitioner desires, and each one will look different according to preference. They can be a small space on a dresser or an elaborate space in a shared living area. As with all aspects of *Urglaawe*, one can practice how they see fit in their own home, but when we come together, we share a common practice.

Private altar

Die Segezweig (Blessing Twig)

A *Segezweig* is chosen from either the altar decorations or from any nearby plant and used to sprinkle ritual participants with the blessed libation from a *Sege*. The *Segezweig* may also be used to draw a rune on the forehead of the participants with the libation or shake a libation at their feet.

Der Zauberzettel (Charm Ticket)

Der Zauber is a spell, a spoken charm, or an incantation. A *Zauberzettel* is a charm or spell that is written onto a piece of paper. The ticket may be used as a talisman that one wears or carries or as a stationary item to protect against negative energy. The most common use of *Zauberzettels* in *Braucherei* and *Hexerei* comes in the form of house blessings, where they are tucked away in windowsills, doors, chimney flues, and any other openings to the outside. These openings include water pipes: The *Zauberzettel* is placed behind the pipe on the inside of the house before the point at which the water opens into a sink or a toilet. Adhesive tape may be used to keep the *Zauberzettel* in place, but it is never to be affixed using any metal, such as a paper clip.

Die Waerrickgawwel (Distaff, Spindle)

With several spindle goddesses in our pantheon, the distaff and the spindle are very sacred, but they are most closely identified with Freid. The spindle is one of the tools used to hallow an altar, particularly for the *Entschtanning* ritual.

Der Hammer (Hammer)

A hammer is the primary tool used to hallow the altar along with a sickle or other tool appropriate to the deity or celebration in question.

Es Hexeschild (Hex Sign)

Hex signs are among the most recognizable forms of *Deitsch* art. In the current era, academics have encouraged the signs to be referred to as *barn stars* or *Scheierschtanne*. Despite the advocacy of the new terminology, though, the use of the term *hex sign* persists, and the historic association between these symbols and the concepts of protection from witchcraft and negative energy persist. While most *Deitsche* believe that the symbols have always had meaning, the academic convention is that the meaning of the signs would be established by the creator of the art rather than by the viewer of the symbol. This has led to some believing that the signs and symbols were merely decorations as opposed to being sacred sigils carried down from antiquity. However, the symbols also appear in many unexpected places, such as carved onto gravestones, drawn on birth certificates and wedding announcements, and even in advertising. As such, many *Deitsche* believe that the symbols are part of our heritage and of our collective unconscious. Hex sign symbols are resurging in frequency and in importance within *Urglaawe* communities. This revival is resulting in an increasing accessibility to the creators' purposes and intentions. While we cannot always be certain of the intentions behind the hex sign creations of the past, we can have better insight going forward and can construct new ways to use them.

Es Drankopfer (Libation)

These are the blessed beverages consumed in ritual and offered to the deities. Typical libations include mead, wine, beer, apple cider or juice, hard cider, various herbal teas, or even water in a pinch. There is always a nonalcoholic option, and if there is only one choice available, it will be nonalcoholic to respect those who do not partake.

Der Eedring (Oath Ring)

Der Eedring is a ring of wood or metal that all *Urglaawer* use to take oaths upon. Not every group will have *der Eedring*, as oaths are not taken in a *Freibesatz*, or freehold. While oaths may not be an every-gathering occurrence, the oath ring will always appear on the altar as a reminder of any oaths already taken. Oaths are very serious and should not be taken lightly.

Es Opfer (Offering)

Es Opfer is an offering made to any entity or deity. An offering is usually placed on the altar by the participant at a specific time during the ritual. Many different types of offerings are given, ranging from food or drink to handmade creations or found natural items like stones or sticks. The offerings are poured into the ground or burned as is appropriate.

Die Roon (Runes)

Runes are letters of an ancient Germanic alphabet. It is often argued by rune enthusiasts that they were never used for magical purposes, but we would challenge that insofar as we have been using them in this manner for a minimum of fifty years and more likely a couple hundred. If we continue to use them for divination and write down our experiences, in another couple hundred years, our own future generations will have far more information than we were able to find in our lifetimes. We are future ancestors; let's leave our next generations more stepping stones to this information.

The runes are not only used for divination, but they are also used in ritual. Intonation of the runes' sounds helps to set the mood of the ritual, and the runes are used to bless the participants at the end of the *Sege* round. Even when not used for divination purposes, many *Urglaawer* use them for meditation, artwork, healing, and spellwork.

Die Sichel (Sickle)

Urglaawe's official symbol is the sickle. The focus of *Urglaawe* is agricultural rather than warrior based. Most people are not directly tied to the land any longer. The connection between seasons and weather and what is or is not available to eat regionally at any given point is knowledge lost by younger generations. The farmer's tools in our ancestors' past were tied both to working the land and protecting it. The sickle, as with most agrarian tools, can serve double duty as a tool of life and an instrument of death. In our rites, it is used to hallow the altar.

Der Getz/Die Getze (Statuary)

Deity representation on the altar can range from looking quite like the deity to more abstract depictions or even everyday objects used to represent the deities of the day. The presence of *Getze* on *Urglaawe* altars is extremely common. We want to stress that a *Getz* is a representation of a deity and that while a deity may occupy a *Getz* during a ritual, the *Getz* itself is not a deity. *Getze* serve as the focal point of the invocations and are treated with great respect since a deity may choose to reside there during ritual. We want to remind you, though, that we are honoring the deity we are calling, not the statuary itself.

Ser Seidel (Stein)

Due to cultural influence, many *Urglaawer* use a stein rather than the horn our Ásatrú or other Heathen counterparts use. While the stein used to be shared as a form of community building, more *Urglaawers* are finding their own smaller steins to use since the COVID pandemic in 2020 in an effort to minimize disposable cups. Regardless of the vessel, the stein and more so its contents are blessed and on the altar, and all other vessels are filled by this one. Again, there is always an alcoholic and nonalcoholic option available, and if we only have one choice, it will usually be of the nonalcoholic variety so that everyone can partake.

Der Dreifuuss (Trivet)

The trivet you will see on an altar is usually the iron one with feet. The trivet represents the hearth on an altar.

We just described many of the tools that you may see on an *Urglaawe* altar. We want to emphasize that if you are starting a practice at home, you do not need fancy tools or expensive items. These things can be gathered over time. Use what you have available to you when starting out. If you only have a sickle or hammer pendant, it will work just as well until you can find other options. If you are starting a practice with others, combining efforts definitely helps.

5

RUNES

The runes are an ancient alphabet, each one representing a vowel or a consonant sound. They were used to write in Germanic languages before the Latin alphabet was adopted, and, afterward, they were used for other purposes, such as religious associations and divination.

The runes turn up in *Deitsch* lore in a few ways, including in artwork and in *Braucherei* and *Hexerei* work. The system was not passed down intact, but we do have letter names, letter shapes, and some sound values that are seemingly unique to our culture. The artwork and hex sign symbols are believed, fairly widely, to have emerged organically from ancient times.

We have no idea how long they have been used by *Deitsch* folks, so we do not claim what we have to be of antiquity. Perhaps someone studied the runes several generations ago and then introduced them to the practices. It matters little if they were used all along or came back into use later; we use them now and continue to do so with great success.

Runes

Basic Rune Meanings

All runes have an upright, or *rechtdaub*, meaning and a reversed, or *driebdaub*, meaning. *Rechtdaub* is the standard upright appearance, and *driebdaub* is the upside-down presentation of the rune. In this case, we consider "upside-down" to be when the rune is sideways rather than flipped completely over.

Some runes, such as *Gewwe* and *Engel*, might be drawn in a way that makes it difficult to distinguish between *rechtdaub* and *driebdaub*. If a *Gewwe* is drawn similar to a capital *X* so that it has more height than width in *rechtdaub*, then the *driebdaub* would have more width than height, like a capital *X* on its side. If a *Gewwe* rune is drawn so that its height and width are the same in *rechtdaub*, then the *driebdaub* would be resting on one foot in a manner similar to a + sign. *Engel* is usually drawn with equal or nearly equal height and width. In that case, *Engel* in *rechtdaub* stands on one of its points, and most people would describe the shape as a diamond. In *driebdaub*, *Engel* rests on one of its sides, and most people would call it a square. If an *Engel* has more height than width in *rechtdaub*, it would rest on one foot, and most people would call it a diamond. In *driebdaub*, it would rest on one of its sides and would have more width than height. Most people would describe it as a rectangle.

There is much information about using the runes, and we could write an entire book just about that! Since we hope to one day write that book, we will just show the names of the runes and a few keywords for each, which can be used for divination, meditation, or creating bindrunes. We also describe how we use them in the rotation of runes through the annual cycle.

ᚠ

Vieh

Pronunciation: FEE

Rechtdaub: Literally translates to "cattle." Portable wealth, prosperity, success

Driebdaub: A block in the ability to achieve or hold on to wealth, loss of wealth

Deity association: Fro

ᚢ

Ur

Pronunciation: OOR

Rechtdaub: Strength, wild power, courage

Driebdaub: Run down, overwhelmed

Deity association: Holler

ᚦ

Dunner

Pronunciation: DOO-nah

Rechtdaub: Conflict, defense, reactive force

Driebdaub: Being prepared, proactive defense

Deity association: Dunner

Antwatt

Pronunciation: AHN-twaht

Rechtdaub: Translates to "answer," messages

Driebdaub: Not listening, ignoring messages

Deity association: Wudan

Reit

Pronunciation: RITE

Rechtdaub: Literally means "ride" and refers to any type of journey either physical or trance work, the journey of life

Driebdaub: Possible bumpy journey, unable to progress

Deity association: Schlumm

Kerze

Pronunciation: KAR-zuh

Rechtdaub: Means "candle" or "flashlight," controlled fire, spark of inspiration, life-force energy within the self

Driebdaub: Being in darkness without light, losing one's spark

Deity association: Zisa

Gewwe

Pronunciation: GAY-veh

Rechtdaub: To give, exchange, gift for a gift, compensation

Driebdaub: A broken gifting cycle, giving too much of one's self or too little

Deity association: Weisskeppichi Frau

Winsch

Pronunciation: VINCH

Rechtdaub: "Wish," joy, optimism, links and bonds among family and friends

Driebdaub: Alienation, deception

Deity associations: Wudan, Holler, Fro, Frouwa

Haagel

Pronunciation: HAW-gl

Rechtdaub: "Hail," major changes (good, bad, or neutral); protection; transformation; often forces are out of our control

Driebdaub: Indication to look around before you are swept away by the hailstorm without warning

Deity association: Holle

Not

Pronunciation: NOTE

Rechtdaub: Need, distress, suffering, but also creativity resulting from conflict

Driebdaub: Beginning to get needs met

Deity associations: Many

Eisich

Pronunciation: EYE-zich

Rechtdaub: Ice, icy, stillness, slow down

Driebdaub: The release of whatever is holding you back or keeping you frozen

Deity association: No specific deity

Yaahr

Pronunciation: YORE

Rechtdaub: Year, cycles, progress

Driebdaub: Going in the wrong direction

Deity associations: Freid, Holle

Eiwe

Pronunciation: EYE-veh

Rechtdaub: "Yew," serpent energies, tree of life, fight fire with fire, strength, and support

Driebdaub: Overthinking, toxicity

Deity association: No specific deity

Peil

Pronunciation: PILE

Rechtdaub: "Arrow," bolt (of lightning), hand on a clock, *Urleeg*, mystery, luck, the unmanifest

Driebdaub: Planning, getting ready

Deity association: No specific deity

Schild

Pronunciation: SHILLD

Rechtdaub: "Shield," protection, safety, awareness, alertness, vigilance

Driebdaub: Exposed, unprotected, jeopardy, hypervigilance

Deity association: Ziu

Sunne

Pronunciation: SOO-neh

Rechtdaub: "Sun," victory, wholeness, guidance, mastery, hope, honor, hitting the mark

Driebdaub: Delusion, false hope, gullibility, hopelessness, missing the mark

Deity association: Sunna

Tuisko

Pronunciation: TWEE-sco

Rechtdaub: Justice, right action, rationality, law, fairness, peacekeeping, clear path, sacrifice, personal or community struggle for just cause.

Driebdaub: Injustice, wrong action, lawlessness, lost causes, irrationality, sacrifice for the wrong reasons or to no avail.

Deity associations: Tuisko, Ziu, Zisa

Baerke

Pronunciation: BEAR-kuh

Rechtdaub: "Birch," birth, rebirth, becoming, life changes (life or death), liberation, sanctity, shelter, the "now," concealment, protection, mental stability

Driebdaub: Lingering, delaying, captivity, exposure, loss of control, mental instability, addiction

Deity associations: Berchta, Freid, lesser association with Holle

Hengscht

Pronunciation: HENG-scht

Rechtdaub: "Stallion," "steed," companion relationships, trust, teamwork, animals, love, partnership, amity

Driebdaub: Duplicity, mistrust, betrayals, nightmares, enmity

Deity association: Alcis

Mann

Pronunciation: MAAHN

Rechtdaub: Evolution of human consciousness, the perfected human, "one" as in an individual

Driebdaub: Resistance to progress and self-improvement

Deity association: Wudan

Loch

Pronunciation: LOK (rhymes with yolk)

Rechtdaub: "Hole," collective unconscious, mirrors, depth of the self

Driebdaub: Depression

Deity association: Schlumm

Engel

Pronunciation: AY-ngl (like the ng in singer not the ng in finger)

Rechtdaub: Fertility, potential

Driebdaub: Barrenness

Deity associations: Fro, Ing

Daag

Pronunciation: DAWG

Rechtdaub: "Day," daybreak, eureka moments

Driebdaub: Confusion, muddled thoughts

Deity association: Helling

Ochdem

Pronunciation: OKH-doom

Rechtdaub: "Breath," wealth that is not easily transferred, family, clan, tribe, nation, humanity

Driebdaub: Isolation

Deity association: Wudan

Now that you have seen all the runes, you can begin learning about them more deeply by perhaps pulling a rune a day. If you pull a rune at the beginning of your day, you can see what the day may be bringing. If you pull the rune at the end of your day, you can see what lesson or message you can take away from your experiences that day. By writing them down, you can see any patterns that may develop.

You can also bring the energy of each rune into your life by keeping it on you during the day. You can carry a rune stone or wood disc or wear a piece of jewelry with the rune on it. There are many ways to bring the runes into your daily practice. Experiment!

Rotation of Runes

One feature at many *Urglaawe* rituals is the presence of colored flags. They each have certain runes and are placed around the sacred space. These flag colors represent the progression of the individual through life, death, and rebirth, and are derived from *Braucherei* funerary rites. *Urglaawe* adds runes to the flags that are consistent with the meaning of each flag. Here are the colors and the seasonal movement of these flags.

White

This color represents the rebirth of the newly integrated soul within a new physical form. The rune associated with this time is *Engel*, which stands for the manifestation of the new soul structure from the remnants of the old soul construct. Considering *Frofescht* as the beginning of our spiritual year, this flag would start in the north at that celebration.

Red

This red is a blood red, and it represents the journey through life, from birth to adulthood to the point of death. It is accompanied by the *Reit* rune.

Green

This color represents the moment of death and the commending of the body back to nature. This flag bears the *Yuuhr* rune, which reflects the cycles, spirals, and helixes that we experience as we move from life to life.

Black

Black represents the time between lives after passing through the Mill. It is a time of mystery, and it is a time that we do not usually remember once reborn. The rune associated with the black flag is *Kerze*, for it represents the self moving through the darkness in between lives.

Purple

To the north, just beyond the circle formed by the placement of the four aforementioned flags, stands a purple flag bearing the *Mann* rune. The color and the rune each bear similar meaning: the pursuit toward self-actualization and the perfected human. The human life wave is still far from reaching this goal, but there is value and purpose in the pursuit of it.

Flag Rotation

On *Zwelfder Daag*, the Twelfth Day of *Yuul* (January 1), at sunset, *Noochyuul* ("After-Yule") begins and continues until *Grundsaudaag*. This is the time that *Urglaawer* "reset" the cycle of the flags to represent the progress of the soul, using the *Yaahrsraad*, or Wheel of the Year, as a reference point. The flags form a compass, with the current "season" of the year being in the north.

At sunset on January 1, this is how the rotating flags would stand

North: White

West: Red

South: Green

East: Black

The flags rotate as described here in a clockwise direction at the following times:

Oschdresege, Spring Equinox

Red moves to the north to represent the soul in the physical body throughout the life of the physical body.

Green moves to the west.

Black moves to the south.

White moves to the east.

We continue to use the *Yaahrsraad* as an allegory for the progress of the soul, so red stays in the north for all of the holidays in which we observe the progress, growth, and change of the physical body.

Hoietfescht

This is the festival of the *Hoiet*, or the haymaking. Different crops are cut for hay at different times throughout the year, and weather and soil conditions can affect when a given crop is ready to be cut. The rule of thumb is that cereal crops should be cut in the "late boot stage," which is the time when the seed head is about to emerge—but has not yet done so—from the leaf sheath. As such, there are actually many haymaking times.

Three crops, though, appear to have set the default timing of the general *Hoiet* observances. Winter wheat is first cut in early May, and the cutting continues through the summer; in Pennsylvania, the crop is most often cut between July 5 and August 10. Spring wheat is typically harvested in Pennsylvania beginning in early August. Flax is sometimes harvested in early July or even in June in Pennsylvania, but the most common time is the last two weeks in July.

The influence of these haymaking harvests has set the general *Hoiet* observance within the *Deitsch* culture to the last two weeks of July and the first two weeks of August. The *Urglaawe* ritual observance of *Hoietfescht* in the Northern Hemisphere typically falls on the last Saturday in July or the first Saturday in August. *Urglaawe* groups outside of Pennsylvania can adjust the timing of the observance to coincide with the major crops of their region. In Australia, for example, this observance would fall by default in February, with different regions of the hemisphere taking crop conditions and hardiness zones into account for the timing of their observances.

Green flag moves to north to represent the harvest, the decline of the body, the transition, and the return to nature.

Black flag moves to the west.

White flag moves to the south.

Red flag moves to the east.

Allelieweziel, October 30

Black flag moves to the north to represent the passing through the Mill and the crushing and "death" of the soul construct.

White flag moves to the west.

Red flag moves to the south.

Green flag moves to the east.

Then, again, on January 2, the pattern repeats, starting with white in the north.

Note: Purple remains to the far north at all times throughout the year.

Runes are used in *Urglaawe* for meditation, prayer, journeying, and in many other ways that expand beyond the reach of this book. Many *Urglaawer* never move beyond the way the runes are used in ritual when gathered with others. Some use them as their main form of divination, others use them as magical bindrunes in energetic workings, and still others embroider them on clothing or charms. The applications are endless.

6

WHEEL OF THE YEAR

The *Urglaawe* Wheel of the Year is our calendar. The term in *Deitsch* is *Yaahrsraad.* In *Urglaawe,* we recognize both seasonal and cultural observances. This chapter isn't exhaustive, and practices may vary depending on how the seasons fall where you live. We encourage aligning your practice with the seasonal changes in your own area. Many of our festivals are twelve days long with observances on different days throughout that festival. Those will be explained soon.

Our observances revolve around the seasons with an emphasis on the agrarian cycles of our forebears. With each worldly reflection, there is a focus on more internal matters as well. Each person should use each observance to acknowledge the impact and reflect on the implications of the corresponding season and all that goes with it. Additionally, it is also a good time to check in with our own personal development spiritually, mentally, and physically.

It should also be noted that the observances as described herein are naturally set against the climate of the *Deitscherei* in the Northern Hemisphere. If you find yourself called to *Urglaawe* and its deities and reside in the Southern Hemisphere, simply adjust the observances by six months in order to coincide with the seasons where you live. Additionally, if you live in a different regional climate—for example, the Southwest of the United States—feel free to make adjustments to your practice to accommodate the nature and plant spirits of your region. In fact, *Urglaawer* in California have developed their own ways to celebrate some of our observances, especially when the diverse growing seasons do not align.

In the *Deitscherei* itself, the USDA hardiness zones seem to be more of a guideline than a hard rule these days. Microclimates and the changing macroclimate mean that, as *Urglaawer*, being attentive to our own personal landscapes is key. Many places still celebrate local harvest festivals at the traditional harvest times, but your harvest may vary. Just because the autumn equinox falls around September 21 every year does not mean that autumn happens on that date in your location. Being attentive to these shifts, and the shifts of the local plant spirits, can make a huge difference in your harvests, whether they be emotional growth or plant-based food. Any recipes shared are either created by us or from our own families, often handed down for generations.

Urglaawe inherited some of the most basic aspects of its calendar from *Braucherei*, including the understanding that the *Yaahrsraad* operates on a tilt; this tilt means that there are multiple "beginnings" to a year, each of which depends on the context in which it is considered. First, there is the "new sun" idea, which begins at *Yuul*. Second is the New Year on the common social and commercial calendar, which begins at the stroke of midnight on January 1. Finally, there is the onset of the new spiritual year, which is the sunset prior to the spring equinox, which can fall on March 19, 20, or 21, depending on the year. This is the time that *Urglaawer* use to begin the year ritually and where we will begin our journey together.

The festivals are as follows:

March: *Oschdresege*

April: *Ziegdaag, Hexenacht/Wonnenacht*

May: *Wonnezeit, Der Grieg Geeich die Reifries*

June: Observance of the Desecrated Shrines, *Summeraafang, Dingsege*

July/August: *Hoietfescht*

September: *Erntfescht, Zisasege*

October: *Allelieweziel*

November: *Ewicher Yeeger/Hollersege, Die Verschimpfing Geeich der Reifkeenich*

December: *Voryuul/Lutzelfraalaaf; Yuulzeit: Yuulsege, Berchtaslaaf*

January: *Yuulzeit* ends/*Frofescht*

February: *Entschtanning, Grundsaudaag, Lichderfescht*

March: *Grumbieredaag/Frouwasege*

Die Oschdre: The Beginning of Spring

The majority of American Easter traditions are directly handed down from *Deitsch* culture. Alfred L. Shoemaker's book *Eastertide in Pennsylvania* provides a great resource for further information and reading on that matter. For *Urglaawer* specifically, the vernal equinox marks our spiritual new year. We celebrate the birth and rebirth of all things. We revel in the joy of color returning to the landscape. This is the time of year we honor our relationships with the animals in our lives, be it our companion animals or those that ultimately sustain us. Hares and eggs, both symbolic of fertility, are sacred to the goddess Oschdra. Her myth goes like this:

> Three sisters, Helling, Nacht, and Oschdra, gathered together at a point on the world they called east. Each sister wore a cloak of transformative power. Helling wore a cloak of light; Nacht, a cloak of darkness; and Oschdra wore a cloak that could not be seen. They decided to meet at this moment because they were bored with the blandness of existence and wished to make it all appear more interesting and exciting.
>
> Nacht stepped forward first, and as she did so, her cloak covered the world and everything beneath her and it became black. Oschdra, seeing what happened when her sister progressed, moved forward next, only Oschdra's cloak seemingly had no effect on the world below. Next, Helling walked forward, and as she did, the world below her and her cloak was cast in white. Most amazingly, as Helling's white touched Nacht's black under where Oschdra stood, Oschdra's cloak and everything below her transformed and could now be seen in a new shade she called "gray."

Oschdra then called upon a pair of finches named Distelfresser and Himmelflucht to fly from her right hand, a place she called north, to her left hand, a place she called south. As they made their flight, everything in their path would be washed in gray. Distelfresser and Himmelflucht agreed but asked Oschdra to grant them a simple request: Himmelflucht's eggs shall also be gray so that she could see them regardless of Helling or Nacht being above them. Oschdra happily granted their request, and the finches began their flight.

The three sisters continued their walk around the world—Nacht providing the black hue, Helling the white, and Oschdra the gray. After nine days, Oschdra became restless once again. She was unhappy that she could only create a tint on the world by standing between her sisters. She wanted to provide her very own hue. She looked upon her cloak and closed her eyes. She imagined one side of the cloak afire with a varied warm glow, and she called it red, orange, and yellow. She imagined the other side luminescent with a cool iridescence, and she called it green, blue, and violet.

Oschdra opened her eyes, and now her cloak bore all these hues, which she called *Farewe*, but in her own tongue. Now, as Oschdra walked from the east to the west, the skies radiated with the new colors. Her sisters saw the change, and they admired Oschdra's craft.

Together, the three sisters of the east, thenceforth known as the Oschdre, decided to do more. Helling added white to the colors and Nacht added black. Oschdra's palette grew, and the sisters loved their work. The colors appeared in the sky but not elsewhere in the world. Oschdra and her sisters wished for the whole world to emerge with the colors of their work, so they sought the assistance of the most prolific of the animal world to help them with their work. They found Haas and asked him to transform the world wherever his tail went by saturating everything in its path with the colors of the ladies' craft. Haas agreed but asked in return that all of his descendants would inherit his role as the bearer of color.

The Oschdre sisters agreed. While Helling and Nacht stood opposite one another, Oschdra sent Haas forth. Haas was directed to begin at the nest of the finches, who, having completed their journey, were now flying south to north. Oschdra declared to Himmelflucht, "With Haas's colors, your eggs will always be in your sight."

Just as Haas painted the last of the eggs, Distelfresser landed in the nest to check on them, and he was pleased. Haas's tail brushed against him as Haas was leaving, and Distelfresser's plumage transformed to vibrant yellow, blue, green, and red.

Haas continued on his way, and to this day, wherever Haas goes, color follows his tail.

Basic Information

Date: Vernal equinox

Observance: *Oschdresege* on the vernal equinox

Honored deities: Helling, Nacht, Oschdra

Runes: *Sunne, Yaahr, Daag, Not*

Tool: Paintbrushes

Colors: All (especially bright) colors

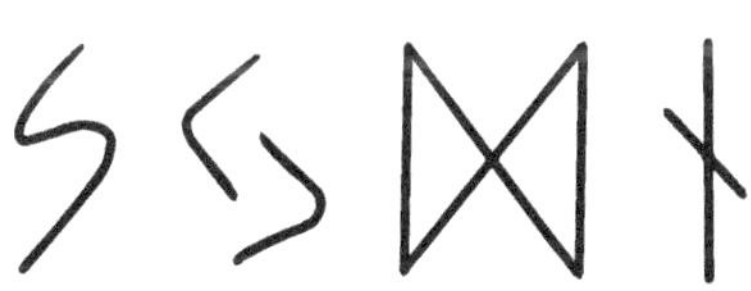

Oschdre runes

Common Foods

Common foods for this holiday include early greens like asparagus, kale, radishes, and spring onions, egg dishes, saffron bread, and dandelion wine.

RECIPE

Dandelion Greens with Hot Bacon Dressing

This is a very common salad and dressing combination in the *Deitscherei.*

Ingredients

Fresh young dandelion greens

6 slices bacon

½ cup cream

2 tablespoons butter

2 eggs

4 tablespoons vinegar (white or apple cider vinegar)

4 tablespoons sugar

Salt and pepper to taste

½ teaspoon paprika

Directions

Pick and wash a large bowl of young dandelion leaves. Wash thoroughly and pat dry. Place back into the bowl. Cut bacon into small pieces and cook until crisp. Use a slotted spoon to remove from the pan and set aside on paper towels. Pour the hot bacon grease over the dandelion greens and return pan to the stove. Add the cream and butter to the pan and melt over low heat. Beat eggs with the vinegar, salt, pepper, sugar, and paprika and then add to the pan. Mix thoroughly and pour over the dandelion greens. Stir well and serve.

Oschdre Activity: Decorating Eggs

Use store-bought kits, or if you are adventurous, dye them using natural methods. The process of using organic materials to dye eggs is as much a science experiment as it is an art form. Part of the fun is finding items that will work when coloring eggs. The following is a guideline, and you should feel free to find other natural ingredients for discovering your own colors! Approximate measurements of material per cup of water:

- 1 cup chopped purple cabbage for blue-green
- 1 cup red or yellow onion skins for rust or orange
- 1 cup shredded beets for pink or red
- 3 tablespoons ground turmeric for yellow
- 2 tablespoons dried hibiscus flowers for pink or red
- 2 sliced large carrots for orange
- 2 cups spinach or 1 bunch parsley for green
- 2 cups strong-brewed coffee for brown

Add one tablespoon of white vinegar to every cup of strained dye liquid.

Place the prepared dye material in a saucepan with the water and bring to a boil, then simmer covered for at least 30 minutes. Strain the liquid through a fine mesh strainer or cheesecloth into a bowl or cup deep enough that the egg will be completely covered with the dye. Mix in the vinegar and let cool to room temperature. Adding eggs to hot liquid will cook them further, and we don't want that! Transfer the eggs in the dye to the refrigerator and chill until the desired color is reached. Colors intensify if they sit for an hour or more. Take them out and let them dry to see how deep your colors are. If needed or desired, dip them again.

Ideas for the Solitary Practitioner

Decorate or dye eggs as described above. Use a clear-wax, food grade crayon on the eggs to draw runes or other symbols that represent rebirth and the return of spring.

Der Ziegdaag: Moving Day—Transformation

Ziegdaag in Pennsylvania Dutch literally means "moving day" and was (and still is, to a drastically reduced level) the day when tenant farmers moved to their new locations in a flurry of activity called a "flitting." *Urglaawe* is the repurposing of this existing event and placing it into the context of change and transformation.

This observance is inspired by the imperfect characters in Germanic and other central European folklore: those who have suffered, those who have made mistakes but have grown from them, those who struggle to find themselves, those who live in the margins of society, those who have to shift their shape in order to move about safely, and those who cast off the burdens of the past to become the people they want to be.

It is about growth and change of all kinds: good and bad. It is about recognizing when it's time to move on and when it's time to fight (it's time to fight!). It is about one's wit, one's ability to survive, and learning to adapt. It is about maturing, evolving, coming out, adopting new names, moving away from toxicity, and self-empowerment.

This is the time of year to recognize the importance that transformation plays in our lives. It's a time to honor all nonbinary energies and entities. We also use this time to acknowledge that even those characters one may consider shady, shifty, or chaotic have contributions to society at large. It is a time to remember that one should not take themselves or life itself too seriously. Learning to explore areas of life outside of what is considered "normal" in today's society expands our minds and allows our consciousness to continue to evolve. It pushes us to try new things and thwarts stagnation. Even if we find that we prefer the comfort of our known world, having an open mind and discovering all the nuances of life affords us the knowledge that we are more alike than different.

Basic Information

Date: April 1

Observance: *Ziegdaag* on April 1

Honored beings: Rips (Riewezaahl), Schlumm, Schaade, the Elbedritsch, es Buckliches Mannli

Runes: None specific for this rite

Tools: None specified

Colors: Bright and neon colors, shades of gray

Common Foods

Common foods for *der Ziegdaag* include bread, cheese, peas, and turnips.

RECIPE

Split Pea Soup

Usually made after cooking a ham, this pea soup is rich and filling!

Ingredients

1 large onion

2 tablespoons oil

3 quarts water

1 pound bag split peas

2 carrots, sliced

1 ham bone

Salt and pepper to taste

Directions

Chop onion and add with oil to bottom of large pot to cook until translucent. Add water, split peas, sliced carrots, and ham bone to the pot and simmer for 3 hours until soup is thick. Remove ham bone and run an immersion blender through the soup to the thickness you prefer. Pick over the bone and add the ham back into the soup and stir. Add salt and pepper to taste and serve.

Ziegdaag Activity: Creating a Shrine

A shrine is like an altar, but it is dedicated to a particular person, deity, or other entity or energy, and it is left up as opposed to being taken down after each use. For this ritual, create a shrine or devotional to your nonbinary forebearers, blood or otherwise. Find a special shelf or space somewhere and gather pictures or symbols of those forebearers you wish to honor. This can include family, friends, or other people that moved you in some way. Cover it with a special handkerchief or other cloth and place items on it that evoke feelings of your forebearers. You can include small flags, pins, flowers, drinks, or any special item that connects you to them.

Ideas for the Solitary Practitioner

Since this observance is all about challenging the status quo and avoiding stagnation, try something new! This could look as simple as going to a movie or lunch by yourself or as complicated as hiking the Appalachian trail or skydiving. Pushing ourselves out of our comfort zone allows us to grow and progress in many ways.

Die Wonnezeit: Time of Joy

This is a twelve-day celebration of the end of the Wild Hunt, marking the goddess Holle's return to our realm. It begins with *Hexenacht*, or Witches' Night, at sunset on April 30; this night is also sometimes called *Wonnenacht*, or the Night of Joy. This is the start of the light half of the year. Spring cleaning must be completed by *Hexenacht* or an offering left for Holle for areas unfinished. She, upon her return from the Hunt, will inspect the homes of her dedicants for tidiness. It is customary to leave windows and doors open (as much as safely and comfortably possible) to allow her and her entourage to pass through the home. This celebration ends with *der Grieg Geeich die Reifries* (the Battle Against the Frost Giants) where Dunner trains all of the activated *Butzemenner* to fight off the frost giants who are trying to thwart the return of the warmth.

This following myth is a product of Robert L. Schreiwer's Folklore Research Project and represents tales and fragments of tales related principally by folks who identified themselves as practitioners of *Hexerei* and *Braucherei*. Some segments of the story were also known to individuals outside of the practices. The term *Wonnenacht* has been seldom used historically, but it has become the principal term for *Walpurgisnacht* in *Urglaawe*. The term *Wonnedanz* ("Dance of Joy") was related by a *Hex* from Montour County, PA, and is a replacement for *Hexedanz* (Witches' Dance), and *Wonnezeit* ("Time of Joy") describes the twelve-day observance.

Wonnezeit represents the transition from the *Dunkelheft* (dark half of the year) to the *Brechtheft* (bright half), and the observance welcomes Holle upon her return from the Wild Hunt.

HEXENACHT AND THE WONNEDANZ

As Sunna's kiss brought increasing warmth and light to the *Hatzholz* (heartwood; the physical realm), Holle sent for her ever-loyal servant, Gedreier Eckhart, whose job it was to walk ahead of the Parade of Spirits to warn the living of the fury behind him. Eckhart's love for Holle is as great in death as it was in life, so he flew into the midst of the host, finding the goddess dressed in white and seated in a wagon being pulled by the souls of nine bulls. The wagon rolled on three great spinning wheels. From each wheel spun a multicolored thread that wove with the thread from the others, forming a sack of infinite size named *Immerraum* ("always-room"). The thunderous voices of many found spirits within the sack resounded across the realms.

"I have filled the sack that cannot be filled, and it is time to bring them home," Holle said. "Go forth to *Mannheem* and tell the living that they may welcome the host and that they should be prepared for the visit. Those who remembered and honored my word will be rewarded. After the visit, they are to light two fires and to pass between them. Through that action, they will be renewed. Then you are to go to the *Mannheem* field, where you will find a lone linden tree under which you may rest until I arrive."

As Eckhart began his journey into the *Hatzholz*, announcing the return of the Great Lady, Holle took her mighty sickle and cut each of the three threads, using the end of the strands to tie the sack shut.

The host crossed from the eastern leaves, or *Oschtbledder*, into the *Hatzholz*. Throngs of people, though scared at first, came out to welcome the parade, honoring the arrival of the wondrous lady. The clamor of spirits filled the high skies as Holle entered *Mannheem*. The bulls pulled her wagon through open windows and doors, seeking those who welcomed her. The orderly homes served as a sign that her command was obeyed. She filled the homes with bright light that brought such joy to the residents that they broke out in song and dance.

Presently the wagon approached the *Mannheem* field called *Hexefeld*, where Holle found Eckhart sleeping within the bark of a linden tree. She sent the southwest wind, Riffel, to awaken him. She instructed Eckhart to lead the host to *Hexefeld* and, upon arrival, to cut loose the spirits in the sack. "It is time to meet my sister," she stated.

Eckhart did as he was told. As the host of the cosmic spirits approached the field, Eckhart saw another parade descending from the clouds, emerging from the forests, and coming from the soil. Ahead of this parade was a brilliant gray light radiating from a beautiful elderly woman who was also dressed in white. Eckhart approached the woman, recognizing her as Berchta, and he bowed before her. He then took the lead through the countryside as the two parades merged together and drew closer to the linden tree where Holle awaited them.

A hush fell upon the host as the two sisters greeted one another. They embraced, and they began to spin in a dance. The dance spun gentle whirlwinds that touched the host, bringing warmth and joy to the spirits of the host, and they, too, began to dance. Some gathered strands and dust from the sack, streaming the strands around trees and scattering the dust on the ground.

The sisters continued to dance with the host dancing behind them, moving from the field and over the rivers and lakes. Every being in the water began to dance for joy. The whirlwinds spawned gentle rains that awakened the spirits in the sleeping plants, and they, too, began to dance for joy.

The dance moved to the foothills, where the frost giants had taken refuge from Sunna's breath. As the host approached, the winter vanished, forcing the frost giants to retreat.

On the twelfth day, Holle instructed Eckhart to sleep in a rock at the base of a mountain pillar while the dance continued up a ridge called *Hexenkopf*. The entourage eventually stopped by a marshy wellspring near the top. The two sisters took rest by the wellspring, and the spirits began to feel drawn to its depths.

Holle and Berchta commanded the host to continue their journey to its end by Holle's home.

Holle led one half of the parade to an elder bush, the roots of which reached beyond the *Hatzholz* and into the dark realms, taking nourishment from three creeks named *Schprudlendi*, *Gwellendi*, and

Fliessendi. Berchta led the other half to the depths of the wellspring, which emptied into the same creeks.

The spirits followed the goddesses into these creeks and surfaced in Holle's meadow, named *Bollwies* (flax meadow), in the *Dunkelgegend*. The spirits followed the goddesses through some woods, passing Holle's home, *es Heisli*. They soon entered an open field called *Weiwerfeld* and soon approached her Mill.

Holle unhitched the bulls from her wagon and yoked them to a giant millstone named *Seelbreecher* ("Soul Breaker"). Behind Berchta, the spirits lined up and entered the Mill, where they would be split apart, never to return in their present form. Holle returned to the joyous *Mannheem*, taking her seat upon the *Hexenkopf* pillar while Eckhart slept in a rock.

On the other end of the Mill, the kernel of the selves of each soul emerged behind Berchta, who then led them up the world tree to the *Unnergegend*. There they take full form and await their return to the living realms.

Der Grieg Geeich die Reifries

Thus, the bright half of the year began, and order was restored to *Mannheem*. *Der Reifkeenich* ("King Frost"), fearful of losing his grip on the valuable realm, sent his armies to attack. *Urglaawe* tradition, based on stories from *Braucherei* lore, holds that, beginning at sunset on May 12 (which is 13. *Wonnet* on the *Urglaawe* calendar), three *Reifries*, or frost giants, and their armies begin to attack the newly awakened lands. The first army was under the leadership of a *Reifries* named Dreizehdax ("Thirteen-Badger"). As all of the *Butzemenner* in the fields observe, Dunner meets Dreizehdax and beats his armies into retreat. On the next night, 14. *Wonnet*, the second army of the *Reifries* Vatzehfedder ("Fourteen-Quill" or "Fourteen-Porcupine") sets in to freeze the land. This time, *Dunner* teaches the *Butzemenner* how to fight the *Reifries*, and Vatzehfedder also retreats. Finally, on 15. *Wonnet*, the third *Reifries* army, under Fuffzehfux ("Fifteen-Fox") arrives in *Mannheem*, and the army of *Butzemenner* thwarts the *Reifries*' advance. As of sunrise on 15. *Wonnet*, or May 15, the planting of tender plants outdoors may begin.

The *Reifries* are in retreat, but they are not defeated; they will return again in November to reclaim the land.

Basic Information

Dates: *Wonnezeit* April 30–May 11; *Der Grieg Geeich die Reifries* 12–15

Observances: *Die Hexenacht*: Night of April 30; *Wonnezeit*: May 1–11; *Der Grieg Geeich die Reifries*: Starts sunset May 12 and lasts through sunrise May 15

Honored deities: Holle, Berchta

Runes: *Haagel, Kerze, Yaahr, Winsch*

Tools: None specified

Color: Cobalt blue

Wonnezeit runes

Common Foods

The common foods for this holiday include green onions, scallions, lettuce, spinach, and rhubarb.

RECIPE

Rhubarb Jam

This jam is wonderful over oatmeal, with yogurt, or in a sandwich with any nut butter.

Ingredients

3 pounds rhubarb

½ cup water

2–3 cups sugar

One orange

Directions

Cut rhubarb into half-inch pieces, removing any extra-fibrous parts. Place in saucepan and add water and two cups sugar. Add the zest from the orange and then slice and add the juice. Cook on low-medium heat until mixture is thick. Taste and adjust sugar to your liking. Keep in fridge for up to a month.

Wonnezeit Activity: Making a "Wilkum, Holle!" Sign

Urglaawer always hang a "Wilkum, Holle!" sign for this holiday to welcome her into their homes upon her return from the Wild Hunt. This can be as easy as a printed paper sign taped to your windows or doors, a small flag for your garden, or a large banner for your porch. Use white or colored paper and draw "Wilkum, Holle!" for each door of your home. You can print it with color or print an outline to color yourself. Hang with tacks or tape before May 1.

"Wilkum, Holle" sign

Ideas for the Solitary Practitioner

Since Holle inspects our homes upon her return, spend some time in the weeks before tidying up your home and then perform a very simple welcoming ceremony. Light a candle, then open your front and back doors (or windows if that is more appropriate/safer) while calling to Holle to be your guest. End the ceremony with a special meal, making a plate for Holle.

Observance of the Desecrated Shrines: Remembering

This observance, which is unique to *Urglaawe*, isn't a celebratory holiday so much as an act of remembrance. It is in honor of the many gods and goddesses whose sacred shrines, temples, and images were desecrated or destroyed through acts of zealotry. Although the original context of this observance was the destruction of Germanic shrines to various deities by Saint Boniface, this *Urglaawe* ritual may be taken and adjusted to meet the needs of other traditions' and pantheons' deities whose shrines and sacred sites were also destroyed.

This date was chosen because it is the feast day of St. Boniface, who was responsible for the destruction of the ancient Thor's Oak (*Dunnereeche*) in Hesse. The church's own lore tells the story:

> There stood at Geismar, not far from Fritzlar and Buraburg, an oak of extraordinary size, which was dedicated to Thor or Thunar, "the god of thunder," and was called Thunar's oak, or Donnereiche, i.e. Thor's oak, or the Thunder oak. Here from time immemorial the Hessians were wont to assemble for the worship of Thor. In the immediate vicinity was Wuodensberg (afterwards called Udenesberg, and later still Gudensberg), a conical hill, on the top of which was a circle of stones, within which the worship of Woden was carried on. Thus the place was the chief sanctuary of the Hessians, and had a character of peculiar sanctity. And as the principal town of the province, Maden or Mattium, where the national assemblies met, was in the neighbourhood, it was the most fitting place that could be selected for an open attack on the popular worship.

> Having made up his mind to fell this oak, Boniface repaired to the spot with his monks, not carrying as usual the Holy Scriptures in his hand, but armed with the formidable German axe. He made no secret of his purpose, and the report of the intended sacrilege quickly spread around. Thousands of Pagans flocked to the place, a few of the most zealous bent on preventing the offence to the god, but by far the greater part trusting to the god to revenge himself by striking his enemy dead on the spot; while others, whose belief in the gods had been shaken, watched anxiously for the result on which their faith was suspended; and others, again, looked confidently for the triumph of their newly found religion. Every eye was riveted on Boniface as he approached the sacred spot and amid solemn, breathless silence raised his arm, and struck a vigorous blow. The mighty trunk quivered, the branches shook, and a deep groan burst from the excited crowd. Then the monks fell to. Blow followed blow, and the trunk was well-nigh half cloven, when suddenly, in the topmost branches, was heard a rushing sound as of a whirlwind, and the giant of the forest toppled over, fell to the earth with a thundering crash which shook the whole forest, and echoed again and again from the Wuodensberg, and in the fall its whole length split into four parts. But Boniface and his little band stood unharmed.[16]

Basic Information

Date: June 5

Observance: Observance of the Desecrated Shrines on June 5

Honored deities: Dunner, Stuffo, Yechaa, Lohra, Reto, Biel, and all deities whose shrines were destroyed

Runes: *Sunne*, *Winsch*, *Daag*, *Tuisko*, *Mann*

Tools: None specified

Colors: None specific

16. Anne Fulton Hope, *Sequel to the Conversion of the Teutonic Race: S. Boniface and the Conversion of Germany*. R. Washbourne. 1872, 88–90.

Observance of the Desecrated Shrines runes

Common Foods

There are no specific foods for this ritual.

Observance of the Desecrated Shrines Activity: Create a Prayer Card

This simple craft can serve as a focus for your ritual. Do a little research into one or more of the locations that Saint Boniface leveled or a name from a possibly forgotten deity. Write the name of the deity, their location, or both (if known) and any referenced symbols that may have survived. Use this card in your ritual. It can be saved and added to each year or burned each year as an offering.

Ideas for the Solitary Practitioner

This ritual is practiced alone in our own homes, so no adjustments need to be made.

Der Summeraafang: Summer Solstice

Celebrating the longest day of the year, this observance acknowledges that light eventually overcomes darkness in the progress of cycles. It is also a time to recognize that we have planted our seeds of growth, both from an agricultural standpoint and from a mental standpoint. It's time to nurture those seeds and watch them grow. It's also time to be social with our friends and family and build community. This is a time to enjoy the warmth and light and understand that even the darkest of days will eventually become brighter. As such, it's a good time to look at aspects of our lives that are not bringing joy. Release the burdens and embrace the happiness that life has to offer, even if just for this one day.

Basic Information

Date: Summer Solstice

Observance: *der Summeraafang* on the summer solstice

Honored deities: Sunna, Volla, Voll

Runes: *Sunne, Winsch, Daag, Tuisko, Mann*

Tools: None specified

Colors: Yellow, red

Summeraafang runes

Common Foods

The foods that are common at this celebration are pies, funnel cake, corn fritters, berries, cherries, grapes, melons, tomatoes, peppers, carrots, cucumbers, beans, garlic, corn, summer squash, and mushrooms.

RECIPE

Elder Blossom Lemonade

This refreshing and fun drink was created by the authors during an herbal class for a project to be shared with the group. It is a perfect summer drink!

Lemonade Ingredients

1 large handful fresh elder flowers

2 large handfuls fresh lemon balm

2 large handfuls fresh lemon verbena

Water

Violet Simple Syrup Ingredients

2 cups violet flowers

2 cups water

1 cup sugar

Directions

Place elder flowers, lemon balm, and lemon verbena into a pot, pitcher, or French press and cover with hot water (just under boiling). Let steep for at least 20 minutes. To make violet simple syrup, gather two cups of sweet violet flowers and boil in two cups of water. Add a cup of sugar and heat over medium heat until dissolved. Strain both the lemon and the violet mixtures. Add the violet simple syrup to the lemonade to taste and cool to serve.

Summeraafang Activity: Make a Flower Wreath

Make a wreath or crown of fresh or fake flowers and greenery. Gather or purchase flowers and greens. If gathering, try to keep stems long enough to braid and find long, vine-like greens to add to the wreath. Start by taking three single-flower stems and offset the ends by a couple of inches each. Begin braiding and add a new stem or green vine when you get close to the flower of each stem. Tuck the last ends in and decorate with ribbon. Use as a decoration for your altar or yourself!

Ideas for the Solitary Practitioner

Invite a friend or friends for a barbecue or out to dinner. This is the time to be social. They need not know it's a religious ceremony (unless you want to let them in on it). After all, everyone enjoys a good meal!

Der Dingsege: The Thing

Across the Germanic cultures, personal disputes and other legal matters were tended to at community gatherings that were overseen by a lawspeaker. In Iceland, this type of governing assembly is still called the *Althing*. For Germans, it was called the *Ding* or *Thing*, and *Dingsege* is the ritual that accompanies the gathering of an *Urglaawe* group for the purposes of sorting out legal matters ranging from personal disputes to land acquisition to end-of-life documents. The deity most associated with this assembly is Ziu, whom English speakers might know better as Tyr or Tiw. As is the case with other Germanic groups, *Urglaawer* associate Ziu with justice, right action, and Tuesday. The *Deitsch* word for that day does indeed reflect this relationship but not by having the day named after the god; instead, the name is drawn from the *Ding: der Dinschdaag.* Optimally and traditionally, our *Dingsege* would take place on a Tuesday and would take place with the lawspeaker seated upon a giant council rock called a *Hottenstein*, but practicality and the reality of the workaday world make these arrangements difficult. *Urglaawe* groups typically hold *der Dingsege* as a business meeting in June, often piggybacking it with their *Summeraafang* ceremony. However, there are times when we gather specifically for the purposes of creating, reviewing, updating, and, when appropriate, sharing our health care documents and end-of-life plans with the community.

Our community has experienced instances in which the next-of-kin did not approve of the decedent's chosen religious identity, and without the proper documentation, we were unable to challenge the next-of-kin's decision to hold funerary rites per the beliefs of a religion with which the decedent actively disagreed. Therefore, we urge everyone, regardless of their religious identity, to ensure that they have a completed will, living will, power of attorney medical, power of attorney financial, and funeral designee form. Different jurisdictions have different laws and require different forms, but, for example, the funeral designee form in Pennsylvania allows one to designate another individual to control the disposition of one's own body, thus overriding the statutory authority of the next-of-kin. Some US states have combined some or all of these documents into a single "advance directive" that can help to simplify the documentation process.

The annual observance of *Dingsege* provides *Urglaawer* with a reminder to be sure these documents are done. Even once these documents are completed, the observance can also serve as an annual checkpoint for *Urglaawer* to be sure that their end-of-life and other important documents are up to date.

Basic Information

Date: June—Any day in June, usually at *Summeraafang*

Observance: Dingsege on chosen day

Honored deity: Ziu

Runes: *Daag, Tuisko, Mann*

Tools: None specified

Color: Red

Dingsege runes

Common Foods

No specific foods related to this observance.

Dingsege Activity: Organize Your Legal Papers

Since this day is dedicated to getting your legal paperwork in order, make it enjoyable by finding or decorating a special folder or box to safely keep your important documents. Add stickers, draw runes, make it yours so that this yearly ritual is perfunctory yet personal.

Ideas for the Solitary Practitioner

With organization being the theme of this holiday, take this opportunity to attend to the more mundane aspects of your home maintenance, your finances, and your health care and end-of-life documents. Perhaps invite family or friends to help you.

Es Hoietfescht: The Haymaking

This observance celebrates what was historically the first harvest with a specific emphasis on haymaking. Spiritually, it's a time to observe and celebrate the circumstances and community that support and nurture us. It's a time to reflect on how our hard work produces results and reap the rewards of that work. This can relate to any number of things in our lives: educational goals, health and wellbeing goals, etc. The possibilities are limitless, as every individual has life goals specific to their world. It's a time to celebrate all the things we plant and nurture. This includes plants and crops but also friendships, loving relationships, partnerships, and communities. The date is dependent on one's region and the readiness of the harvest. In Pennsylvania and Ohio, for example, haymaking virtually always falls sometime between the last two weeks of July and first two weeks of August.

One unique aspect of *Hoietfescht* is the honoring of the Grain Spirits, like *Fraa Weeze* ("Lady Wheat") or *Harr Rocke* ("Lord Rye"), for example. These spirits are the deities of the grains themselves. There is a common thought stemming from some animistic beliefs in *Hexerei* that, much like humans have deities, plants, animals, and even minerals have their own deities. This belief is most pronounced and central at *Hoietfescht* because of the *Deitsche* focus on grain harvests, but the belief in everything having a spirit—and in constructed things forming a merged spirit consisting of the spirits of their components—is pervasive.

After the hallowing during this ritual, all metals are removed from the sacred space, and the statuary or symbols of Erda, Nehalennia, and the Grain Spirits are brought into the space by way of a small wagon processional. It is decorated with flowers, streamers, grains, beads, and whatever other seasonal decorations you like. It is pulled up to the altar, and the statues are brought out and placed on the altar. They are removed in the same manner in reverse at the end of the ritual.

Basic Information

Date: Varies but usually falls between July 15 and August 14

Observance: *Hoietfescht* on chosen day

Honored deities: Erda, Fro, Frouwa, Nehalennia, Grain Spirits

Runes: *Engel*, *Yaahr*, *Winsch*, *Loch*

Tools: None specified

Colors: Browns

Hoietfescht runes

Common Foods

The common foods you will see for this ceremony include fruits like berries, melons, peaches, apricots, and plums. You will also see peas, eggplants, beans, potatoes, celery, leeks, and grains.

RECIPE

Homemade Egg Noodles with Buttered Breadcrumbs

This is a simple yet filling meal that is requested again and again!

Ingredients

2 eggs

½ teaspoon salt

Sifted flour (author's note: I have used up to 2 cups)

½ stick butter or 4 tablespoons

Breadcrumbs

Directions

Mix eggs in a bowl and add salt. Sift flour and add half a cup at a time until a stiff dough is achieved. Knead well and divide into two portions. Roll each as thin as possible on a floured surface and let sit for half an hour to dry. Fold up the dough from the bottom a couple of times and slice into ¼–½-inch strips. Lay on parchment paper to dry completely.

Cook the noodles in boiling water, strain, and place in a bowl. Melt butter in a saucepan and mix in breadcrumbs a tablespoon at a time to make a thin "sauce." When the breadcrumbs are browned, add to the top of noodles just before serving.

Hoietfescht Activity: Create a Hoietfescht Wagon

This craft can be as easy or as complicated as your skill and energy allow. We have a wooden cart for our kindred, but you could fashion one from a shoe box or other small cardboard box that can hold your statuary or symbols.

Your wheels can be wooden discs, empty spools of thread, or large buttons. You can use paint, markers, colored paper, felt, fabric, or any other way to cover the outside of the wagon. Add a string or rope pull for your procession.

Ideas for the Solitary Practitioner

Since this is the first harvest, have a Reap Rewards Ceremony. Think of all the things you've put your time and effort into nurturing this year; gather representations of the results of that work (for example, photos of friends, vegetables from your garden, something you created, a slip of paper that has written on it what you may have accomplished with your exercise goals, etc.) and focus on the tangible rewards produced by your nurturing. Celebrate these. Honor yourself for accomplishing them. And then, reflect on how you'd like to continue to cultivate these goals.

Es Erntfescht: Harvest Home

Traditionally, in *Deitsch* culture this was known as Harvest Home and was *the* Thanksgiving. So prevalent was this holiday in *Deitsch* minds that there was a shunning of the national holiday for many years. To this day, many Protestant churches observe this holiday during a Sunday service in September when the sanctuaries are filled with donated food. *Urglaawe* continues and extends this time-honored cultural tradition. It is a time to reflect on our blessings and express our gratitude for them. When possible, it's appropriate to share one's good fortune. This is a time to ensure that the community is prepared for the imminent winter. In the past, it was a time to exchange, barter, or donate provisions to family, friends, and neighbors. As the time when we reap the bounty of the preceding months, this is the time to accept the oaths of associate kindred members who have participated through the year and wish to become full members. This is also a time of balance, where there are equal amounts of light and dark. As such, it's a good time to take stock of what circumstances and relationships are working in your life and what may need adjustment.

Basic Information

Date: Autumn equinox

Observance: *Erntfescht* on autumn equinox

Honored deity: Dunner

Runes: *Dunner, Yaahr, Not, Winsch, Peil, Tuisko*

Tools: None specified

Color: Orange

Erntfescht runes

Common Foods

The common foods for this holiday are turkey, brussels sprouts, cabbage, chicory, onion, celery, potatoes, sweet potatoes, and pumpkins.

RECIPE

Potato Filling

This is a regular side dish on *Deitsch* tables at this time of the year!

Ingredients

5 pounds russet or gold potatoes

5 celery stalks, chopped

1 medium onion, chopped

Butter or bacon fat (author's note: I use about 2 tablespoons)

5 pieces white bread, ripped into 1-inch pieces

Additional butter and milk, as desired

Salt and pepper to taste

Pinch of saffron (optional)

Directions

Boil potatoes until soft.

While potatoes are boiling, sauté celery and onion in fat until translucent, about 5 minutes. Add bread and sauté until brown. Set aside.

Mash potatoes, adding butter and milk until desired consistency. Add salt and pepper to taste. Add pinch of saffron.

Fold celery and onion mixture into potatoes. Spread into a greased baking dish. Distribute several pats of butter or brush melted butter over the top and bake at 350 degrees F for 30 minutes or until top is golden brown.

RECIPE

Pumpkin Chiffon Pie

A tasty variation on pumpkin pie that is perfect for this celebration.

Ingredients

¾ cup brown sugar
1 envelope unflavored gelatin
½ tsp salt (for preservative)
½–1 tsp cinnamon
½ tsp nutmeg (optional)
¼ tsp ginger (optional)
3 slightly beaten egg yolks
¾ cup milk
1¼ cup canned pumpkin
3 egg whites
⅓ cup sugar
Graham cracker crust (premade or homemade)

Directions

In saucepan, combine brown sugar, gelatin, salt, cinnamon, nutmeg, and ginger. Combine egg yolks and milk, and add to brown sugar mixture. Cook and stir until boiling. Remove from heat. Stir in pumpkin. Chill until it mounds (stiffens) slightly. Beat egg whites and add sugar, beating to stiff peaks. Fold pumpkin mixture into egg whites. Put into crust. Chill until firm.

Erntfescht Activity: Create a Gratitude Jar

Find a special jar and some favorite pens and paper. Create slips of paper indicating what you are grateful for. You can write them in your own handwriting, use special calligraphy, or decorate the slips with pictures, stamps, or stickers. Keep the jar in a location you see regularly so you can fill it when a circumstance occurs that you feel blessed to experience, or you can take a slip out to read when you need a reminder of your blessings.

Ideas for the Solitary Practitioner

Erntfescht is a time for bounty, but not everyone has enough. If you are in a position to do so, donate food to a local food pantry or shelter. Better yet, if you have the ability, go volunteer to help them out. This holiday is one of celebrating with community and making sure everyone has what they need going into the colder months coming.

Zisasege: Honoring the Undoer of Knots

Although we often combine *Zisasege* with *Erntfescht* due to practicality and time constraints, we have two separate altars for each observance. Our *Zisasege* altar is very much red in color with pine cones and knotted strings on the table. As part of the ritual, participants are invited to take a string home with them and to meditate upon the knots in their lives. Once the meditation is completed, they can sympathetically undo the knot while appealing to Zisa for aid. Remember, the basis needs to be right action coming from a right mind.

Also, some knots are better off left tied, and sometimes loose strings need a knot. If you come to Zisa for aid, be sure you understand the potential consequences of untying your knots. Many times we think our actions are pure, but they are often agenda-driven, and it is important to be honest with ourselves about that fact.

Basic Information

Date: September 28

Observance: *Zisasege* on September 28

Honored deity: Zisa

Runes: *Kerze*, *Tuisko*

Tools: None specified

Color: Red

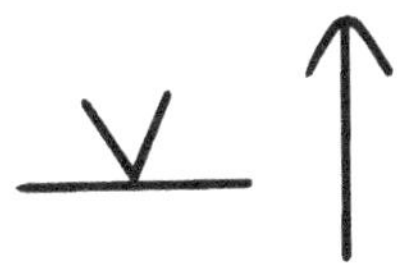

Zisasege runes

Common Foods

The only regular food for this specific celebration is pine cone jam or syrup and foods that use them or go with them. The pine cone syrup can sometimes be found online by searching for pine cone jam. Generally found in Eastern European markets in person, it may be easier to make your own if you have trees nearby that you know have not been sprayed with pesticides and you have the time to invest.

RECIPE

Spice Cake

Full of warming spices, this cake is perfect for this season. Combined with the pine cone syrup, it becomes the perfect *Zisasege* dessert!

Ingredients

2½ cups all-purpose flour

¼ cup cornstarch

4 teaspoons baking powder

2 teaspoons ground ginger

1 teaspoon ground cinnamon

½ teaspoon ground nutmeg

½ teaspoon ground allspice

½ teaspoon ground cloves

½ teaspoon salt

1 cup milk

3 large eggs

2 teaspoons vanilla extract

1 cup (16 tablespoons) butter, softened until easily spreadable

2 cups dark brown sugar, tightly packed

⅓ cup (approximately) pine cone syrup

Directions

Adjust oven rack to the middle position; preheat to 350 degrees F. Grease and lightly flour a metal 9 × 13-inch pan. Whisk flour, cornstarch, baking powder, spices, and salt together in a large bowl. Mix milk, eggs, and vanilla in a 2-cup measuring cup. Using an electric mixer, beat softened butter into the flour mixture, first on low, then medium, until mixture forms pebble-sized pieces. Add about ⅓ of milk mixture and beat on low until smooth. Add remaining milk mixture in two stages, and beat on medium until mixture is just smooth. Do not overbeat. Add brown sugar, beat until just incorporated (about 30–45 seconds).

Pour batter into prepared pan. Bake in preheated oven until a toothpick inserted in center comes out clean, about 40 minutes. Cool briefly in pan on a wire cooling rack, then run a butter knife around the edges of the pan to loosen. Invert carefully onto the serving plate and let cool completely. Poke holes in top of cake with chopstick or dowel, and pour pine cone syrup on top to cover the top of the cake so it can soak through.

RECIPE

Pine Cone Syrup or Jam

It is hard to find pine cone syrup or jam for sale, so we have included this recipe to make your own at home.

Ingredients

¼ cup young green pine cones (should be no larger than an average adult thumbnail—any larger and they'll be very bitter) (Young pine cones should be green and identified as an edible species. Toxic species such as ponderosa, yew, Norfolk, and lodgepole pines should be avoided.)

½–¾ gallon unfiltered apple cider or apple juice (¾ gallon will give more syrup)

¼-inch stick cinnamon

2 whole cloves

Pinch of salt

Directions

Rinse the pine cones to remove any loose dust or debris. Blanch the pine cones in a few cups of water for 1–2 minutes, then remove to a plate. Using a 1-gallon pot (you will need the headspace), combine the cider, spices, salt, and pine cones. Bring to a boil, then turn down the heat to a simmer, and let simmer for an hour. After the hour has passed, evaluate how much reduction has occurred. The goal is to reach about 1½ cups of syrup. At this stage, the pot must be watched constantly. Continue reducing until bubbles are reaching up the sides of the pot and the consistency is that of warm honey. Transfer cones and syrup to a preheated Mason jar and allow to cool for 30 minutes before putting a lid on and transferring to the refrigerator. After chilling, evaluate consistency and adjust if needed. If it's too thick, pour into a bain-marie and thin it out with 1 tablespoon of cider, then cool and re-refrigerate. Should keep in the refrigerator for 4–6 months.

Zisasege Activity: String Art

Work some of Zisa's magic while creating a protection wreath for your home or room. You will need a 6–8-inch grapevine wreath available at craft stores, or you can fashion one yourself by using vines and twigs. Cut nine strips of fabric 1½ inches thick by about 12 inches long. Take them one at a time, and as you tie each one in a knot around the bottom of the wreath, focus on your intention and ask Zisa for protection. Tie a string around the top of the wreath and hang on or near the front or back door in your home.

Zisasege wreath

Ideas for the Solitary Practitioner

This time is perfect for working with Zisa on areas where you may be feeling stifled or held back. Create a cord spell with red string by tying a loose knot while concentrating on your problem. Meditate on the knot you just made, thinking about where you want things to progress. When ready, untie the knot while thinking about the road to your goals being cleared for you. Your string can be burned, buried, or saved for future use.

Es Alleliewezeil and Ewicher Yeeger Sege/Hollersege: The Last Harvest

This is a high holy observance and the last harvest of the growing season. This twelve-day observance marks the end of our spiritual year. It begins with *Alleliewezeil* on October 31 and ends with *Ewicher Yeeger Sege* on November 11. This is also when we burn the *Butzemann* that we created at *Entschtanning*. This is historically the culling time, and it marks the start of the dark half of the year. We honor and celebrate the masculine energies and spirits. All *Butzemenner* must be burned before this observance begins, i.e., sundown on October 30, as it marks the start of the Wild Hunt. Holle collects the souls of the departed to take with her, including the souls of the *Butzemenner*. Therefore, if the *Butzemann* is not burned, it would leave an empty shell for negative entities to inhabit and use to wreak havoc across the land. This is a good time to also ask your *Butzemann* to carry unwanted and undesired aspects with him. This can be accomplished by attaching banishing tickets with a brief explanation of what you want to banish before burning him.

This is also the time to Rail Against the Frost King. The frost giants are aware of Holle's departure on the Wild Hunt, and they begin their advancement toward the *Hatzholz* from the northern leaves. In some versions of the King Frost tale, the giants' army includes some familiar names: Dreizehdax, Vatzehvedder, and Fuffzehfux. These are the giants who come in May in an attempt to destroy the expanding fertility of the land. Their visit at this time of year prepares the way for the arrival of King Frost, who brings the killing frost to the land.

While the giants ultimately take the land in Holle's absence, the railing weakens their ranks and allows more time for Holler to direct their souls to the Wild Hunt.

Winter is natural and necessary for many regions. Some seeds need extended time in frozen temperatures, etc. Thus, the best way to frame this entire effort is to focus on winter's grasp over us as individuals. Each of us can assert our authority over ourselves not to become sullen from the heavy snows or the cabin fever. Thus, we are railing against our own reactions to winter too. The tool we use is a *schtaab*, or staff, or, not so ironically, a *Riggel*, or rail. Defensive words are spoken into the end of the staff.

The contents of what is said are pretty much up to the individual, and some cannot be written down. One thing, though, that can be said into both ends of the staff liberally is "Zing!" This is likely a contraction of "zieh dei(n) Gift" ("move thy poison"). It is said like "TSEENG."

After the words are spoken into the staff, the staff is then lifted above the head and then wielded, shaken, or swung in the dominant hand in a sympathetic striking of the target of the rail. Words may also be uttered during this process. When one feels they have sufficiently made a statement, the rail is lowered. It can later be stood in a doorway or hung on a wall for at least three, six, or nine nights. After nine nights, it may be removed at any time.

We are keeping this defensive. The act of cursing is very dangerous, as the energies it creates can harm the self and witnesses. There may be times when cursing is necessary against truly destructive forces, but the coming of winter in the era of modern conveniences is not worth a stain on our *Wurt*. By framing this as a struggle against ourselves, we have no need to curse and can instead focus on defending ourselves against our own reactions. This means that one makes clear their intentions for dealing with the impending winter and its weather.

The Story of Ewicher Yeeger

This is an old *Deitsch* myth from all across the *Blobarrick*.[17]

Deitsch colonists settled in the area now known as Lynn Township (Lehigh County), Pennsylvania, by about 1732. They must have forgotten their knowledge of farming because they quickly cleared large plots of all vegetation while building their farms and homes at the base of the *Blobarrick*, or the Blue Mountain, and thought nothing more of it.

The soil they worked, however, was not as fertile as other places close by, and when they did plant, they experienced a drought. When rain finally came, it washed away the seeds along with the topsoil, and very few of the seedlings could cling to anything, let alone grow. The settlers were devastated and named their land *Allemaengel*, which means "all deficiencies."

Of course, the wildlife that had lived in the areas they cleared with a heavy hand found new homes in the still-standing forests. The settlers worried as early snowstorms began to threaten in autumn. After the snowfall, they were unable to leave *Allemaengel* to try to hunt or get supplies. They worried and prayed. They also set out a meager offering of hay and cloth.

They were struggling with sickness and starvation when, on a mid-autumn evening, they heard a booming sound and the loud barking of hounds coming from everywhere and yet nowhere at the same time. The sound persisted periodically through the night while the settlers cowered in their homes, frightened and hungry.

When the sun started to rise, the settlers came out of their homes to a wonderful surprise. The wildlife had been driven back over the *Blobarrick* into *Allemaengel*. They saw deer and rabbits and were overjoyed. They were able to hunt and preserve the meat for the winter.

The sound of the hounds was heard in the *Blobarrick* that first winter, letting the people know that Ewicher Yeeger, the Eternal Hunter, had sent the wildlife back over the mountain to save them.

17. This is an old story with variations all throughout the *Deitscherei*. One published variation may be found in Jane Polley, ed., *American Folklore and Legend* (Reader's Digest, 1978), 28–29.

Even today in parts of the Blue Mountain, when the *Deitsch* folk hear the barking howls of Ewicher Yeeger's hounds, they know he is keeping the lands full of wildlife.

Basic Information

Dates: October 31, November 11

Observances: *Allelieweziel* on October 31; *Ewicher Yeeger Sege/Hollersege* on November 11; *Die Verschimpfing Geeich der Reifkeenich*, or the Railing Against King Frost, on November 11

Honored deities: Wudan, Holle, Ewicher Yeeger

Runes: *Reit, Yaahr, Kerze, Engel, Mann* for *Allelieweziel*; *Dunner, Eiwe, Hengscht, Loch* for Ewicher Yeeger

Tools: None specified

Colors: Orange, purple, black

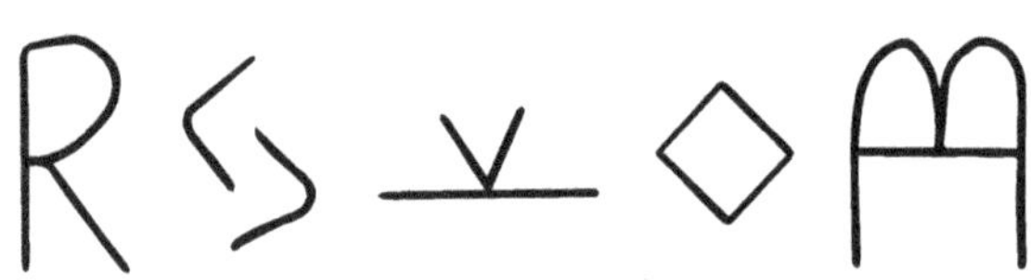

Allelieweziel runes

Ewicher Yeeger runes

Common Foods

The common foods seen at this celebration are scrapple, hog maw, pumpkin, winter squash, garlic, fennel, and cranberries.

RECIPE

Homemade Sauerkraut

So many of us *Urglaawer* make our own kraut at home! It's very easy and a great way to make the most of your harvest if you grow your own cabbage. If you don't grow your own, that's fine too.

Ingredients

Organic green cabbage

Fine sea salt

Directions

Before you start, weigh your cabbage and measure your salt. Using fine sea salt, you will need 1–1½ teaspoons of salt per pound of cabbage. Take your cabbage and remove the outer leaf if damaged. The outer green leaves contain lactic acid that helps the fermentation process.

Cut the cabbage into quarters and then use a knife, mandoline, or special kraut knife to make long, thin ribbons. Thin cabbage will ferment better than thick slices. Do not waste that core! It can be shredded into the sauerkraut for a real boost of vitamin C. Take a Mason jar and fill it halfway with the cabbage and sprinkle some of the salt over it. Close the jar and shake it a little to spread the salt around. Using a solid wood masher, tamp the cabbage down until it creates enough liquid to cover the cabbage. Add more salt and repeat the mashing process until you have the cabbage covered with liquid about an inch or two from the top of the jar.

It is important to make sure that the cabbage stays under the water in the jar. You can use glass or stone weights to keep the cabbage submerged. If using metal lids, acquiring a Burp Lid is very handy. It is a silicone top that has a raised bump with a slit that fits into the ring, and you can release the built-up pressure by squeezing or "burping" it. If you don't have one, a plastic lid will work.

Set your container in a corner of your counter that is not in direct sunlight, that is not near the stove, and where you will not forget about it. The best temperature for fermentation is approximately 66–72 degrees. You will check on your jar daily for the first week to let out any built-up gas. Either use the burp lid or open your jar and tap on the weights. This should release any bubbles of gas.

After the first week, you can lift out the weights and taste the sauerkraut. It should take about three to four weeks to fully ferment, give or take a few days on either side depending on your home's temperature during the fermentation process. This is when your tasting is important. You'll want to home in on your favorite texture and flavor by tasting every few days. Once you are happy with the flavor of your sauerkraut, you can put it in the fridge, where it will keep for up to a year—if you can manage not to eat it right away!

RECIPE

Scrapple and Sauerkraut Balls

This recipe was created for this observance to blend two of the most well-known *Deitsch* foods. It was a huge hit!

Ingredients

Store-bought scrapple, or make your own from one of the many recipes online

Sauerkraut, homemade or store bought

Butter or oil to cover bottom of pan

Breadcrumbs

Salt and pepper to taste

Directions

Take scrapple and sauerkraut and mix together in a bowl until well blended. Place butter or oil in a pan on medium heat to melt. Take a spoon and scoop out some of the mixture, roll into a ball, roll in breadcrumbs, and place in the pan to brown all sides. Drain on a paper towel and salt and pepper to taste. Serve hot.

Alleliewweziel Activity: Fall Foliage Mandala

Since this is the last harvest, this project is perfect to capture the abundance of color and variety in the outdoor spaces you frequent. Take a walk and find as many different shapes, colors, and textures as you can. Leaves, seedpods, bark, berries, vines, rocks, flowers—all of these items will make great art! Gather and set out your items on the table. Then, on white or colored paper, arrange your items in a pleasing design, perhaps round with a flower in the middle and leaves around it. Take pictures of your favorites and return the natural items to nature.

Ideas for the Solitary Practitioner

This is the last harvest, and we are moving into the darker, more introspective time of year. If you created a *Butzemann*, have a burning ceremony for him. You can include aspects you wish to banish from your life by tucking slips of paper with those things written on them into his clothes or tie them on with string. If you did not create a *Butzemann*, have a simple banishing ceremony by writing out the things that no longer serve you or that you wish to banish from your life and burn the slip(s).

Voryuul: Fore-Yule—The Coming Winter Solstice

Voryuul, as a distinct observance, is relatively new, though it is drawn from very old traditions. In the cycle of life, death, and rebirth, *Voryuul* is the time between death and rebirth. It is the time we do not remember, the mystical time when our divinity is awaiting the formation of a new soul construct before being reborn. The light from the last life is fading, and the darkest of times is yet to come.

Voryuul pretty much starts when *Allelieweziel* ends (sunset on November 11), but as a discrete observance, it begins on the night of December 8 (which is December 9 by *Urglaawe* lunar reckoning). That night, we light twelve candles, engage in a meditation, and then snuff one out. On the second night, we light eleven candles and then blow one out. Each night through December 19, we light one fewer candle and blow out one more. This brings us up to the night of December 20, which is the beginning of *Yuul* and the rebirth, when the last candle is blown out and then, after a period in the darkness, is relit to represent the return of light.

Lutzelfraaslaaf: The Progression of the Lantern Lady

While observing the *Voryuul* nights, we also have *Lutzelfraaslaaf* on the fifth night. The *Lutzelfraa*, or Lantern Lady, is believed to be Berchta in the guise of a beggar woman. She is out on this night usually asking for clothing or food. If one has the means and is helpful to her, they are rewarded with good luck. If one does not have the means but shows compassion for the *Lutzelfraa*, they, too, will be rewarded. But should those with the means ignore her, they will find themselves with their "belly slit," a metaphor for bad luck or health. This night is a turning point in the meditations, where one shifts from inner evaluation to integration of what one has learned.

There is a lot more going on within the *Voryuul* nights, but this is the basic process. It helps us to focus ourselves on what is working for us—and what is not working for us. Many of us base New Year's resolutions on the results of our *Voryuul* meditations.

Voryuul can be rough. Answering to the meditations honestly can bring about a lot of churning emotions and uncertainties. It is a time of introspective exploration that can lead to unpleasant conclusions or unhappiness. There is a fine line between confronting and embracing the realities about ourselves and falling into despair. These introspections are not required, so only engage in them if you feel you are ready to deal with the answers. The results of *Voryuul* meditations can be upsetting; if you feel overwhelmed by them, please discontinue the meditations immediately and seek the assistance of a trusted friend or counselor.

Voryuul Meditations

These are the standard meditations we have used over the years. We added a more gentle affirmation set of prompts as well, and one can use either of these options or create their own.

December 8:

Voryuul night 1 (begins sunset local time)

Meditation topic: What did I learn in the past year?

December 9:

Voryuul night 2 (begins sunset local time)

Meditation topic: Who am I these days? Am I happy? Am I content?

December 10:

Voryuul night 3 (begins sunset local time)

Meditation topic: Am I stuck in a rut? If there was one thing I could change in my life, what would that be? Why? How? To what end?

December 11:

Voryuul night 4 (begins sunset local time)

Meditation topic: What are my true motivators? What are the real causes of my actions?

December 12:

Voryuul night 5 and *Lutzelfraaslaaf* (begins sunset local time). This is an auspicious time to make donations to food banks or shelters.

Meditation topic: What do I do when I win the battle but lose the war?

December 13: (2024 Lutzelfraaslaaf observed)

Voryuul night 6 (begins sunset local time; observance of *Lutzelfraaslaaf*)

Meditation topic: Mindset and relationship around giving and generosity.

December 14:

Voryuul night 7 (begins sunset local time)

Meditation topic: How do I find balance and contentment between what I want and what is available?

December 15:

Voryuul night 8 (begins sunset local time)

Meditation topic: How can I leverage the shadowy aspects of myself? What positive things do useless hopes and wishful thinking bring to me?

December 16:

Voryuul night 9 (begins sunset local time)

Meditation topic: Status of open projects: What is worth finishing? What is weighing me down?

December 17:

Voryuul night 10 (begins sunset local time)

Meditation topic: Were there patterns of behavior that have served me or others well? What behaviors or actions were detrimental and should not be engaged in again?

December 18:

Voryuul night 11 (begins sunset local time)

Meditation topic: How am I affected by the company I choose to keep? How can I affect the world around me?

December 19:

Voryuul night 12 (begins sunset local time)

Meditation topic: What can I do differently in the new year that will take me out of my comfort zone?

December 20:

Voryuul ends at sunset local time and *Yuul* begins.

Some of us may not be in a position to do a deep dive or even wade into shadow work this year. If that is the case for you, we invite you to try the more gentle affirmations here, which are formed with the same underlying intent and focus.

December 8:

Voryuul night 1 (begins sunset local time)

Affirmation: I am learning about myself every day. I am discovering who I am.

December 9:

Voryuul night 2 (begins sunset local time)

Affirmation: I am evaluating where I put my energy. I am working on creating firm boundaries.

December 10:

Voryuul night 3 (begins sunset local time)

Affirmation: I am growing and changing every year.

December 11:

Voryuul night 4 (begins sunset local time)

Affirmation: I move forward with intent.

December 12:

Voryuul night 5 and *Lutzelfraaslaaf* (begins sunset local time).

Affirmation: I am resilient.

December 13: (2024 Lutzelfraaslaaf observed)

Voryuul night 6 (begins sunset local time; observance of *Lutzelfraaslaaf*)

Affirmation: I am able to receive help when I need it, and I will offer help to others when I am in a position to.

December 14:

Voryuul night 7 (begins sunset local time)

Affirmation: I seek balance and contentment.

December 15:

Voryuul night 8 (begins sunset local time)

Affirmation: I seek to know myself better.

December 16:

Voryuul night 9 (begins sunset local time)

Affirmation: I am able to step away from that which is not feeding me spiritually.

December 17:

Voryuul night 10 (begins sunset local time)

Affirmation: I focus on my own actions and intentions.

December 18:

Voryuul night 11 (begins sunset local time)

Affirmation: I am aware of my impact on the world around me.

December 19:

Voryuul night 12 (begins sunset local time)

Affirmation: I will move into the new year with confidence.

December 20:

Voryuul ends at sunset local time, and *Yuul* night 1 begins sunset local time

This is a solemn period to acknowledge the liminal times and spaces in our lives. Examining one's shadow side is the focus of this time. It's a time to prepare ourselves to enter the introspection period of *Yuul.* We use this time to take a breath and ground ourselves after the busyness of the harvest seasons and observances but before entering the hectic period of the end-of-the-calendar-year holidays and start of the new spiritual year. One could consider it a sort of reset button.

Basic Information

Dates: December 8–20

Observances: *Voryuul* on December 8–20; *Lutzelfraaslaaf,* Progression of the Lantern Lady, on December 13

Honored deities: Lutzefraa, Wudan

Runes: *Dunner, Eiwe, Hengscht, Loch, Baerke*

Tool: Sun wheel

Colors: Gray, silver

Voryuul runes

Common Foods

There are no common foods associated with this observance; however, we are including a recipe that is enjoyed at all of our autumn and winter gatherings.

RECIPE

Mulled Cider

There is never enough of this cider at any celebration! A definite favorite during the cooler months at the end of the calendar year.

Ingredients

Mulling spices: cinnamon sticks, whole cloves, star anise, allspice, nutmeg

2 large handfuls mugwort

2 quarts apple cider

1 8-ounce package fresh cranberries

1 handful dried cranberries

Directions

The exact amount of the spices will be determined by your personal taste. Mugwort can be bitter tasting, and some people may not like that. Start with 1–3 whole cinnamon sticks, 3–5 whole cloves, 1 star anise seed pod, and 1 teaspoon each of the dried allspice and nutmeg. Take the mugwort and all the spices and wrap them in cheesecloth or put in a large tea ball. Pour the cider into either a slow cooker or large pot on the stove and add fresh cranberries. Let simmer for 15 minutes on low-medium heat (or for 20–30 minutes on high in a slow cooker) and begin tasting. Add more spices if desired and the dried cranberries. Simmer for another fifteen minutes on the stove (or set slow cooker to warm) before serving.

Voryuul Activity: Pine Cone Ornaments

Make pine cone decorations for your *Yuul* tree. Take a walk where there are pine trees and find some fallen pine cones. Back at home, place them on a baking sheet and place in your oven for 3 hours at 200 degrees F to kill any unwanted mildew or bugs. Once cooled, you can paint your pine cones with silver or gold paint or brush with glue and add glitter. For a more natural look, leave them untouched. Tie ribbons or string to the top end and hang on your *Yuul* tree.

Ideas for the Solitary Practitioner

This is a time of deep introspection and self-reflection. Journal with the prompts given or find another set of shadow work prompts that speak to you. Keep this journal to use next year and to see how you are changing year to year.

Die Yuulzeit: The Beginning of Winter

This observance lasts for twelve nights and twelve days and marks a time of introspection, contemplation, and addressing our shadow sides. It begins with the *Yuulsege* at sunset on December 20, and ends with the *Frofescht* on January 1, or the feast of the god Fro. While we celebrate that the shortest day is past us, it is also important to acknowledge that we all have work to do.

Historically, all spinning work was set down for the *Yuulzeit* period, and as part of that mental orderliness, the goddess Berchta requires that projects are completed prior to the start of *Yuul. Urglaawer* who practice the fiber arts particularly pay attention to this requirement, as it is an easy way to honor her. Berchta requires tidiness of mind.

As the time of new light in the world, this is the time for new members to take the kindred oaths as associates; they are not yet voting members. As this is a time when most make New Year's resolutions, it's important to understand the implications of oath taking. Generally speaking, we want to see everyone succeed when they are motivated to set a goal for themselves. It's encouraged to set multiple small goals to achieve an overall outcome rather than one large undertaking. A perfect example of this is that a lot of folks desire to become healthier in the new year. Many people will set a goal of "I'm going to go to the gym every day and throw out all of the junk food in my house." Instead, a reasonable goal may be "During the first week of the new year, I'm going to spend ten minutes a day walking around the block and give up soda." Goals should be specific, attainable, and within your power to do. Have a plan for completing the goal or oath. We must also acknowledge that when made in the presence of our gods, our oaths carry a weight of obligation. If we cannot fulfill our oaths, then we must be ready to make a concession, and that concession should be considered during the time the oath is made. As fellow kindred members, it is our responsibility to encourage and support our kinsfolk in their desire to fulfill their oaths.

Just like the American Easter traditions, many of the American Christmas traditions take their lead from *Deitsch* culture, including baking and distributing cookies and candy.

Berchtaslaaf: The Progression of Berchta

Berchtaslaaf, or the Progression of Berchta, begins at sunset on December 31, which is Yule's *Zwelfdi Nacht* ("Twelfth Night") and ends at sunrise on *Zwelfder Daag* ("Twelfth Day"), or January 1. This observance relates to legends of the goddess roaming through towns and villages on her feast day, sometimes appearing as a beggar (see also *Lutzelfraalaaf* above). This observance features a meal that, according to Grimm, traditionally consisted of gruel and fish, typically herring.[18] The *Deitsch* expression of this prescribed meal survives in the form of oyster stew and crackers on New Year's Eve. Either form of the meal is fine. Some folks, particularly in Canada, also make simple pancakes of only flour and water, or *Zammede*, as part of Berchta's meal. *Zammede* turn up in a number of practices among the *Deitsch* too, and we include them in our Twelfth Night observances.

This meal is a meal of subsistence, perhaps reflecting the starving away of the old year. It stands in contrast to the lavish meal of *Frofescht* on January 1. It is said that if the meal is not consumed and offered to Berchta on her

18. Jacbon Grimm, *Teutonic Mythology*, vol. 1, trans., James Steven Stallybrass (Dover Publications, 166), 273.

feast day, she will slit open the bellies of those who partake of other foods while ignoring hers, and she will replace the contents with straw. While this certainly may be read literally, it may also be a metaphor for a loss of luck or of food or wealth in the upcoming year. It is also important to note that *Urglaawe* is a religion of conscience and voluntary participation, not of force. If one cannot or does not wish to partake of this meal, it is not compulsory to do so. One may make adjustments as needed or desired. What practicing *Urglaawer* have found is that she is understanding of dietary and cost restrictions, and as long as a genuine attempt is made to follow an austere meal (or including the required meal as part of a larger celebration), no punishment occurs.

Frofescht: Feast of Fro

Frofescht ends the twelve-day observance of *Yuul*. This meal, in contrast to the scarcity of Berchta's meal, is a meal of abundance. This is the New Year's Day dinner of pork and sauerkraut that is highly common in the *Deitscherei*. You will often find lore relating to these foods being eaten because pork is associated with progress, as the pig roots forward in the ground, and cabbage is associated with fortune because of its green color. However, in *Urglaawe* (and in Germanic Heathen lore in general), boars and pigs are sacred to Fro, and cabbage is associated with prosperity. Therefore, we see this as a remnant of old Germanic belief and tradition surviving within the living *Deitsch* culture.

Basic Information

Dates: December 20–January 1

Observances: *Yuulsege* on December 21; *Berchtaslaaf* on the night of December 31; *Frofescht* on January 1

Honored deities: Wudan, Berchta, Fro

Runes: *Antwatt, Haagel, Eisich, Sunne, Eiwe*

Tools: Hammer, sickle, goose prod (specifically for *Berchtaslaaf*)

Color: White

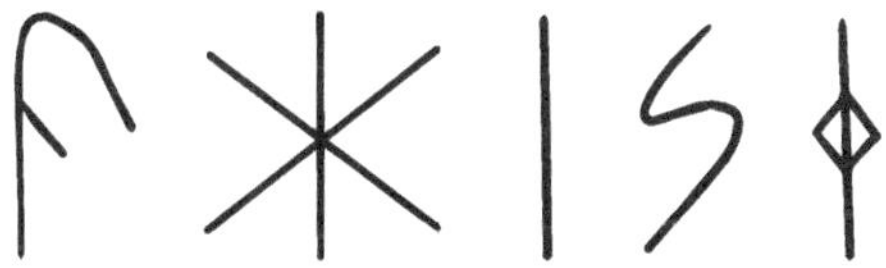

Yuul runes

Common Foods

Common foods for *Yuul* include goose, oysters and crackers, or herring and gruel, prepared any way. Other appropriate foods are cabbage, pork, potatoes and sweet potatoes, and, of course, gingerbread and other holiday cookies.

RECIPE

Pork and Sauerkraut

You will find pork and sauerkraut in most *Deitsch* homes from *Yuul* through the New Year's Day celebration. It is one of the most common holiday celebration foods this time of year.

Ingredients

Pork tenderloin or chops, ½ pound per person recommended portion size

Sauerkraut, as much or as little you prefer

Directions

Place pork loin into a Dutch oven or slow cooker. Cover with prepared sauerkraut (including juice) and cook for several hours. If using a slow cooker, cook on high for 4–6 hours or low for 6–8 hours. Pork is ready when it reaches an internal temperature of 145 degrees F.

Serve with a side of mashed potatoes.

RECIPE

Drop Sand Tarts

This is Michelle Jones's family recipe passed on by her Mom-Mom Reber.

Ingredients

½ pound butter (2 sticks or 16 tablespoons)

1 pound sugar (2 cups)

3 eggs (separate)

3 cups flour

1 egg white

Cinnamon sugar

Pecan halves

Directions

Cream butter, add sugar, then add egg yolks and flour, alternating with beaten egg whites. Drop by spoonful onto cookie sheet and flatten slightly. Brush with egg white, sprinkle each cookie with cinnamon sugar, and place a pecan half on each cookie. Bake at 375 degrees F for 9 minutes or until golden brown. Makes about 4 dozen cookies.

Yuul Activity: The Sunwheel

Create a sunwheel, either with a real source of fire like candles or with a simulated source like battery-operated tea lights. You can also use a representative image to help you focus on the observance. Gather pine branches, holly, or other available winter greens and make a circle on your altar or table. Place a lantern or candle in the center as a focal point for your ritual.

One style of a sunwheel

Ideas for the Solitary Practitioner

Set aside 15 minutes each day of *Yuul* to reflect on the day's value(s), how you are implementing it in your own life, where you could improve yourself with respect to the value, and how you can exemplify the core value in your interactions with the world at large. All twelve days have an overarching theme of introspection. Value(s) by night:

Entire period: *Der Selbschtreiguck* (introspection)

First night: *Die Schaffichheit* (industriousness) and *die Verwalting* (stewardship)

Second night: *Die Neigierheit* (curiosity)

Third night: *Der Mut* (courage)

Fourth night: *Der Edelmut* (generosity)

Fifth night: *Die Uffwaarting* (hospitality) and *die Ehr* (honor)

Sixth night: *Es Mitleid* (compassion)

Seventh night: *Die Addning* (discipline)

Eighth night: *Die Gschwisichabhenkichkeet* (interdependence)

Ninth night: *Die Treie* (troth/loyalty) and *die Waarheit* (truth)

Tenth night: *Die Ausdauer* (perseverance) and *die Verwandschaft* (kinship)

Eleventh night: *Die Selbschtverbessering* (self-improvement)

Twelfth night: *Die Weisheit* (wisdom) and *die Geischtlichkeet* (spirituality)

At the close of *Yuul*, after your Feast of Fro, burn your sunwheel candles to symbolize leaving the past to the past. You can attach slips of paper with your hopes for the new year or with the things you'd like to remove or refresh for the new year.

Die Entschtanning: Emergence

This is a high holy twelve-night, twelve-day observance starting with Groundhog Day, or *der Grundsaudaag*, and ending with the Feast of Light, or *es Lichderfescht*. Considered to be the "baby bump" phase of the year, it celebrates emergence, new beginnings, and seeds of inspiration. This is a celebration of feminine energies and spirits, including the *Idise*. Traditionally, this is a time to begin spring cleaning. And what better way to start than by cleaning out our hearths? It is during this time that hearths, firepits, or candleholders are cleaned of any remnants of the previous year's fires and a new fire is started with birch.

During this time, we also make and activate our scarecrows, or *Butzemenner*. The *Butzemann* is an activated scarecrow that is given the breath of life at Groundhog Day, or *Grundsaudaag*. He is the "father" of this year's crop, and he guards his designated area throughout the growing season. He is made from plant material saved from last year's harvest and should be dressed in organic materials so that he can be safely burned later. Anything he is dressed in or that is given to him becomes his and must be burned with him. This burning must happen no later than *Allelieweziel* or bad luck is sure to follow. Leaving an unburned *Butzemann* will attract all manner of negative beings.

If we follow our word and treat our *Butzemann* well, he will become a symbol of the plant world around us, especially in our own gardens which he is set out to guard. He embodies the souls of all the plants and serves as a focal point for *Blanzegschwetz*, or speaking to plants. Although we tend to expand traditions in many ways, the *Braucherei* traditions report that the scarecrow contains male energies in order to fulfill the seeding of the soil and the sacrifice later in the season.[19]

Es Lichderfescht: Festival of Lights

The last night of *Entschtanning* is celebrated with lights that represent the promise of the growing sunlight. Houses are adorned with lights, most commonly green and white in color, and many *Urglaawer* set off fireworks to celebrate the promise of new life and renewal.

Basic Information

Dates: February 2–14

Observances: *Grundsaudaag* on February 2; *Lichderfescht* on February 14

Honored deities: Freid, Sunna

Runes: *Baerke, Gewwe, Ochdem, Loch*

Tools: None specified

Colors: Green and white; pale blue (for Freid)

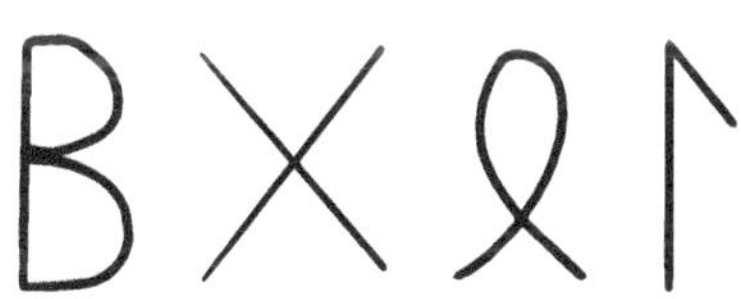

Entschtanning runes

Common Foods

Common foods for this celebration include *Fettekuche* (referred to as *Faschnachts* or *Fastnachts* in common cultural language); early greens and root vegetables like broccoli, cauliflower, cabbage, turnips, and winter squash; and fermented vegetables.

19. Amos Long Jr., "Dutch Country Scarecrows," *Pennsylvania Folklife* 12, no. 3 (1961): 54–59.

RECIPE

Fastnachts (Fettekuche)

This is Michelle Jones's family recipe passed down by her aunt Janet. The note on the recipe passed down reads "Real German, I believe."

Ingredients

1 cup mashed potatoes

1 cup lukewarm water

1 cup sugar

1 yeast cake (3¼ ounce packets of yeast = 1 yeast cake)

1 cup sugar

1 pint scalded milk (chilled)

Salt (optional)

¾ cup lard

3 eggs

Flour, enough to stiffen

Pinch of nutmeg

Directions

Mix the first four ingredients around 5 p.m. At 11 p.m., add 1 cup of sugar and 1 pint scalded milk (after chilled). Add salt (for preservative, optional), ¾ cup lard, and 3 eggs. Add enough flour to stiffen and a bit of nutmeg. Let dough rise overnight. (Volume doubles, so be sure to use a sufficiently large bowl.)

In the morning, knead in enough flour until hands remain free of flour and dough. Roll out dough, cut in squares, and let stand until dough doubles in size (about 1 or 2 hours).

Cut slits into top of each square. Fry in lard until golden brown. (Make sure fat reaches 350 degrees F. They will puff up as they're being fried.) Makes about 5 dozen.

RECIPE

Cauliflower and Broccoli Au Gratin

Another favorite dish in our homes.

Ingredients

1 head cauliflower

1 head broccoli

¾ stick unsalted butter

6 tablespoons all-purpose flour

3 cups whole milk

¼ teaspoon nutmeg

16 ounces shredded Gruyère cheese (cheddar or Swiss could also be used)

Kosher salt and pepper to taste

¼ cup each flax seed and breadcrumbs for topping

Directions

Preheat oven to 350 degrees F. Butter or grease a 9 x 13-baking dish. Core and slice the cauliflower and trim and slice the broccoli and arrange in dish. Melt ½ stick butter in a medium saucepan over medium heat. Add flour and cook, stirring for 2 minutes. (Do not let it darken.) Slowly whisk in milk. Simmer, whisking occasionally, until slightly thickened, 3–4 minutes. Remove from heat and stir in nutmeg and 1¼ cups cheese. Season with salt and pepper. Pour over vegetables. Sprinkle with remaining ¾ cup cheese. Mix flax seed and breadcrumbs and sprinkle over cheese. Melt remaining butter and pour over breadcrumb mix. Cover loosely with aluminum foil and bake for 15 minutes. Remove foil; bake until vegetables are tender and the top is golden brown, 20–25 minutes. Let stand 10 minutes before serving. Serves 8–10.

Entschtanning Activity: The Butzemann

This is the time we build a *Butzemann* and perform a Ceremony of the Corn, or *Kannsege*, to activate him. The base for the *Butzemann* is plant matter from your own garden or yard that should be collected at the end of the growing season and stored for the following year. This can be put into something as simple as a small linen drawstring bag or as elaborate as a full-sized scarecrow dressed in adult-sized clothing. Most are somewhere in between.

Everything that is used to make the *Butzemann* must be organic, as he will be burned later. Everything given to him, like a chair or stool to sit on, should also be able to be burned.

Before the *Butzemann* is completed or sewn up, insert a heart cut from paper or cardboard. You could also use a representation of a heart such as an acorn or seed. You can add prayer slips with expressions of goodwill and prosperity or rune slips for a specific focus.

You will need

Your finished *Butzemann*

A copy of the following ritual

Access to your property

Directions

The *Butzemann* should already be constructed out of plant remnants from the prior season. If you use only one type of plant for the construction (e.g., corn), you may edit the calls to relate only to that specific plant. We use many different plant remnants, so the calls refer to "plants."

The next segment is the incantation that places the speaker out onto the world tree to serve as a bridge for the plant spirits to come into this realm in order to awaken the dormant plant spirits within the *Butzemann*'s shell. There is a pronunciation guide in appendix A for all *Deitsch* in this ritual.

Butzemann

Incantation

[English]

I begin the Ceremony of the Corn.

This Earth, this Air

This Earth, this Air

This Earth, this Air

I bid of the deities the permission to step into the heavenly partition.

I stand with one foot in the Hatzholz and step with the second into the western leaves.

I call to the compassionate Plant Spirits to come hither to come to the aid of their descendants.

I am the Bridge.

I am the Bridge.

I am the Bridge.

[Deitsch]
Ich fang der Kannsege aa.
Daer Bau, die do Luft
Daer Bau, die do Luft
Daer Bau, die do Luft
Ich bitt vun de Ziewe die Erlaawing, fer in die hallich Scheid neizuschteige.
Ich schteh mit eem Fuuss uff em Hatzholz un schteig mit zweddem in die Weschtbledder nei.
Ich ruf zu de mitleidiche Blanzeseele, fer die haerzukumme, fer ihre Noochkummer auszuhelfe.
Ich bin die Brick.
Ich bin die Brick.
Ich bin die Brick.

Note that the word Bau is transcribed as Bow and is pronounced like English bough. The phrases of "Ich bin die Brick," or "I am the Bridge," may be repeated in triplets for as long as needed in order for the speaker to become a figurative link between the ancestral plant spirits in the western leaves of the world tree and the dormant plant spirits within the Butzemann.

At this point, you do not want to close out your connection to the western leaves, but you can speak freely in *Deitsch* or English. Here is where you can state in more detail to the spirits what your purpose is (for them to meld with the static spirits in order to awaken them within the plant material of the *Butzemann*, to give the breath of life to the *Butzemann*, etc.).

Your Commitment

Your promise is to name and to take care of the *Butzemann*, to honor his purpose, to make offerings to the spirits within him, to aid him in the care of his "children," etc. This is an oath, and you must abide by your words. Most importantly, you must promise to relieve him of his duties at an appropriate time, usually by sunset on October 30, in order to help the melded spirit within him to return to the otherworld of the western leaves through respectful immolation.

The Activation: Butzemannsege

You will now activate the *Butzemann* with the following words.

[English]
So begins the Butzemann Blessing.
I give to thee the breath of life. Let the main of life awaken thee!

[Deitsch]
So beginnt der Butzemannsege.
Ich geb zu dir der Ochdem. Loss der Megge dich uffwecke!

Breathe onto the "mouth" of the *Butzemann*.

Antwatt rune

Intone the *Antwatt* rune and draw the rune with your right thumb over where the mind's eye would be on the *Butzemann*. If skilled in otherworldly experiences or in runes, do this repeatedly until you sense that you have received the rune back in response from the now-activated spirit.

Now, give a name to the *Butzemann*. There is a traditional naming convention. A first-generation *Butzemann* has the appellation of "der Nei" following his name to indicate the first of his line. If his name is Arnold, he'd be "Arnold der Nei." Following *Butzemanner* would have the first name as the last name; in this case, "Arnoldson."

Be sure to keep a record of his name. You will need it when he is burned. In fact, consider calling him by his full name frequently. The naming serves as recognition of, and respect for, the plant spirits as beings. When the rite is completed, close it out by saying the following:

[English]
The Butzemannsege is closed.

[Deitsch]
Der Butzemannsege watt gschlosse.

After the activation rite is completed, it is important to serve as a bridge back. Speak the following:

[English]
I thank the deities and the compassionate Plant Spirits. I still stand between the Hatzholz and the western leaves so the Plant Spirits may return.
I am the Bridge.
I am the Bridge.
I am the Bridge.
The Ceremony of the Corn is closed.

[Deitsch]
Ich bedank mich zu de Ziewe un de mitleidiche Blanzeseele. Ich schteh noch gschwisich em Hatzholz un de Weschtbledder, fer die Blanzeseele zerickzuschteige.
Ich bin die Brick.
Ich bin die Brick.
Ich bin die Brick.
Der Kannsege watt gschlosse.

Your *Butzemann* is now ready to be shown where he is to guard. This is done by showing him around the entire border of the land you own or, at the very least, your garden that he is to protect. If you have only indoor plants, show him those and let him know what his job is. Then, find a place where he can stay while he guards your land until he is burned. This can be a windowsill inside, a pole or perch in a tree outside, or a chair in your garden. Remember, if you gift him the chair, it will need to be burned. This can be circumvented by telling him you are letting him sit in your chair while he does his job.

Ideas for the Solitary Practitioner

Since we are clearing out the hearth and making way for new things to come, have a Hearth (or Firepit or Candleholder) Cleaning Day followed by a celebratory first lighting of new fire and a feast. Clean out your fireplace, firepit, or even your stove. Many *Urglaawer* also use this time to clean all candleholders and discard all unused candles. When clean, start a new fire using birch to light the fire or candles.

Der Frouwasege un der Grumbieredaag: Frouwa's Blessing and Potatoes Day

This observance pairs with the traditional *Deitsch* holiday of St. Gertrude's Day, which falls on March 17. It is also known in wider *Deitsch* culture by the name *Grumbieredaag*, or Potatoes Day, which is the term we use in *Urglaawe*. On this day, we honor Frouwa. This is one tradition that the Christians have inadvertently kept alive, and we benefit from it. The Christian expression has been edited to reflect the needs of the *Urglaawe* tradition and to return this observance to its older roots.

Since the *Deitsch* population overwhelmingly identifies as Protestant or Anabaptist, the survival of this Catholic observance within the wider culture is interesting in its own right, even if it has been diminishing over time. Even many Christians acknowledge the heathen roots of the observance.

Potatoes have become a staple crop for the *Deitsch* since arrival, and tradition is that March 17 is the day to put potatoes in the ground. There are rituals to feed the household spirits, called *Heinzelmenner*, or other *Kowwolds* and to bring fertility to the garden. Specific foods include *Datsch* (a type of almost granola-like potato bread) and spring onions.

It is important to note that this observance is the completion of the potato cycle. Potato bread from last year's harvest is consumed and offered to the land at the time that this year's crop is being planted.

Basic Information

Date: March 17

Observances: *Frouwasege* and *Grumbieredaag* on March 17

Honored deity: Frouwa

Runes: None specific for this rite

Tools: None specified

Color: Emerald green

Common Foods

The most common foods for this day are potatoes, spring onions, and *Datsch*.

RECIPE

Hot Potato Salad

This recipe is always well received when shared at a ritual, and there are never any leftovers!

Ingredients

5-pound bag of Yukon Gold or other yellow potatoes

Salt

½ pound of bacon

1 medium yellow onion

2–3 tablespoons water

1–2 tablespoons sugar

1/3 cup white vinegar

Fresh parsley

Directions

Peel and cut potatoes into even chunks. Place potatoes in large pot and cover with salted water. Boil until potatoes are soft when pierced with a fork. While potatoes are cooking, cook the bacon in a large, deep pan until very crispy. Place the cooked bacon on a paper-towel-covered paper plate. Do not discard the bacon grease! Finely dice the onion and cook in the bacon grease until translucent. Add water, sugar, and vinegar to the pan and bring to a boil. When boiling, add potatoes to the pan and crumble half the bacon into the potatoes. Stir to mix and heat thoroughly. Transfer to a serving bowl and garnish with the rest of the crumbled bacon and freshly chopped parsley.

Frouwasege Activity: Making Toys for Cats

Cats are sacred to Frouwa, so this is a perfect time to make toys and treats for cats. Gather fabric or felt squares and sew shut on three sides. Place a spoonful of dried catnip inside and sew the final side and toss around with your cat. If desired, make some in a fun shape like a fish.

Cat toy

Ideas for the Solitary Practitioner

If you do not have cats of your own, you can donate food or other items to a cat rescue. If you are able, donations of time are often an option as well.

Other Cultural Observances

Throughout the generations all over the *Deitscherei*, and even today, one can find any number of festivals tied to the agricultural calendar. Strawberry and peach festivals abound in the summer. Billboards advertising pork and sauerkraut dinners proliferate the towns in the autumn.

Der Deitschedaag

In English, this day is referred to as Deitsch Day, Pennsylvania German Day, and Pennsylvania Dutch Day. This celebration occurs on 6. *Gehling*, or October 6. Although organizers were already in Philadelphia prior to settlement, on this date in 1683, the first German arrivals from Krefeld in the Holy Roman Empire arrived at the port at Philadelphia, thus beginning a great migration that eventually led to the creation of the *Deitsche* as an ethnic group.

While the first families were Christians (Mennonites and Quakers), the subsequent waves consisted of people of all backgrounds. The largest portion of the settlers came from the German Palatinate, leading the English to refer to all of the settlers as "Palatines." Some of the early settlers originally dwelled in caves along the Delaware River. Economic refugees became an increasingly larger element, particularly as the economies of the German states suffered hardships in the early 1700s.[20] The British authorities eventually removed the settlers and filled the caves in due to the rowdy behavior of some of the Palatine settlers.

Die Fasching

The festivities of modern Shrove Tuesday and Mardis Gras, known in *Deitsche* as *Fasching* or *Fastnacht*, are almost certainly related to *Grundsaudaag*. The Heathen practices of what is now *Grundsaudaag* were originally tied to lunar calendar observances but eventually became associated with February 2. The timing of Shrove Tuesday comes from the Christian calendar and moves in accordance with the computus determination of the timing of Christian Easter.

20. William T. Parsons, *The Pennsylvania Dutch: A Persistent Minority*, The Immigrant Heritage of America Series (Twayne, 1976), 40.

In the *Deitscherei*, the most famous method of observing *Fasching* is the consumption of deep-fried doughnuts called *Fastnachts* or *Faschtnachtskuche*. The likely origin in this case are the Passover and Lent constructs of Judaism and Christianity.

Parade of Spirits

The Parade of Spirits, or *der Geischderschtrutz* in *Deitsch*, serves as a depiction of the Wild Hunt from Germanic mythology and features liminal and shadow-side entities, such as Belsnickel, Krampus, and the souls of the recently departed.

The parade is an *Urglaawe*-informed, grassroots, family-friendly, community-based, participatory parade that takes place in the Northern Liberties neighborhood of Philadelphia, Pennsylvania. Originally founded as Krampuslauf Philadelphia in 2011, the event has expanded its focus to include more folkloric features. Traditionally, the time in mid-December prior to the winter solstice (Yule) was when the Pennsylvania Dutch held spooky parades and when children donned costumes and went "Belsnickeling," or trick-or-treating. The Parade of Spirits is a modern expression of that old tradition.

Although the basic functions of the parade are based in German and Pennsylvania Dutch myth and folklore, this is a secular event. All shadowy-side, shady-side, and dark-side traditions from all cultural backgrounds are welcomed and encouraged. This is an inclusive event and welcomes participants of all backgrounds; no bigotry is tolerated.

While some costumes may be commercially produced (particularly Krampus, Perchten, or other traditional Alpine costumes), most are handmade, from the simple to the complex. Simply putting green or gray makeup on one's face and participating as a ghoul on the Wild Hunt is fantastic. If there isn't a Wild Hunt parade near you, consider gathering some friends and starting one!

Many different observances can be developed in the *Urglaawe* context, whether based specifically on the *Deitsch* culture or not. Individual practitioners can celebrate their ancestors' birth dates or even death dates, since there are old *Deitsch* traditions of remembering the date of someone's passing because that was the date upon which they had accomplished all they would in life. Observances can also include community endeavors, such as cleaning creeks or taking up food drives during harvest times. The intention behind the observance is as important as the observance itself.

7

STANDARD FORMAT OF AN OBSERVANCE

This chapter provides a representation of a typical group celebration. Smaller groups like a family or couple at home may look different, especially if children are involved or if you share your home with someone of another faith. Suggestions are also provided for solitary practitioners. This format is used for all observances with just the details being changed, such as the hallowing tool or the colors of the altar cloth depending on the observance. A practitioner should consult chapter 6 on our observances to obtain those details.

This is the way an observance, which often takes a few hours, is conducted from beginning to end. Generally, we gather, set up the altar, and then feast during discussion time. There are two parts of the observance, called *Sege* and *Sammel*, which are the meat and bones of the observance, and that is where we honor deities, ancestors, and others. After, the libations are poured out and the last closing of the rite happens.

Set Up the Altar

Setting up the altar is typically done as a community effort for *Urglaawe* observances so that everyone can be involved. There are no specific decorations required, but typically, altar decorations consist of tablecloths in colors associated with the observance and seasonally appropriate flowers and plant material. There is usually a stein on the altar as well as an offering bowl. There can also be candles, statuary, and other items.

Kindred altars are most often folding tables, picnic tables at a park, or tables in the home (see the illustration on page 78 for one representation). If you are a solitary practitioner, create your altar where and how you feel most comfortable. This could look like a folding table, coffee table, or a space on your dresser.

Die Farewe (Colors)

In traditional *Deitsch* culture, *die Farewe*, colors, have certain associations and significance. These are commonly known and widely used in hex sign design and other folk art, while specific colors—crimson, yellow-green, black, and white—show up in *Urglaawe* funerary rites. In all *Urglaawe* rituals, these colors are used to inform our choices for altar decorations. We also consider them when designing runes for magical working and creating hex signs for specific uses. They even influence the clothing we wear for our rituals.

Black, *es Schwatz*: Important in processing of souls between lives, protection, used in binding

Bloodred, *es Blutrot*: Blood and war

Blue, *es Blo*: Calm, spirituality, peace

Brown, *es Brau*: Earth, strength, soil

Crimson, *es Karminrot*: Death, also important in processing of souls

Gold, *es Gold*: Fortune, luxury

Gray, *es Gro*: Trickster energy, uncertainty

Green, *es Grie*: Fertility, growth, bounty

Orange, *es Arrensch*: Adds extra energy to all endeavors to allow for success

Red, *es Rot*: Passion, marriage, lust, blood, charisma

Slate, *es Schifferich*: Provides a connection to rocks and minerals

Tan, *es Gehlbrau*: Provides a connection to creation, animals

Violet, Purple, *es Veilich*: Mystery, cosmic energy, sacredness, completeness of the soul

White, *es Weiss*: Power of the moon, illumination, the flow of energy, rebirth

Yellow, *es Gehl*: Mind and body health, connection to divinity and spirit, power of the sun

Yellow-Green, *es Gehlgrie*: Fading (as greens beginning to yellow as plants die), in funerary rites, this color is used to represent commending the body to the soil

Feast and Observance Discussion Time

After the altar is set up, attendees spend time enjoying a meal together. Sometimes a member of the community offers to prepare the meal, but, most times, it is a potluck where everyone contributes to the meal. Either during the meal or immediately after, time is set aside to discuss the observance and its components and share individual insights and experiences.

If you are a solitary practitioner, make yourself a meal using the list of common foods found in the respective observance section in the chapter on observances. This is the time to also read up on the observance and lore related to it.

Offerings to the Land Spirits

An offering of food and beverage is left out for the land spirits. The offering is a plate made up from foods shared during the feast. This holds regardless of if you are celebrating with a group or are a solitary practitioner. The plate stays on the altar until later on in the ritual. When leaving food on an altar or outside as an offering, consider local animals: No toxic foods should be left for them to get to.

Bless the Libations

Libations are used as a sacred medium to connect community and deity and can be either alcoholic or nonalcoholic based on the decisions of the group gathering. The *Urglaawe* standard is that there will always be a nonalcoholic offering; the alcoholic option is optional. The libations may remain in their original vessel or be poured into a stein or steins to be passed around the community during the ritual. We have also always had sick cups available for attendees who are not feeling well or prefer to not drink from the same cup as the community. The libations are blessed by one of the Godspeople, or *Ziewer*, by intoning the runes of the celebration over the vessel containing the libation.

If you are a solitary practitioner, you may bless the libation yourself.

Die Aarufing (Convocation or Call to Worship)

This is a chant that is used before some more formal ceremonies, like a wedding. The chant calls to the land spirits of the four directions and the spirits of above and below. It also serves as a call to worship for participants to gather for the celebration. This can be done by a *Ziewermensch*, a chosen participant, or the solitary practitioner. Often done for outdoor rituals, this chant, while beautiful, is optional. Note that this entire chant is in *Deitsch*. A pronunciation guide is in appendix A at the back of the book.

Ich ruf zu mitleidiche Grefde vun der Nadde,
vun der Erd, vun em Schtee
Mit der Ruhzeit im Hatz
Kummt doch her, gebt uns Helf un Verwaahring
Losset uns mitschtimmlich mit Erdgraft sei
Liewe Ziewe! Fliesst darrich Naddwind in uns!

Ich ruf zu mitleidiche Grefde vun em Oscht,
vun der Luft, un em Sunnuff
Mit Yungezeit im Hatz
Kummt doch her, gebt uns Helf un Verwaahring
Losset uns mitschtimmlich mit Luftgraft sei
Liewe Ziewe! Fliesst darrich Oschtwind in uns!

Ich ruf zu mitleidiche Grefde vun der Sudde,
vun em Summer, un em Feier
mit Leidenschaft im Hatz
Kummt doch her, gebt uns Helf un Verwaahring
Losset uns mitschtimmlich e mit Feier sei
Liewe Ziewe! Fliesst darrich Suddwind in uns!

Ich ruf zu mitleidiche Grefde vun em Wescht,
vun em Wasser, un Schpotyaahr
Mit Heemgehzeit im Hatz
Kummt doch her gebt uns Helf un Verwaahring
Losset uns mitschtimmlich mit em Wasser sei
Liewe Ziewe! Fliesst darrich Weschtwind in uns!

Ich ruf zu mitleidiche Grefde vun em Himmel,
vun Schepfer, vun die Schtanne
Mit der Umwandleheet im Hatz
Kumm doch her, gebt uns Helf un Verwaahring
Losset uns mitschtimmlich mit em Himmel sei
Liewe Ziewe! Fliesst darrich Himmelwind in uns!

Ich ruf zu mitleidiche Grefde vun der Erd,
vun die Blanze, vun de Vorgenger
Mit Freindschaft im Hatz
Kummt doch her, gebt uns Helf un Verwaahring
Losset uns mitschtimmlich mit de Voreldere sei
Liewe Ziewe! Fliesst darrich es Gebliet in uns!

Intonation of the Runes

As stated, each observance has specific runes associated with it. Each rune is intoned three times, led by one of the *Ziewer* in charge of the ritual. When practicing as a solitary practitioner, the individual may intone the runes themself.

Runes

Hallowing

This is a blessing of the altar and ceremony space using the ritual tool or tools that are associated with the observance. If a deity has an associated tool, such as Dunner with the hammer, that tool would be used in the opening of the ritual. Some *Urglaawer* write their own openings. For our group rituals, we change the text of our hallowing to meet the circumstances of the ritual. For example, since Dunner is one of the featured deities of our *Erntfescht* observance, the hammer would be a tool called upon in the hallowing. If there is no specific tool associated with the deity or particular purpose of the ritual, the default is the sickle, as it is a primary tool used in *Urglaawe*. The manner of choosing the tool holds regardless of if you are practicing with a group or as a solitary practitioner.

Der Zweck (Purpose)

This is when we state the purpose of our gathering. We spend time together to share stories and lore about the ceremony or the honored deities. The ritual leader describes why the ritual is being held. Often, the purpose is to honor a particular deity, celebrate the turning of the seasons, or to build connections to a lesser-known deity.

Solitary practitioners can benefit from identifying the purpose as well. It helps to set the intention behind the ritual, and it makes it easier to be sure the purpose was met by the time the ritual is completed.

Der Aaruf (Invocation)

This is a call to the deity or deities of the day, inviting them to be part of the ritual. This can be spoken off the cuff or written ahead of time. While the inclusion of statuary on the altar is up to the leader of the ritual or solitary practitioner, most *Urglaawer* find statuary to be useful as a focal point. The statuary can also serve as a reserved place for the deity to occupy during the ritual time.

Readings as Appropriate

These are poems, stories, myths, or even songs that are related to the observance. They are read or sung by the *Ziewer*, participants, or the solitary practitioner.

Der Sege (The Spoken Blessing Rite)

The *Sege* is the reverent time of ceremony when the deity or deities of the day are honored and worshiped. This is one of the primary rites in *Urglaawe* observances. This consists of a libation into which the ritual leader has spoken words of blessings to all who partake of the drink or who respectfully dispose of a portion of the drink during the rite. The libation is typically inside a stein. Prior to the outbreak of COVID-19 in 2020, most of our rituals featured the stein being passed from person to person, and each would say words of blessings to the deity or deities of the day. Since the pandemic, though, we pour a portion of the libation from the *Seidel* into individual cups, and each participant uses their own cup when it is their turn to say a hail or a blessing. Once all participants have spoken their piece, each pours some of the contents of their individual cup into a larger libation bowl, which, in turn, is used in the distribution, or *Ausdeeling*, rite that comes a little later.

Solitary practitioners can conduct this rite by themselves by selecting a libation to share with deity. The practitioner can then set the libation into a vessel and may speak hails or blessings to the deity or deities of choice. The practitioner can then take a sip from the vessel.

Die Opfer un die Eede (Offerings and Oaths)

This time is set aside to present offerings to the deities and to hear any oaths that are to be spoken. Oaths are typically preapproved by the leader or leaders of the ritual before they are stated in the ritual itself. Anyone who has an offering would come up and place it on the altar now. If working alone, the offering can start off on the altar ready to be hallowed.

Hallowing of the Offerings

This is when the offerings are blessed. A twig or a flower from the altar is used to sprinkle some of the libation from the libation bowl onto the offerings. This is most common in group rituals because the libation is infused by the energies of multiple individuals, but solitary practitioners can also find value in this act as an extra level of ritual and emphasis behind the presentation of the offerings.

Die Ausdeeling and der Sege (Distribution and Blessing)

At the end of the one round of *Sege*, the steins are poured into the libation bowl. (When conducting this rite alone, there is no need for the distribution rite to follow, so the practitioner can continue to the pouring of libations.) The libation is then distributed by sprinkling onto or at the feet of the participants or by the drawing of a rune onto their forehead. This is the portion for which the rite is named. The ritual leader may either use their dominant hand by dipping their thumb into the libation or choose a leaf, flower, or stem from the altar to dip in. They then draw a rune over each participant's third eye on their forehead. In larger public rituals, they may simply sprinkle each participant either on the forehead or at the feet. This is the participants' reception of the spoken blessing, which has been infused into the libation.

Die Ausschitting (Pouring of Libations)

To the best of the participants' abilities, whether it is a solitary or a group of people, find an appropriate place where the libation can be poured from the bowl. The location is usually determined by the host of the ritual or by the leader of the ritual, but, in some circumstances, such as rituals conducted in institutional settings, the choices are limited by the participants' levels of access to the outside. For most *Urglaawer*, the base of a tree or a natural body of water will work. There have been occasions within institutionalized settings when inmates or patients have had to use a window to pour a libation into the ground, and, in one case, the participants had to resort to using the drain in order to release the libation. If there is no other option, this is acceptable, albeit not preferable.

When pouring the libation, all who are present are encouraged to speak these words. The English words are common to most Heathen denominations. Either language, or both, may be used in *Urglaawe* ritual:

> [English]
> *From the gods to the earth to us,*
> *From us to the earth to the gods.*
> *A gift for a gift.*
> *Hail!*[21]

> [Deitsch]
> *Vun de Ziewe zu der Erd zu uns,*
> *Vun uns zu der Erd zu de Ziewe,*
> *'N Gschenk fer 'n Gschenk.*
> *Heele!*

Closing of the Sege

The ceremony leader closes the *Sege* rite by taking the tool used to open the ritual and closes the ritual by stating:

> [English]
> *This Sege is closed!*

> [Deitsch]
> *Daer Sege iss gschlosse!*

21. This is a derivation of a blessing that originated in Ár nDraíocht Féin (ADF: A Druid Fellowship) and was adopted by Lewis Stead and The Raven Kindreds. Lewis Stead, *The Raven Kindred Ritual Book*. The Raven Kindreds, 1993. Accessed May 29, 2025, from https://www.sacred-texts.com/bos/bos623.htm.

Es Sammel (The Gathering)

This is a community rite that allows each participant to share their feelings, life situations, and celebrations with the other participants. It typically consists of three rounds: The first is to any of the deities of the *Urglaawe* pantheon; the second is for heroes, ancestors, forebears, descendants, and those who inspire you; and the third is an open round. Each person present takes their turn with their stein for each round.

This portion of the ceremony tends to be a bonding experience for a kindred and the participants, because information shared is sometimes of a personal nature (although this is not required). However, it is still a useful ritual for the solitary practitioner to use the time to hail the same entities as one would in a group.

Closing of the Sammel

The ceremony leader closes the *Sammel* rite in a manner similar to the closing of the *Sege* rite. The verbiage is:

> [English]
> *This Sammel is closed!*
>
> [Deitsch]
> *Die do Sammel iss gschlosse!*

Time for Fellowship (Optional)

Attendees sometimes stay after the ritual to socialize, or if we are in a park or other public area, a visit to a local restaurant can be arranged. The breaking of bread with your group is an important community-building activity.

This chapter shows the basic structure of an *Urglaawe* rite and what the various parts entail. This general outline is used as the basis for all *Urglaawe* rituals, including ones you will see in the next chapter on life cycles. While this is what we do when we are together, your practice can be any variation that you find works for you.

8

LIFE CYCLES AND RITES OF PASSAGE

Es Lewesraad is the cycle of life, from birth to death, beyond death, and then rebirth. In *Urglaawe*, we see all of existence in a pattern of cycles, as opposed to a linear timeline that has a beginning and end. Actually, it is more like a pattern of spirals that we traverse on our path to becoming elevated to where the gods are when they started their next journey. This view is shared across much of *Deitsch* society, regardless of religion because of its alignment with the cycles of the crops and raised farm animals. It is, for example, a core component of Amish culture and other Plain sects.[22] In *Urglaawe*, this concept includes not only the cycle of the individual, but also the cycles of all things on earth, the earth itself, the universe, and all of existence. Holle and Freid are the keepers of the order of the cycles in our current universe, with the other *Wurthexe* executing the progression of time, space, and *Wurt*.

22. John W. Friesen, "The Myth of the Ideal Folk Society versus the Reality of Amish Life," *Pennsylvania Folklife* 43, no. 3 (1994): 140–45.

In this chapter, we share several outlines of rituals that mark different rites of passage that one can experience during a lifetime. Most of these rites are based on the generic ceremony outlined in the last chapter. Since they are for use either with your own family or your own group, each one will have a basic outline so you can add your personal flair. If you are looking at starting or leading a group, keep all these things in mind as you approach people, and listen to them and their wishes. Keep them involved in the planning as much as possible.

Birth

Each pregnancy and birth are unique, as is each baby, birthing parent, partner, sibling, and situation. When planning a rite to honor this time, always make sure the honorees are centered. They should not be ignored for the baby bump they may still be carrying or have just delivered. The honoree may be experiencing body dysmorphia, difficult hormonal changes, or other things going on in their lives. Please be mindful.

Der Aerscht Sege (The First Rite)

This rite is to be used shortly after a newborn enters this world. This can be as early as three days or as late as six weeks but usually before their first birthday, when the Child Blessing takes place. This is a short-term protection and blessing intended to cover the time from birth until the Child Blessing, or *der Wasserdaafiwwergangsgebrauch*. At this point, the baby's legal name might not even have been decided upon. It is fine to use a temporary name. Speak these words:

> [English]
> *Hail [name or temporary name]!*
> *Welcome to the world!*
> *May your journey be smooth and even.*
>
> [Deitsch]
> *Heel zu dir*
> *Wilkum in die Welt!*
> *Meeg dir die Rees blatt sei.*

Next, draw the *Reit* rune on the child's forehead. This rune is drawn once using the thumb of the application hand (typically the dominant hand) when the hand is in the thumbs-up form.

This short and simple rite can be completed by the parents on their own or by a Godsperson if desired.

Der Wasserdaafiwwergangsgebrauch (Child Blessing)

Many cultures around the world have rituals for the acknowledgment or the welcoming of newborn children. In *Urglaawe*, we have *die Daaf*, or, in English, baptism, which can be performed, with parental or guardian permission, on any child. This word in English aligns more with the Christian practice, but the *Deitsch* meaning with its significance and nuance deserves to be restored. The *Deitsch* word hints at using a liquid, like a libation, to sprinkle, and this hearkens to an old Heathen right similar to the Anglo-Saxon *Vatni Ausa*. In that tradition, the father sprinkles sacred water onto the child's head and the child is then given a name.

The *Urglaawe* cognate of this ritual is a featured rite in a larger welcoming ritual called *der Wasserdaafiwwergangsgebrauch*, which literally means a "water-sprinkling custom of passage." This rite typically features one or both parents or guardians presenting the child to a Godsperson, or *Ziewer*, and to the assembled community. The *Ziewer* sprinkles sacred water from *Hexenkopf* or blessed water from a nearby stream or from some other water source on the child's head while speaking blessings or intoning runes. Often, the child is given a *Hollesichel* pendant as a gift from the community. (The sickle is Holle's sacred tool.) There is actually no rule, though, that specifies that a *Ziewer* or other clergy is needed to perform this rite. A parent, friend, or other community member may conduct this ritual.

Items needed

Hexenkopf water or other sacred or blessed water

Statuary or image, if available (Holle, Weisskeppichi, Waahra)

Libation of choice (nonalcoholic option must be available)

Stein or steins and individual cups for those who do not drink from the communal steins

Libation bowl, *Hollesichel* pendant, altar cloth, altar items of choice

[Child]'s *Hollesichel* will be placed into the bowl containing the *Hexenkopf* water

The Ceremony

Begin with the intonation of the runes. Each rune is intoned thrice: *Kerze, Engel, Yaahr, Reit, Mann.*

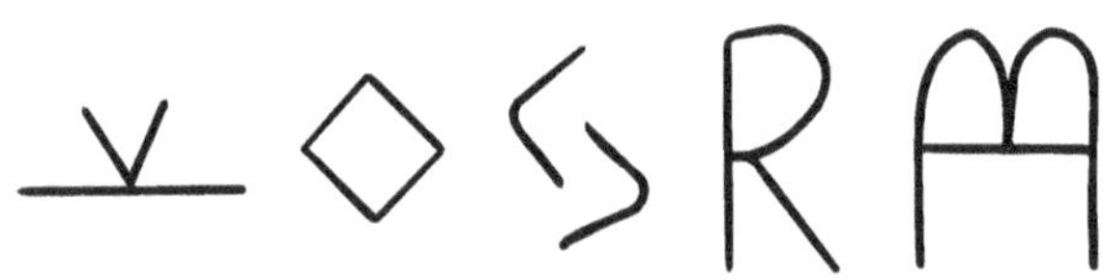

Child blessing runes

Unser Zweck (Our Purpose)

Ziewer or lead speaks the following:

Heit sammle mir fer [em/der] [em Kind sei Naame] [sei/ihre] Wasserdaaf zu feiere.

Today is a day to celebrate the birth, naming, and entry into the community of [child's name].

Waer bringt [em Kind sei Naame] heit zu der Gmeeschaft vorher?

Who brings [child's name] before the community today?

(Parents or representatives may respond in Deitsch, *"Mir duhne,"* or in Engish, *"We do."*)

Please state your names.

(Parents or representatives state names.)

Please bring [child's name] into the center of the circle.

Der Wasserdaafiwwergangsgebrauch (Water Consecration Rite)

Parents come forth and stand in center of circle with [child]. Everyone comes into a close circle around them.

Die Heiliching (Hallowing of the Site)

Ziewer or lead speaks the following:

[English]
Sickle of Holle, bless this altar and this site!
Protect us with the power of our great goddesses:
By Fraa Holle, to renew the folk;
By the White-Haired Woman, to bestow might and main upon us;
By Waahra, to hear our words today.
The Hammer forges the Sickle,
And the Sickle feeds the Hammer.
Forebears have gone.
We are walking,
And the descendants are drawing nigh.
Birth, life, death, rebirth:
It is the Wheel of Life, to sow and to cut.
Sickle of Holle, bless this altar and this site!
Hail! Hail! Hail!

[Deitsch]
Sichel vun der Holle, verweiht daer Aldaar un die Schtell!
Beschitz uns mit der Graft vun unsere grossi Ziebinne:
Bei der Fraa Holle fer es Volk zu erneire
Bei der Weisskeppiche Fraa fer Macht un Megge uns zu verleihe;
Bei der Waahra, fer unsere Wadde heit zu heere.
Der Hammer schmittet die Sichel,
Un die Sichel fiedert der Hammer.
Voreldre sinn gange.
Mir sinn am Laafe,
un Noochgenger kumme naah.
Geburt, Lewe, Dod, Widdergebur
'Siss es Lewesraad, zu saehe un zu schneide.
Sichel vun der Holle, verweiht daer Aldaar un die Schtell!
Heel! Heel! Heel!

Der Aaruf (Invocation)

Ziewer or lead speaks the following:

I hail thee, Holle!
Mother of Urglaawe!
Leader of the Hunt!
Guardian of Order,
and Protector of Children!
Come today to our celebration of life and love, and be our honored guest.
I hail thee, Weisskeppichi!
Mother of Braucherei!
Giver of Life and Life Force!
Generous, supreme Healer!
Come today to our celebration of life and love, and be our honored guest.
I hail thee, Waahra!
Witness to Oaths and Promises!
She who guides and holds people to their Word!
Come today to our celebration of life and love, and be our honored guest.
I hail the compassionate ancestors of [child]!
Please bear witness to the events today!
Come to celebrate [pronoun] life and the love that surrounds [pronoun].
Be our honored guests!
I hail the compassionate land spirits from all directions, above and below, to come to our celebration today. Be our honored guests!

Sege (Blessing)

This is one round of hailing the three invoked deities and asking their blessings on [child]. After the round is completed and the blessing distributed to the participants, [child]'s *Hollessichel* may be removed from the bowl containing *Hexenkopf* water, and the libation will be poured into the bowl. *Ziewer* or Godsperson joins [child] and parents in the center of the circle along with the bowl containing the libation and the *Hexenkopf* water. Parents take some of the water and sprinkle it on [child's] head, repeating the child's full name three times. After the third sprinkle, the parent(s) or representative(s) bestow upon the child the sickle that will be the child's name fastener (*Befeschdicher*). *Ziewer* or lead draws runes upon [child's] forehead and presents [child] to their new community.

Die Begriessing (Welcoming)

With parental consent, community members in the circle may, one by one, express wishes of luck, prosperity, long life, etc., to the child.

Zum Schluss (Closing)

Deities, ancestors, and land spirits are thanked for their presence.

This ceremony can be adapted if you are adopting an infant or child. When possible, involve siblings in the planning and the ceremony as their level of comfort allows.

Coming of Age

Coming-of-age ceremonies have all but disappeared in standard American culture. There are several subcultures that still mark the occasion: the Amish Rumspringa, the Jewish Bat or Bar Mitzvah, the Latino quinceañera. Various Americans may have sweet sixteen parties, but the focus is more general celebration and less moving from one phase of life into the next. Coming-of-age rituals often mean a change in responsibility for the teen(s), and often the ceremony would have shows of skill or strength. In preindustrial communities, these ceremonies were important to make sure young adults could continue meeting the hunting, gathering, home, and community needs.

From the *Urglaawe* perspective, marking this time is very personal. Many things must be considered. For certain cultures, the ceremonies for boys and girls are different, marking the social norms of that community and what was expected of them as a grown man or woman. In our current society, we are pushing to redefine those norms. We try to expand the idea of what a girl or boy can do and not have their entire future predefined by their presenting sex alone. For some girls, celebrating their menstruation would be fine, but for many, it may be a source of stress or confusion. A young boy who more identifies with the cooks of the family may feel out of place in a competitive sports-like celebration. The ceremony must be created individually to celebrate each individual's process, not just "You're a boy; you get this!" A ceremony can be as complicated or as simple as the young person desires.

Stacey's daughter, when she came of age, opted for a simple gathering of our grove of women at the time. Each woman present made a little disk of wood with a word or phrase on it and put it in a box decorated for her. She reached into the box, picked a disk, and read the empowering word or phrase, and then the woman who created it shared a story of something she either wanted the honoree to know or something she wished she knew at that age. The ceremony was done during a nice but casual luncheon. This was way more meaningful to Stacey's daughter, and she still has that box.

Some Guidelines for Creating a Coming-of-Age Ceremony

Involve the young person for whom this ceremony is being created. Determine who they feel comfortable having present. Be mindful of their comfort level throughout the entire planning process and the ceremony itself. There is no standard ritual format, as this ritual should be built around the honored young person's preferences.

Pet Blessings

Pets are members of our families and dearly loved companions. Pets of all kinds can be honored with blessings as well! The following ritual was done on *Ewicher Yeeger* in 2022 for several pups in our kindred. *Grumbieredaag/ Frouwasege* would be the appropriate time for a "Blessing of the Cats."

This would also be an appropriate time for honoring pets that have passed. The ritual format would be the same, with the honored pet being represented by a photo, special toy, collar, or their cremated remains.

Items needed

Hexenkopf water or other sacred or blessed water

Your pet or a representation of them if they are not present

The Ceremony

Anyone can speak the following.

Leader: *Today is the day to celebrate and bless the lives of our canine companions. Just as Ewicher Yeeger's hounds accompany him on his annual errands and herald promise to all who hear them, and Holle's hounds join her on the Hunt, our dogs provide companionship, loyalty, and love in our lives. Their presence is a comfort in a world fraught with stress and hardships. We honor their existence in general and in our lives, specifically, today. Who brings their dog(s) or an item of representation in front of the community and Ewicher Yeeger?*

Pet parents come forward with their dog(s) and respond: *"[I/We] do."*

Leader: *What [is/are] your dog(s) name(s)?*

Pet parents respond accordingly.

Leader:
I hail you, Eternal Hunter!
Leader of Hounds,
Be here in this moment to bless our dogs with stamina, agility, and strength.
I hail you, Fraa Holle!
Leader of the Hunt,
Be here in this moment to bless our dogs with perception, joyfulness, and affection.
I hail you, White-Haired Woman!
Giver of life and life force,
Be here in this moment to bless our dogs with long and healthy lives.
[Name of dog], may you be blessed. May you and [the name(s) of the pet parent(s)] enjoy life together and find joy in this life with the guidance and protection of the deities.

Sprinkle *Hexenkopf* water on each of the dogs or their item of representation.

Leader:
Hail [each dog's name]! Hail Weisskeppichi!
Hail Holle!
Hail Ewicher Yeeger!

Marriage

As with most of the life ceremonies we have discussed so far, marriage is yet another time for one's uniqueness to show. Whether we call it *marriage, jumping the broom, tying the knot,* or anything else, it all represents a commitment of two or more parties to one another. This can be done legally or not per the preference of those getting married. This ritual can be performed by the people getting married alone, by a family member or friend, or by a *Ziewer* and should be designed with the input of all parties involved.

If this is a ceremony that will have a legal element, make sure you (if you are performing the ceremony) or your officiant (if you are designing your ceremony with someone else) is legally recognized in the place you live or the location at which you will be married. At the current writing of this book, many LGBTQIA+ people are finding their rights to legally marry each other being challenged in some places. It is a sincere hope that this trend takes a plunge in the coming years. In any case, make sure you are aware of the laws in your area that relate to what is required for a legal marriage.

Keep in mind that there is no reason a commitment needs to have a legal stamp of approval from the government if all parties involved are in agreement. A marriage in the eyes of the gods is sacred, but it does not protect a domestic partnership when it comes to insurance, taxes, and medical emergencies. Some employers allow domestic partners to be covered by insurance, but if you are with an employer that does not offer this, you and your partner can choose to make each other medical power of attorney in case medical decisions need to be made. If you do get legally married, your taxes will change, and if one of you is disabled, your benefits can change. This decision is never to be made lightly. Like any other oath, it needs to be considered very carefully before committing.

While we have provided our general outline based on our generic ritual structure, this is your day, make it your own!

Die Vordraagung (Processional)

The partners enter together and approach the altar.

Die Aarufing (Convocation or Call to Worship)

As with other rites, the Aarufing is optional but can be sung if the participants wish.

Griesse (Greeting of Guests)

The partners, or the officiant, will state their intention to be married before the gods and those gathered.

Die Heiliching (The Hallowing)

Performed by either the couple or the officiant.

Die Aaruf (The Invocations)

The partners' choice of honored deities would be called upon to bless the marriage. Freid and Dunner are a common choice for this ceremony.

Die Aadacht zu der Waahra (Devotional to Waahra)

The partners or officiant recognize Waahra in her role of "Keeper of Oaths."

Die Hochzicheed (The Vows)

These are spoken by the partners to each other while holding the oath ring.

Sege (Sege to the Deities)

This is a toast to honor the chosen deities of the ceremony.

Zum Schluss (In Closing)

The partners or officiant makes closing remarks and closes the rite.

Der Auszuck (Recessional)

The partners leave the altar and exit from the ritual area.

Der Infehr (The Reception)

The sharing of food, drink, fellowship, conversation, dancing, etc. with all present.

Der Letscht Sege (Last Rite)

This ritual is used when someone is approaching death. It could be done bedside if the person is home on hospice or in a hospital or other care facility. Make sure if you are using this ritual in one of those places, you inform the health care professionals of your plans and the person's wishes if they haven't already told them.

As the ritual begins, the runes are drawn once on the forehead using the thumb of the application hand (typically the dominant hand) when the hand is in the thumbs-up form. Speak the following:

[English]
May your journey be smooth and even. (Reit)
May the stream waters be warm for you. (Loch)
May the walk through the wilderness be safe. (Baerke)
And may the hands of Holle guide you to the Mill. (Yaahr)
May your actions build you a good Urleeg. (Engel)
May your name long be spoken. (Gewwe)
With a good reputation and with love. (Winsch)
May the forebears smile upon you. (Ochdem)
As you leave this life, (Haagel)
Know that you have left behind your imprint. (Eisich)
Forward toward the Mill! (Reit)
Forward toward infinity! (Yaahr)
Hail to the traveler! (Kerze)
Make it always better! (Engel)
Make it always so! (Mann)

[Deitsch]
Meeg dir die Rees blatt sei. (Reit)
Meeg fer dich es Schtromwasser waarem sei. (Loch)
Meeg dir der Laaf darrich der Busch sicher sei. (Baerke)

Un meege der Holle ihre Hend dich darrich die Miehl voraafiehre.
(Yaahr)
Meeg dei Warick dir en guder Urleeg baue. (Engel)
Meeg dei Naame lang gschproche warre. (Gewwe)
Mit gudem Lob un mit Liewe. (Winsch)
Meeg dich die Vorgenger aalache. (Ochdem)
Weil du des Lewe verlosscht, (Haagel)
Weess as du dei Abdruck hinterlosse hoscht. (Eisich)
Vorwaerts noch die Miehl! (Reit)
Vorwaerts noch Endlosichkeet! (Yaahr)
Heele [zum Reeser/zur Reesern]. (Kerze)
Mach's immer besser! (Engel)
Mach's immer so! (Mann)

Die Reiniching (Cleansing)

This is a Pennsylvania Dutch tradition coming from the practice of *Braucherei*. When someone passes away, a strong tea of birch is decocted by the community elders for use during the memorial or funerary rites. The participants all drink a bit of the tea or have some dabbed on the forehead. Those closest to the one who passed are given extra and later are bathed or rinsed in the tea. Grief is seen as a visceral fire, and birch has the property of being able to halt fires and is also one of the trees best adapted to post-fire growth. It is thus said to remove the energetic imprint of the loss and to begin the renewal and recovery process. It is also strongly associated with the *Urglaawe* goddess Berchta, who has stability of the mind as one of her areas of concern, and with Freid, who has stability and security of the home as one of her areas of concern.

Die Richtschnier (Rules of Action)

A tradition received from *Braucherei* is that of resolving unfinished business with the deceased. This tradition, called *die Gedechtniszettel*, dictates that any person with a grievance toward the deceased must make peace at the time of the funeral. There are many methods to accomplish this, but *Urglaawe* has chosen to use paper to use in a fire. This can also be used to express unsure feelings during grief.

Hearkening back to our definition of *Fruchsfriede*, the concept of *die Richtschnier*, or the rules of action, includes morals, rules, protocols, and both the written laws and the unwritten morals of the community or greater society. In this example, the participants must resolve any unfinished business or disputes with the deceased. They can do so by writing down a resolution to the dispute on a slip of paper that is provided. This message can be private or shared with the *Ziewe*. The papers are either put into the actual fire or into the *Barick*, or barrow, which is similar to a casket with no top or a wheelbarrow with no wheel.

Die Bekehrung (The Conversion)

The subject of conversion can be sensitive, particularly since each person's experiences with religion and spirituality differ from those of anyone else. At its simplest form, though, taking on an *Urglaawe* identity can begin by saying the words, "I am an *Urglaawer*." There are, however, other considerations related to the conversion. For many, this means that conversion is not as much a single act as it is a process.

Simply changing our identity from one religion to another without changing our mentality can lead to a cognitive dissonance within the self from holding the values of one religion while bearing the trappings of another. This is particularly true in the United States, where Christianity's influence runs very deep, but it can certainly apply elsewhere. Some people cannot imagine that understanding and embracing the darker aspects of our minds can lead to enlightenment. Perhaps even more people cannot fathom the presence of multiple deities, much less multiple deities that are not omniscient, omnipresent, and infallible.

Urglaawe's lack of a single, designated sacred text has caused confusion among Christian chaplains in institutionalized settings, and the grassroots aspects of the establishment of *Urglaawe* have also brought about some criticism of it not being a real religion because there is no seminary. It is interesting that the rigidity of the orthodoxy of the dominant religion has led to so many people being unable to comprehend that a spiritual system can arise from within a community and without leaders with divinity degrees—just like Christianity itself began. This dissonance indicates that one's mindset and definitions of what a religion is are dictated by the prior religion, and that means that the new *Urglaawer* would benefit from the experience of a mindshift. Enter the *Umdenk*.

Es Umdenk (The Mindshift)

We often speak about the *Umdenk* when one converts from monotheism (particularly Christianity) to Heathenry. Within the *Urglaawe* community, this shift was first expressed by our kinsman Daniel Riegel prior to his passing in 2011. During a conversation after one of our celebrations, he described the mindshift in the context of embracing the dark half of the year, which was consistent with many others' experiences of recognizing the totality of the self, shadow and all. This recognition of our whole being is not the same as accepting ourselves "as is" and not striving to be better. Instead, it is using the totality of ourselves in order to become the best we can be.

There is a tendency in our society to pretend the shadowy sides of ourselves do not exist. We bury them deeply, and we are ashamed of them. This attitude is pervasive in some Plain sectarian communities, and it is rooted in Christian orthodoxy. Shadow sides are generally viewed as being evil or profane. Orthodoxy, meaning that one is required to believe a certain way, trumps orthopraxy, meaning that one is required only to practice the same way within a group. Orthodoxy leads to dogma, and dogma leads to suppression of variant ideas.

One of the more common beliefs within *Urglaawe* is that the deities want for us to be at the end of this cosmic cycle where they were at the beginning of it. To achieve this, we have to grow as a race of beings. Such growth, particularly an evolution of consciousness, is very difficult when the largest religions in the world actively attempt to limit questioning and independent thought.

Maintaining perspectives from Christianity while practicing Heathenry can result in confusion. Our relationships to the deities and to our ancestors differ from that of the Christian understanding. Our relationship to the world around us differs. It is difficult to wrap one's head around the idea that there may be multiple truths or that our deities have individual personalities that may lead them even into conflict with each other.

The lore is not gospel, and to treat the myths as such can lead one to a state of cognitive dissonance in which the baggage of orthodoxy remains even though the trappings of the religion have changed. Germanic Heathenry has never (at least within the period in which history has been written down) been monolithic. Different tribes knew different deities in different ways... and that is wonderful!

Ditching the mindset of Christianity is critical. We are not fallen. We do not need an intercessor to remove the stain of sin. We have the ability and responsibility to improve ourselves, yes, but we do so to create a better future for ourselves and for our descendants, not because we have a bill to pay from the past.

We have recently seen an uptick in people inquiring about our "unbaptism" information. For many *Urglaawer*, the "unbaptism" is an integral part of the mindshift. Addressing binding circumstances from previous religious identities and putting old business in order might help to make a cleaner break from one's religious past. We live in a society dominated by Christianity, and it is going to be nigh impossible to completely remove its influences from our lives (and, since a great many people whom we love are Christians, we want to keep them living long, happy, and healthy lives).

However, we can strive to remove the toxicity of the "only one way" mindset, and we can work with our deities, our ancestors and forebears, and (most importantly) our communities and selves to make the world a better place for ourselves and for those to come.

For some *Urglaawer*, part of the mindshift includes addressing any earlier religious commitments we made to other belief systems. For most of us, this has been Christianity's sacraments of baptism and confirmation.

Baptism and Confirmation Considerations

There is no requirement in *Urglaawe* to terminate relationships with any previous religion or religious organization (although we do ask that elements from other religions not be presented as being part of *Urglaawe*). Some *Urglaawer* follow another tradition in addition to ours, such as Wicca, Norse Paganism, or Christianity. Thus, for some folks, this is a nonissue. For others, breaking free from the bonds of other religious associations, particularly those that clash with the polytheistic nature of *Urglaawe*, was a critical and sacred act. This subject has come up frequently since its first appearance in 2013, when Rob was assisting prison inmates with spiritual questions as part of In-Reach Heathen Prison Services.

The original question from an inmate was whether there was a specific ritual that existed to be able to deal with one's prior baptism into Christianity. While we do not have a standard ritual per se, *Urglaawer* do have options to consider for the renunciation of a baptism, and, by extension, a confirmation.[23]

Die Uudaaf ("Unbaptism")

There are several ways to view this question, and how one deals with the baptism would depend on which of the following is most relevant:

- If one comes to the conclusion that Jehovah does not exist, then this presents no problem, right? However, if one still made an oath, does nonbelief in the entity that the oath was made to excuse one from that oath? Is one automatically released from their word in this situation? Is an oath ever irrelevant? As Heathens, we generally believe an oath is an extension of self and in it lies one's character.
- If one decides that their entire experience with Jehovah is based on lies, the oath itself is then invalid and can be ignored. We again run into having an unfulfilled oath here.
- One may understand right away that the oath needs to be addressed if one is to move forward. A visit to a church with an offering and an explanation as to why you are ending the oath is an acceptable way to deal with that loose end.
- Another way to resolve the issue would be to appeal to the goddess Zisa and the god Ziu with offerings and ask for help in resolving this unfair oath. Waahra, the deity that hears our oaths, can also help in this endeavor, handling this nullification of the oath from the Heathen side of things and with our own deities.

23. Robert L. Schreiwer, "Urglaawe | Baptism Renunciation | Heathen Traditions," The Troth, June 26, 2023, https://thetroth.org/resource/uglaawe-baptism-renunciation-heathen-traditions/.

- The final way is a very simple verbal pronouncement that can be done anywhere and anytime. One can simply state their desire to terminate the oath to Jehovah specifically and the Christian church in general.[24]

An individual may choose any of these actions as part of their individual spiritual evolution. Other resolutions to this question may certainly be considered and acted upon as warranted.

Other Oath and Binding Considerations

It is important to bear in mind that Heathens of all stripes need to watch for the pressures of oaths in other circumstances. The Pledge of Allegiance is an oath that students are compelled to recite even if they do not understand exactly what they are saying. Thus, they might learn the wrong lesson: that oaths are really not that important and we just say them because we have to. We must assert our rights to sovereignty of consciousness and belief whenever oaths, pledges, and the like turn up in the public sphere.

This chapter was a journey through the cycle of life, from birth through death, and how we create rituals to honor each step of the way. Ritual, at its core, is a way to bring about connection—with deity, with family, with community. These rites of passage are a way to celebrate with family and community during our most meaningful transitions. If you are solitary in your practice, the deities will happily partake in your celebrations.

24. Schreiwer, "Urglaawe | Baptism Renunciation."

9

BIRTH, LIFE, DEATH, REBIRTH

By Larry L. Goble Jr. and Ralph Hutt Young

Death is scary. Death is unwanted. Yet Death comes to all of us at some point. One of the lessons of *Allelieweziel* is that we live in a society that likes to pretend that death does not exist, but death is an integral part of life itself. And yet, due to our fear of it, we are obsessed with death. We depict death so cavalierly in movies and on television, yet because of this fear, we try to avoid planning for the end of the lives of our loved ones or of ourselves.

Urglaawer believe in rebirth. This is not to say that *Urglaawer* believe in the most commonly known Eastern style of complete soul rebirth. It's a bit more complicated than that. The gods' goal for humanity is that, at the end of this cosmic cycle, we will be where the deities were at the beginning of it. Our corporeal forms have limits to our lifetimes, but each soul's experience in this physical realm affords us the opportunity to advance toward that goal.

Due to this goal, death is not to be feared per se; instead, it is part of the continuity of life and the evolution of existence. We are to embrace our lives and to make the most of them, but the eventuality of death is something with which we all must reconcile ourselves.

Death is a gateway to a time of many complex emotions. Sadness, grief, anger, pain, fear, and regret are among the most common feelings. But there is also a place for relief and happiness. In *Urglaawe*, we embrace and encourage expressing the full spectrum of emotions we experience during this period. We explore this more in *die Gedechtnisleicht*, the celebration of life.

Deities and Observances Associated with Death

Holle, Berchta, and Ewicher Yeeger are our deities most closely associated with death. This is very appropriate, as they work in concert by keeping the cycle of death and rebirth flowing. While each has their own separate role in keeping that cycle flowing smoothly, they also work very closely together.

This can first be seen by looking at *der Lewesbaam*, the world tree. *Unnergegend*, the realm of earth-based spirits, evolving ancestors, and those waiting to be born or reborn, is the realm of Berchta. *Dunkelgegend*, the realm of destruction and transformation, is the realm of Holle, and this is where her Mill is located. The soul will pass through both realms in the course of this life cycle. Ewicher Yeeger, as our god of death itself, bridges between the two sisters.

As with death itself, there is uncertainty surrounding what happens with the soul upon death. There are various forms of the myth that influence our belief on this. One version is that if a person dies during the time when Holle is leading the Hunt, their soul construct joins Berchta and stays here in this realm (*es Hatzholz*). Berchta's parade of the recently deceased then joins Holle's Parade of Spirits on *Wonnenacht*. Another form of our myth is that souls immediately go to the *Miehl*, or Mill, in *Dunkelgegend* and wait for Holle to arrive there. Other versions state that they roam among the living until *Wonnenacht*. And still other stories state that they stray and will need to be found when the Hunt begins again. In reality, it is most likely a combination of these myths that actually happens (wandering spirits are often considered to be ghosts). This leads us to our observances associated with this cycle between *Allelieweziel* and *Wonnenacht*.

The Deity of Death

The observance of *Allelieweziel* ("the goal of all love") begins at sundown on October 30. It is at this time that a changing of the guard takes place as Holle leaves this realm (*es Hatzholz*) to lead the Wild Hunt and Berchta leaves her realm (*die Unnergegend*) to oversee the activities of *es Hatzholz*. It is during the Wild Hunt that Holle travels across all realms to collect the souls of those who have passed since the last Hunt. During this time, Berchta also assumes the responsibility of collecting the souls of those who pass in this realm in Holle's absence.

Wonnenacht is celebrated on the night of April 30 into May 1 and ends the dark half of the year. This is the observance of Holle's return from the Wild Hunt. The culmination of this celebration is the Parade of Spirits. It is during this parade that Holle and Berchta meet again, each with their collection of souls in tow, and at this reunion, a great celebration ensues. At the end of this celebration, the collected souls are directed to Holle's Mill where they will be processed into their individual parts and released to serve their next purpose.

Once in the Mill, the soul construct of the deceased is ground down and separated into its constituent parts, which are collected with the soul parts of the others that have died. Imagine, if you will, a stew pot full of parts of thousands of souls. When it is time for a new soul construct to be created, it can be described as ladling out "soul goop" or "soul soup." Every human soul construct (individual person) has individual experiences and lessons learned in each lifetime. Only by joining together and collecting these varied experiences can humans strive to advance humanity to where it needs to be by the end of this cosmic cycle. This blending of parts of disparate souls may also explain knowledge or past memories that seem illogical (remembering things that happened before we were born, the phenomenon of past lives, etc.). This blending is also part of why community on a larger scale is so important—we are literally all one and the same in some regards.

Another major deity in the celebration of *Allelieweziel* is Holler, Holle's consort. The last night and day (November 10 into November 11) are reserved for the observance of the holiday *Ewicher Yeeger Sege*. Ewicher Yeeger is another name for Holler. This god is strongly associated with death (if not Death itself personified). He is a complicated figure, as one would expect Death to be, but his role in the ongoing cycle of life, death, and rebirth is critical. Holler as der Ewicher Yeeger is a spirit known in English as the Eternal Hunter. He is credited with rescuing the early *Deitsch* settlements on the south side of the Blue Mountain. A crop failure had threatened to starve the settlements over the winter. That crop failure also resulted in deer and rabbits migrating to the south to find food. Ewicher Yeeger saved the folk by driving the game over the ridge toward the villages.

Dying a Good Death

Dying a good death means coming to terms and being at peace with your impending mortality as much as possible. This can encompass a wide range of things from resolving conflicts with friends, family, and community to planning so that your final days and funeral are handled the way you want. We will address the planning part of this in more detail in the Legal Considerations section of this chapter.

One of the most important things that we can do to prepare for a good death is to lead a good life. This does not mean that we must be perfect and never do anything wrong. This does mean living a life that you are at peace with. It also means resolving conflicts when they happen rather than letting hard feelings linger. Forgiveness or acceptance on another party's part is not always necessary for personal resolution when an honest effort is made. Also, an oft-overlooked part of living a good life is being very conscientious when making oaths, regardless of whether they be to deities or other people. You don't want the *Wyrd* of an unfulfilled oath looming over you in your ending days. Make oaths that are accomplishable in a reasonable time frame and be prepared to make good on the terms of any *Schuld*, or reconciliation.

Another thing we can do (and this is much more difficult for some of us) is to accept the inevitability of death. Just as the aging process brings us to struggle with the changes in our physical body, death leads us to struggle with the changes that come when we, or a loved one, are no longer embodied.

The physical aspects of the transition of life to post-life varies for almost everyone. Some people may need extensive medical equipment at the end of their physical journey or even a hospital stay. Others may decide to remove themselves from that type of equipment and choose to pass at their home or the home of a loved one. *Urglaawe* does not view either type of decision as "better" than the other. It is up to that individual (and their loved ones) to make that choice. The community's obligation is to support that person so that they can make such decisions honestly.

That said, the traditional way in the *Deitscherei* is to die at home with family surrounding the dying person. It can oftentimes be more soothing and peaceful if the illness or injuries causing transition can be handled in one's comfort zone. Hospice programs and death midwives can aid in this, as hospice nurses can assist with any needed medical assistance, and death midwives emotionally support the person who is passing as well as their loved ones. Dying in one's own home also makes it easier for loved ones to care for the body after death in the traditional manner, such as washing the body and sitting with the body for a day or two to help the soul transition to being disembodied.

Often in modern culture we think of mourning as something that happens only after a death and not also before death. There are a multitude of times that mourning before a death occurs, and it is completely understandable and very healthy. If one has to deal with a decline in health, such as becoming paralyzed or losing vision or hearing, it is healthy to mourn those losses. Mourning and the grief process do not follow a straight line; there is no "right way" to process grief, and *Urglaawe* realizes that. This influences our funerary rite, *die Gedechtnisleicht.*

Die Gedechtnisleicht (The Celebration of Life)

Our funerary rite is called *die Gedechtnisleicht*, the celebration of life. The overall ceremony is split into several parts: the hailing, the feast, and the procession of the barrow. The barrow (with a photograph, drawing, or other symbol of the deceased) stands as a symbol of the journey that the deceased is making.

Sammel (Hailing Rite)

The first part of this ceremony is a hailing rite. This is similar to the most common hailing rite (*Sammel*); we stand in a circle and pass the stein from one person to the next. However, in *die Gedechtnisleicht*, the stein remains on the altar. People are encouraged to approach the altar one at a time, to take the stein, and to share their memories or thoughts in a hailing rite to the deceased's memory. As these thoughts and memories are shared, we not only cry together, but also often laugh together. As a person we love will make us smile and laugh in life, it is appropriate to allow memories of those times to make us smile and laugh at this celebration of their life.

Additionally, slips of paper are provided for the attendees. This is an opportunity for individuals to express in writing any private prayers, thoughts, or unresolved issues that are for the deceased but not the general gathering. Instructions are on the slips of paper.

Schmaus (Feast)

An important part of all of our rites is to also enjoy a feast together while the deceased's representation is present. A place will be left for them and a plate prepared. This reminds us that while they are no longer among us in body, they remain with us in our memories. During this feast, we encourage those gathered to feel free to continue sharing memories of the deceased.

RECIPE

Urglaawischi Drauersupp (Grief Soup)

It is customary to share grief soup during this funerary feast. This soup is imbued with blessings to bestow comfort on those affected by the passing of the deceased. The following is the recipe that has been developed for this purpose.

Over several iterations of needing to prepare this soup, we wanted to develop a standard of sorts. While marjoram with a little rosemary is the main constant, there didn't seem to be a recipe from our research or lore. So, when we committed to developing a recipe, we set out to find a recipe with meaning and symbolism.

At the outset, we knew we wanted to use earthy ingredients. And, secondly, since the soup is meant to be comforting and supportive, we felt like something cream based would be appropriate because it would be thick and filling. We found a recipe that included root vegetables and marjoram and tweaked it from there. The recipe includes leek, potato, and onion; these are appropriate because they represent that which thrives in realms below ground. It includes mushroom, which is appropriate because mushrooms use decaying matter to grow and emerge from the ground and provide nutrients when eaten. The cream in the recipe represents new life and the nourishment given by it. Even the preparation method is indicative of the time and process of our death and dying cycle. There's a point at which you must blend the ingredients, which could be seen as symbolic of the Mill.

The recipe is also easily modified for increased portions, and some ingredients could be changed to accommodate dietary restrictions. For example, one could use coconut milk, almond milk, or cashew milk as a nondairy substitute for the sour cream, and one could substitute vegetable stock for chicken stock as a vegetarian option. Makes 6–8 servings.

Ingredients

1 leek, white portion only, sliced

1 potato, peeled and cubed

1 medium-sized white or yellow onion, chopped

2 tablespoons fat (bacon fat, lard, or vegetable oil are all acceptable)

1 cup (8 ounces) mushrooms, sliced (a mixture of a variety of mushrooms or a single variety)

4 cups of broth (chicken or vegetable)

Marjoram, one good handful fresh, or 1/8 cup dried

2 tablespoons butter (could use vegetable oil)

1 cup sour cream (or nondairy substitute)

Additional marjoram, sprig of rosemary, salt, and pepper to taste

Directions

Combine leek, potato, and onion with fat in a Dutch oven (or slow cooker). Cook on high until vegetables soften.

Add mushrooms and broth to mixture. Toss in the marjoram. Let simmer for several hours.

Turn the heat to the lowest setting. Use an immersion blender to smooth out the soup. Whisk in butter and sour cream. Add additional marjoram, rosemary, salt, and pepper to taste.

Before serving, a blessing should be said over the soup, bestowing comfort on those who partake. (It would also be appropriate to say a blessing over each step in the process and especially during the blending process.) Some may find this soup a little bland. Feel free to play around with additional seasoning. Just be sure that the marjoram is not overpowered.

Die Leichtlaaf (The Procession of the Barrow)

After the hailing rite is completed and appropriate offerings are made, the attendees receive the *Sege*, or blessing. After the *Sege* has finished, *die Leichtlaaf*, or the procession, commences, at which time the folk will stand, forming the processional path along which the *barick*, or barrow travels. Attendees are invited to place onto the barrow as it passes their slips of paper, flowers, and any other gifts that will accompany the deceased on their journey.

The barrow will then be wrapped in four colors of cloth in an age-old Pennsylvania German *Braucherei* custom: Red represents the journey of life; green or yellow-green represent the commending of the physical form back to nature; black represents the mysterious afterlife, which is seen in *Deitsch* myth as being when one passes through the Mill; and white represents the spark of the Divine found in all of us that continues to live on.

After the barrow is wrapped, it is ceremonially burned along with lavender and cornflower, signifying the release of the deceased soul, enabling it to return to be milled and rejoin the cycle of life once again.

We observe moments of silence and contemplation as we remember them during their journey to the ancestors.

We then receive *die Reiniching*, or cleansing. After the *Reiniching*, we then cut the sacred space. Guests are encouraged to engage in a time of fellowship.

Legal Considerations

We have been focusing on the spiritual aspects of death, but there are also mundane aspects that must be given consideration. Without the proper legal documents in order, things may not be handled as you would like during your final days and upon your transition. While laws differ from state to state, there is generally one form or another of documents listed below.

There are many books available to help you with preparing to fill out these documents. Two of which are *Peace of Mind Planner: Important Information about My Belongings, Business Affairs, and Wishes* and *I'm Dead. Now What? Important Information about My Belongings, Business Affairs, and Wishes*, both by Peter Pauper Press. Working with books like these will give you a chance to take your time and gather the information you need in a more relaxed atmosphere. These books also give you the chance to document things that are not covered in the typical legal documents, such as care for pets and the handling of social media accounts.

The best place to store these documents is in a waterproof and fireproof lock box or safe in your home. Also make sure that your executor and other designees know where it is and how to access it, such as keys and combinations. We want to make sure that people in the community are buried as they wish to be.

Here is a list of documents:

- **Durable power of attorney for health care:** This document will legally designate who can make medical decisions on your behalf in the event that you are unable to.
- **Advance directive:** An advance directive is where you outline the medical decisions the medical power of attorney must follow. Two of these directives are the DNR, or "do not resuscitate," and the DNI, or "do not intubate." It would also include the extent of interventions you wish to undergo should you be unable to make those decisions yourself.
- **Practitioner orders for life-sustaining treatment** (**POLST**)**:** POLST complements an advance directive but is more geared toward decisions surrounding eminent end of life rather than general procedures during a time when one might be unconscious or unable to make those decisions. If your family member is on hospice, this would be a valuable form to have. It is valid in any health care situation, not just the primary hospital or with the care team of the patient. Of all the important paperwork, this and the advance directive are the ones most important to have quick access to if your family member still lives at home. If you ever needed to call for emergency medical services, these will be needed to show them what they can and cannot do per the wishes of your family member.
- **Authorization to release medical information:** This is a document that needs to be on file with your health insurance company. This will allow the person designated on the form to have access to your medical

information. While the durable power of attorney for health care will allow the designee to make medical decisions for you, this document is often not honored by insurance companies and expires upon your passing. This will be very important for family members trying to settle remaining medical bills.

- **Designated agent for body disposition:** This document designates who will be responsible for making your funeral arrangements. This document becomes particularly important if you and your next of kin follow different paths. Without this document, your body and all decisions regarding your interment are defaulted to your next of kin. We have had several members of our community pass without having this document, and in some situations, it was difficult if not impossible to give them the funeral that they would have wanted. In some states this is an addendum to your will and in others it is a stand-alone document.
- **Last will and testament:** A legal document by which a person expresses their wishes as to how their property is to be distributed at death and names one or more persons, the executor(s), to manage the estate until its final distribution.

Templates for many if not all of these documents are available online at minimal or no cost. Some, like the POLST and authorization to release medical information, you need to obtain from your physician or health insurance provider. Depending on the laws in your state, most of these documents do not require a lawyer to fill them out, but it may be in your best interest to consult with one to make sure that all considerations are taken into account. Additionally, depending on the laws in your state, some of these documents may need to be notarized. This service is often offered free of charge by many banks.

This is not an easy subject to broach or discuss, but it should not be avoided. It isn't something that should wait until you are older or closer to death. Everyone can benefit from organizing their end-of-life wishes well and early. It is a way to not only make your wishes known, but it will give your living family and friends the gift of not having to make difficult decisions when planning after your passing.

CONCLUSION

We just tried to put the entirety of our practice into a single book, and that is a difficult task, and in some ways impossible. The very interaction of those practicing *Urglaawe* is what gives our tradition the *Gemietlichkeet*, that sense of belonging, we are so often searching for.

In this digital age, geographical barriers need not restrict our spiritual pursuits. One of the first steps toward creating an *Urglaawe* community, and perhaps a freehold outside of Pennsylvania, is by joining and actively participating in the main *Urglaawe* Facebook group. Here, you can connect with like-minded individuals, learn from experienced practitioners, and share your own insights and ask questions. There is also a map on the page that shows the locations of many of the members of the *Urglaawe* community. One can connect with those local to you that might be interested in meeting up with you.

Another way to meet those who might be interested is to organize monthly fellowship gatherings, called *pubmoots*, at restaurants or taverns, or at other friendly, inclusive venues, where people can come together, socialize, and discuss their interest in *Urglaawe*. Creating a meetup group is one way to advertise the pubmoot or parkmoot.

Of course, it is also possible to be a solitary *Urglaawe* practitioner. We have given you all you need to start your solitary practice in this book. Feel free to use as much or as little of it as you wish. While you may wish to practice alone, we hope you also join the main Facebook page so that we can support you on your journey!

Urglaawe is a rich and full tradition. Above all, it is a living tradition that continues to evolve, just as we ourselves evolve. We constantly uncover new information and connect new dots. Old stories come to light, and new connections get made, which bring new insights to our existing base of knowledge. We welcome you to join us on this journey.

APPENDIX A

DEITSCH LANGUAGE AND PRONUNCIATION GUIDE

One of the challenges to taking on the study of *Urglaawe* is the use of the *Deitsch* language. Learning the language is not a prerequisite to practicing the religion. Many *Urglaawer* use only English in their daily practice. However, it is encouraged to use *Deitsch* as frequently as possible because it is the language from which these practices originally arose. The demise of *Deitsch* has been predicted since the colonial era, yet, even with a history of bigotry behind it and without the support of any government entity, the number of native speakers continues to grow. Younger generations wish to learn the language of their forebears. *Urglaawe*'s use of *Deitsch* as an official language helps to bolster the adoption of modern vocabulary throughout communities, and it keeps the language relevant in the communities' daily lives.

Pronunciation Guide for Deitsch Words

Below is a pronunciation guide for the *Deitsch* language. *Deitsch* spelling is not standardized across all regions, even among academics. In 2023, *Urglaawe* adopted the spelling system that is used on PADutchDictionary.com because that website is readily accessible to *Deitsch* speakers and students alike, and the online dictionary can be updated easily. Prior to 2023, *Urglaawe* used the spelling system of Eugene Stine's *Pennsylvania German Dictionary*. The change between the two is not a major transition, but there are some words that do differ between these dictionaries.

Useful Tips

All nouns, whether common, proper, or abstract, are capitalized in *Deitsch* no matter where they appear in a sentence. All pronouns are in lowercase unless they appear as the first word in a sentence. Stress in *Deitsch* is usually on the first syllable of the word. Some verbs keep their stress on the root even when a prefix is added. For example, the stress on the verb *verschteh* falls on the second syllable because *-schteh* is the root of the verb.

Alphabet

The *Deitsch* alphabet consists of the following letters:

A, B, C, D, E, F, G, H, I, K, L, M, N, O, P, R, S, T, U, V, W, X, Y, Z, plus Ä, Ö, Ü, ß, which appear in old texts, some surnames, and in Fraktur fonts, particularly when used in religious contexts. All letters have both upper- and lowercases with the exception of ß, which has traditionally only been used in lowercase.

The letters J and Q are only used in foreign words, and the sounds they represent in English do not exist in *Deitsch*.

Vowels

Deitsch vowels, like English vowels, are categorized as being either short or long.

Short Vowels

A: Pronounced as English "o" in "pot"; *Deitsch* example: *alt*

AE: Pronounced like English "a" in "match"; *Deitsch* example: *Maetsch*

E: Pronounced like English "e" in "met"; *Deitsch* example: *zwett*

I: Pronounced like English "i" in "fit"; *Deitsch* example: *Kind*

O: Pronounced like English "u" in "hut"; *Deitsch* example: *hocke*

U: Pronounced like English "u" in "put"; *Deitsch* example: *Sunn*

Long Vowels

AA or AAH: This sound does not exist in English but is approximated by the English "aw" in "law"; *Deitsch* example: *Fraa.*

E, EE, EEH, EH, OE: Pronounced like English "ai" in "rain"; *Deitsch* examples: *fehle, lese.*

AE: Pronounced like an extended or drawled English "ai" in "hair"; *Deitsch* example: *gaern.*

IH, IE, IEH: Pronounced as "ie" in English "believe"; *Deitsch* examples: *dihr, Fiess.*

O, OO, OH: Pronounced like English "o" in "go" but held longer and with no slide to a diphthongal "u"; *Deitsch* examples: *rot, froh.*

U, UU, UH: Pronounced like English "oo" in "coo"; UU is drawn out in northern variants; *Deitsch* examples: *zu, Fuuss, Schtuhl.*

Diphthongs

AI: Pronounced like English "y" in "my"; used mostly in place names and surnames; *Deitsch* example: *Mainz*

AU: Pronounced like English "ou" in "mouse"; *Deitsch* example: *Maus*

EI: Pronounced like English "ie" in "pie"; *Deitsch* example: *drei*

OI: Pronounced like English "oi" in "oil"; *Deitsch* example: *Moi*

Front vs. Back Vowels

Like English vowels, *Deitsch* vowels are also categorized as front or back vowels, depending on where the tongue is placed during utterance. In *Deitsch*, the location of the vowel can affect the pronunciation of the adjacent consonants, particularly in the case of the letter L and the digraph CH.

Front Vowels

The front vowels are A, AE (short and long), E, EE, EEH, EH, I, IH, IE, IEH, OE, U, and the diphthongs EI and OI.

Back Vowels

The back vowels are AA, AAH, O, OH, OO, UH, UU, and the diphthong AU.

Consonants

B, D, F, G, H, K, L, M, N, P, S, T, and Y are pronounced very similarly to English with the following exceptions:

B: At the end of a word, "b" approximates English "p"

D: At the end of a word, "d" approximates English "t"

G: At the end of a word, "g" approximates English "k"; in the middle of a word, "g" approximates English "y"

H: In the middle or at the end of a word, "h" is not pronounced; it indicates that the preceding vowel is long

L: At the beginning of a word or after front vowels (a, ae, ai, e, ee, i, ie, oe, u), "l" is created by touching the tongue on the rising part of the hard palate above the rear of the upper teeth; after back vowels (aa, au, o, oo, uu), "l" is very similar to English "l"

S: Most commonly, "s" is pronounced like English "s," but it also can be pronounced like English "z," particularly at the beginning of words when followed by long vowels

C, R, V, W, and Z are pronounced differently from English.

C: This letter rarely appears by itself in *Deitsch* words, and even in those cases, they are mostly surnames or place names; "c" is mostly written as part of one of two digraphs: CH or CK

R: This sound is created by trilling or flapping the tongue once; in some northern variants, a uvular "r," which sounds similar to gargling, occurs at the beginning of words when followed by the short vowels "o" and "u." The combination of the letters "er" is pronounced like the "a" in English "father." "R" at the end of a word, in between a vowel and a consonant, or in between a diphthong and a consonant, is also pronounced like the "a" in English "father."

V: This letter is always pronounced like English "f"; it is never pronounced like English "v"

W: This letter is most frequently pronounced like English "v"; some variants do pronounce it like English "w," particularly at the beginnings of words. *Urglaawe* uses the English "v" pronunciation as standard for ritual use.

Z: In *Deitsch*, this letter is never pronounced like English "z"; the sound is a "ts" or a "tz" no matter where in the word the letter falls. If one can say "tsetse fly" in English, then the correct pronunciation has been accomplished.

Digraphs, Trigraphs, and Quadgraphs

BB: The digraph "bb" never begins a word. It makes the sound of an unaspirated English "p"; it is similar to saying the English word "pop" but keeping the lips together at the end of the word so that it is not followed by the puff of air that is part of English pronunciation.

BH: The digraph "bh" makes the sound of a lightly aspirated English "p." The sound is closely approximated by whispering the English word "pop." This digraph never appears at the end of a word.

CH: The "ch" digraph does not occur at the beginning of words, and it is never pronounced like English "ch"; after the vowels "a," "aa," "o," "u," it makes a sound similar to that made by clearing the throat. After any other vowel or consonant (except for "s") it is similar to an exaggerated "h" in the English word "huge" and reminiscent of a cat's hiss.

CK and GH: The "ck" and "gh" digraphs' pronunciations and uses are identical to the "ck" digraph in English. *Deitsch* "gh" is never silent like the "gh" digraph in English. These digraphs never occur at the beginning of a word.

GW: The digraph "gw" is the cognate of English "q," but there is no "k" sound in the beginning, and the "w" portion is pronounced like an English "v." Thus, the sound the digraph makes would sound like "gv" in English.

NG: The digraph "ng" is always pronounced like the "ng" in English "singer" and never like the "ng" in English "finger." The "n" and the "g" make one sound together, so no individual "n" or "g" sound should be audible.

SS: The digraph "ss" is always pronounced like "ss" in English, never like English "z."

SCH: The trigraph "sch" makes the English "sh" sound. This is the only way to represent the English "sh" sound using *Deitsch* orthography.

When the letters "s" and "h" appear beside one another in *Deitsch* words such as *bisher*, they are parts of different syllables and are pronounced individually, as is "bis her."

TSCH: The quadgraph "tsch" approximates the hard, first "ch" in English "church" but never sounds like the second, softer English "ch" in the same word. The English "j" sound does not exist in *Deitsch*, so names like Johnny are rendered as Tschanni.

Older Letters

Ä still appears in some surnames when written in *Deitsch*, old texts, or artistic works utilizing Fraktur fonts but is otherwise rendered as "ae" or, less frequently, as "ee."

Ö is very rarely encountered in old texts. It has been almost wholly replaced by "e" and "ee," though some surnames have replaced it with "oe." The letter is used in artistic works using Fraktur fonts but only in the rare circumstance in which "oe" still appears in a *Deitsch* word.

Ü appears in some old texts and in some surnames when written in *Deitsch*. The letter has been almost wholly replaced by "ie" in *Deitsch* words, so it is only rarely used in artistic works using Fraktur fonts,

ß is rendered as "ss" in *Deitsch*, though this letter is still frequently used in place of "ss" in artistic works that use Fraktur fonts, particularly within the *Urglaawe* community.

APPENDIX B

URGLAAWE QUICK REFERENCES

This appendix is meant to be a quick reference guide with keywords for the concepts and beings in the book. If you remember a part of a name or need to look up a color reference, this will be the place to come search!

Beings and Deities

These are the deities and beings we introduced you to in the book with simple descriptions.

For more information, see the Ase and Wane information on page 43.

die Alcis (pl.): Brother gods of the *Ase* who protect brothers during wartime.

der As (masc.), die Asin (fem.), die Ase (pl.): Tribe of deities known in Scandinavian lore as the Aesir.

die Baricke Mariche: Maria Jung, also known as "Mountain Mary." Legendary figure in *Deitsch* folklore, who associated with *Braucherei*.

die Berchta: Goddess of the *Wane*, sister of Holle. Strongly associated with order of the mind and the completion arc of cycles.

Buckliches Mannli: "the Buckled Man," a goblin spirit who takes over the empty *Butzemenner* if not burned at *Allelieweziel*.

der Butzemann (masc), die Butzemenner (pl.): A spiritually activated scarecrow.

der Dunner: *Ase* god associated with thunder, the working class, and courage.

die Eppeldraagerin (Idunn): The Apple Carrier; while the sacredness of apples is visible throughout Germanic lore, the name of the goddess associated with apples was unknown to *Deitsch* lore. *Urglaawe* has adopted the name *Idunn* from other Heathen traditions.

die Erda: *Wane* goddess of the earth and soil.

die Elwe: Elves, several tribes of beings from different realms on the *Lewesbaam.*

Ewicher Yeeger: The Eternal Hunter; also known as der Holler. God of the *Wane* and consort to Holle and brother of Schlumm; associated with death, pestilence, and plague, yet also with second chances, transformations, and growth through strife.

die Feierries: Fire giants; live in the *Suddbledder* realm on the *Lewesbaam.* Considered enemies of the deities.

die Freid: *Ase* goddess of hearth, home, safety, security, motherhood; consort to Wudan and sister of Voll and Volla.

der Fro: *Wane* god of bounty, fertility, and fecundity; brother to Frouwa.

die Frouwa: *Wane* goddess associated with bounty, wealth, sexuality, and business acumen; sister to Fro.

Gedreier Eckhart: Folk hero who runs ahead of the Wild Hunt to announce the coming fury; loyal servant to Holle.

die Helling: One of the Oschdre sisters. Associated with the daytime sky, daylight, white, and bright colors.

die Holle: *Wane* goddess and mother of *Urglaawe*; chiefess of the *Urglaawe* pantheon; oversees cycles of life, death, and rebirth. Consort to Ewicher Yeeger.

der Holler: See Ewicher Yeeger.

der Holzhacker: The Woodchopper. Shapeshifting entity who tries to distract the souls of the departing from arriving at *Holle*'s *Miehl.*

die Idis (sing.), die Idise (pl.): Female guides, advisors, and protectors of subsequent generations; origin of the concept of the fairy godmother.

die Kowwold (pl.): Kobolds, a particular type of house elf also associated with the mining industry.

der Luul: God of the *Wane*; doula to the yearly cycle of nature, particularly in protecting young spring greens from freezing.

die Mariyeschtann: Goddess of the *Wane* associated with the Morning Star (Venus); sister to Sunna.

der Macher: The Maker. An aspect of *Wurt* that set the process of creation into motion.

der Muun: God of the *Wane* associated with the moon, with tides, and with eclipses; star-crossed lover of Sunna.

die Melkern: The Milkmaid. A shapeshifting being who tries to distract newly assembled souls from their route from the *Dunkelgegend* to the *Unnergegend*.

die Nacht: One of the Oschdre sisters. Goddess of the *Wane* associated with night, darkness, dark colors, the night sky, and space.

die Nehalennia: Goddess of the *Wane* associated with safe passage over water.

die Neine Winde (pl.): Nine Winds, children of Holle: Gibbel (north), Bodde (south), Schteig (east), Setz (west), Schnall (northeast), Warrem (southeast), Kalt (northwest), Riffel (southwest), Wärwel (whirlwind).

die Oschdra: One of the Oschdre sisters. Goddess of the *Wane* who transforms grays into colors; associated with the dawn, the east, and new beginnings.

die Oschdre (pl.): Three sister goddesses of the *Wane*, who introduced color, cardinal directions, bird migrations, and the rotation of earth to the Hatzholz. See also die Helling, die Nacht, and die Oschdra.

die Reifries (pl.): Frost giants, whose realm is in the *Naddbledder* of the *Lewesbaam*. Their power grows by weakening the order of the other realms.

der Ries (masc.), die Riesin (fem.), die Ries (pl.): Giants from several related races of beings who are perceived as much larger than humans and who possess ancient knowledge and fierce power, and who are generally considered antipathetic toward humans.

die Saaga: Goddess of the *Ase*; the keeper of stories; maintainer of language; inspiration behind ideas, concepts, and great works.

der Schadde: Of unknown family origin. *Deitsch* trickster figure.

der Schlumm: God of the *Wane* associated with sleep, dreams, altered states, visions; brother of Ewicher Yeeger.

die Siwwa: Goddess of the *Ase*; strongly associated with grains and grain harvests.

die Sunna: Goddess of the *Wane* associated with enlightenment; personification of the sun; star-crossed lover of Muun and sister of Mariyeschtann.

der Tuisko: *Wane* god, son of Zisa and Ziu.

der Voll: *Ase* god of abundance; twin of *Volla*, brother of *Freid.*

die Volla: *Ase* goddess of abundance; twin of *Voll*, sister of *Freid.*

die Waahra: Goddess of the *Ase* who oversees the taking and maintaining of oaths.

der Wan (masc.), die Wanin (fem.) (sing.), die Wane (pl.): Tribe of deities known to the Scandinavians as the Vanir.

Weisskeppichi Fraa: The White-Haired Lady or White-Haired Woman; goddess of the *Wane*; strongly associated with *Braucherei* and *Megge* (life-force energy).

der Wudan: *Ase* god associated with fury, pursuits of higher consciousness, the collection of knowledge, warfare, and "thinking outside the box" solutions; consort to Freid.

der Wurt: The Maker of creation and the ensuing threads that weave all of creation together.

die Wurthexe: Goddesses who weave and manage everyone's *Wurt*; believed by many *Urglaawer* to be manifestations of *Wurt* itself; there are an unknown number of these goddesses, but *Deitsch* oral tradition holds that there is at least one for every verb tense and mood.

die Ziewe: Neologism to serve as a nonbinary term for "deities."

die Zisa: *Ase* goddess associated with doing or undoing "knots" or placing or removing obstacles in order to guide one's right action. Associated with the South Star (Vega).

der Ziu: *Ase* sky god associated with justice and right action. Overseer of the *Ding*. Associated with the North Star (Polaris).

die Zwarich: Dwarves, whose home realm on the *Lewesbaam* is in the *Unnergegend.* Created by the deities before humans.

Colors

Colors are used for altar decorations, clothing choices for rituals as well as for specific rites.

For a further discussion on colors, see page 166. Unless otherwise noted, all of the entries below are nouns.

es Arrensch: Orange, adds extra strength.

es Blo: Blue, represents calmness and clarity.

es Blutrot: Blood red, represents the blood.

es Brau: Brown, represents soil.

die Farewe: Colors, hues.

es Gehl: Yellow, represents connection to divinity.

es Gehlbrau: Tan, represents connection to animals.

es Gehlgrie: Yellow-Green, represents fading or dying.

es Gold: Gold, represents opulence and fortune.

es Grie: Green, represents fertility and bounty.

es Gro: Gray, represents uncertainty and liminality.

es Karminrot: Crimson, represents death.

es Rot: Red, represents passion, the body, and justice.

es Schifferich: Slate, represents connection to minerals.

es Schwatz: Black, represents protection.

es Veilich: Purple, violet, represents cosmic energy and nobility.

es Weiss: White, represents illumination, brilliance, inspiration, and knowledge.

Core Values

The core values are our guiding principles that we aspire to. They are intertwined with our everyday lives, providing spiritual guidance and connection to the living world around us. For a further discussion on the core values, see page 33.

die Addning: Discipline
die Ausdauer: Perseverance
der Edelmut: Generosity
die Ehr: Honor
die Geischtlichkeet: Spirituality
die Gschwisichabhenkichkeet: Interdependence
es Mitleid: Compassion
der Mut: Courage
die Neigierheit: Curiosity
die Schaffichheit: Industriousness
der Selbschtreiguck: Introspection
die Selbschtverbessering: Self-Improvement
die Treie: Troth/Loyalty
die Uffwaarting: Hospitality
die Verwalting: Stewardship
die Verwandschaft: Kinship
die Waahrheit: Truth
die Weisheit: Wisdom

Holidays

Our Wheel of the Year is here both by month and by alphabetical order. For a further discussion on the holidays, see page 99.

By Month

March (at the spring equinox): *Oschdresege*
April: *Ziegdaag, Hexenacht/Wonnenacht*

May: *Wonnezeit, Der Grieg Geeich die Reifries*

June: Observance of the Desecrated Shrines, *Summeraafang, Dingsege*

July/August: *Hoietfescht*

September: *Erntfescht, Zisasege*

October: *Allelieweziel*

November: *Ewicher Yeeger/Hollersege, Die Verschimpfing Geeich der Reifkeenich*

December: *Voryuul/Lutzelfraalaaf; Yuulzeit: Yuulsege, Berchtaslaaf*

January: *Yuulzeit* ends/*Frofescht*

February: *Entschtanning, Grundsaudaag, Lichderfescht*

March: *Grumbieredaag/Frouwasege*

Alphabetized

Alleliewezie!: Sunset October 30–November 11; major observance of the final harvest, the culling of herds, and Holle's departure onto the Wild Hunt.

Berchtaslaaf: Sunset December 31–sunrise January 1; recognition of the end of the year, of the limits of existence within time. Traditional meal consists of oysters and crackers or of herring and gruel.

Dingsege: Ritual that accompanies the gathering of a *Ding*; often to handle legal matters, paperwork, and deity blessings within the community.

Entschtanning: February 2–14; the emergence from winter and the celebration of potential life.

Erntfescht: "Harvest Home"; the high harvest on the autumn equinox and celebration of the *Ase* deities.

Ewicher Yeeger Sege: Also known as *Hollersege*, November 11; end of *Allelieweziel.*

Frofescht: Feast of Fro, January 1; traditional pork and sauerkraut feast of abundance.

Frouwasege: Frouwa's blessing day, March 17; end of the potato cycle, when the remnants of last year's potato crops are used to bake bread to honor Frouwa. Potatoes are planted to begin the planting season for hardy crops.

Geischderschtrutz: Parade of Spirits: Mid-December; this is a cultural parade through the streets of Philadelphia that echoes the parades of the *Deitsche* in earlier eras. This is the time of *Belsnickeling*, or *Deitsch* tricks-or-treats.

der Grieg Geeich die Reifries: The Battle Against the Frost Giants in May, when the army of *Butzemenner* rises to beat back the frost giants.

Grumbieredaag: Potatoes Day, March 17; see *Frouwasege*.

Grundsaudaag: Groundhog Day; time to make and activate *Butzemenner*, or scarecrows.

Hexenacht: Witches' Night, sundown April 30; the beginning of *Wonnezeit*.

Hoietfescht: Haymaking festival; late July or early August at the first harvest. Celebration for the *Wane* deities.

Hollersege: November 11. See *Ewicher Yeeger Sege*.

Kannsege: Ceremony of the Corn to activate the *Butzemann* at *Entschtanning*.

Lichderfescht: Festival of Lights; celebrated the last night of *Entschtanning*. Celebrates the promise of new life and renewal.

Lutzelfraaslaaf: Progression of the Lantern Lady on the fifth night of *Voryuul*, December 13.

Observance of the Desecrated Shrines: Day of remembrance, June 5, to honor the deities whose sacred shrines were destroyed through the acts of religious terrorism.

Oschdresege: Spring equinox celebration of birth and rebirth.

Summeraafang: The summer solstice, longest day of the year, representing more active participation in community events.

die Verschimpfing Geeich der Reifkeenich: Railing Against King Frost; spellwork from *Hexerei* held in November to disavow any hold that *der Reifkeenich*, or King Frost, and winter will have over one's well-being.

Voryuul: The twelve nights before the winter solstice, a time for introspection of one's own motivations and of the integration of the shadow side.

Wonnenacht: see *Hexenacht*.

Wonnezeit: Time of Joy, observance that begins at sunset on April 30 (1. Wonnet on the *Urglaawe* calendar) and runs for twelve nights and twelve days. This is the time of honoring trees that are significant to the economies of the local area and of recognizing the reawakening of the dormant plants.

Yuul: Winter solstice, representing both a new sun for the upcoming year and the new soul construct being assembled.

Yuulsege: Winter solstice ritual, typically involving the burning of a large log or the lighting of a burning sunwheel.

Yuulzeit: Yule time sundown December 20–December 31, represents the time between lives prior to the soul's next conception. Observance features meditations on *Urglaawe*'s core values.

Ziegdaag: April 1, Moving Day. Honors the shadowy, shady, and trickster figures in our lore.

Zisasege: Feast of Zisa, September 28. Originally a harvest festival celebrated by the ancient Suevi tribe, this observance is part of the *Erntfescht* celebrations.

Zwelfder Daag: Twelfth Day of *Yuul*, running from sunrise to sunset on January 1; date of *es Frofescht* and the end of *die Yuulzeit*.

Months

These are the months of the year as used in *Urglaawe* practice. They differ from the typical *Deitsch* month names.

die Hadding: January

die Hanning: February

die Lenzing: March

die Oschdret: April

die Wonnet: May

die Broochet: June

die Hoiet: July

die Aernet: August

die Scheiding: September

die Gehling: October

die Newweling: November

die Yuuling: December

Days of the Week

Urglaawe uses the same names as the general *Deitsche* do for the days of the week.

Muundaag: Monday

Dinschdaag: Tuesday

Mittwoch: Wednesday

Dunnerschdaag: Thursday

Freidaag: Friday

Samschdaag: Saturday

Suundaag: Sunday

Parts of the Soul

Below is a quick reference for the parts of the soul and their associations. For a further discussion on parts of the soul, see page 29.

der Folyer (masc.), die Folyerin (fem.) (sing.), die Folyer (pl.): Fetch, also called the *Guardian Spirit* or the *Journeyer*.

die Leich: Space in which the soul permeates the physical body.

der Geischt is a subset of the soul that has ten parts:

- **es Gemiet:** This is the complete self, including one's shadows and temperament.
- **die Gewut:** The center of one's desires, passions, and aspirations.
- **es Glick:** This is where one collects and calls upon their own personal power and builds up their stores of luck.

der Hoch: This part of the soul processes and analyzes the experiences of the entirety of the human being.

die Megge: The energy that is in all life, what some might call *universal energy*. This energy is what is called upon for healing in *Braucherei*.

der Meind or der Sinn: The part of the soul where your memories are stored, both the ones you make during your own lifetime and your ancestral memories from generation to generation.

der Ochdem: The literal breath of life given to humanity by Wudan at the time of our creation.

der Seelhaut: The part most often recognized as "ghost." This is the soul skin, which is an ethereal mold of the physical body.

es Urleeg: The most primal layer of the soul. This is where our actions from our lifetime are recorded, the reverberations of which will follow us into our next incarnation.

der Wille: Literally translates to "our will." The capacity to make things happen.

Runes

The *Urglaawe* runes here are shown with their deity association and one- or two-word meanings. For a further discussion on runes, see page 86.

Vieh: FEE, Fro, wealth

Ur: OOR, Holler, strength

Dunner: DOO-nah, Dunner, defense

Antwatt: AHN-twaht, Wudan, messages

Reit: RITE, Schlumm, journey

Kerze: KAR-zuh, Zisa, spark of inspiration

Gewwe: GAY-veh, Weisskeppichi Fraa, exchange

Winsch: VINCH, Wudan, Holler, Fro, Frouwa, wish

Haagel: HAW-gl, Holle, major changes

Not: NOTE, many deities, need

Eisich: EYE-zich, no specific deity, stillness

Yaahr: YORE, Freid, Holle, cycles

Eiwe: EYE-veh, no specific deity, tree of life

Peil: PILE, no specific deity, mystery

Schild: SHILLD, Ziu, protection

Sunne: SOO-neh, Sunna, victory

Tuisko: TWEE-sco, Tuisko, Ziu, Zisa, justice

Baerke: BEAR-kuh, Berchta, Freid, lesser association with Holle, rebirth

Hengscht: HENG-scht, Alcis, companion relationships

Mann: MAAHN, Wudan, perfected human

Loch: LOK (rhymes with yolk), Schlumm, mirrors

Engel: AY-ngl (the ng as in singer not finger), Fro, Ing, potential

Daag: DAWG, Helling, daybreak

Ochdem: OKH-doom, Wudan, ancestral wealth

Worlds and Locations of the Tree

This is a quick reference to our *Lewesbaam*, or tree of life. For a further discussion on the world tree and its locations, see page 14.

die Bollwies: Flax meadow, located by Holle's home in the *Dunkelgegend.*

die Dunkelgegend: Realm located at the roots of the *Lewesbaam*. This is a world of destruction and transformation, and it is the domain of the goddess Holle.

der Ebbelwald: A forest of apple trees located near Holle's home in the *Dunkelgegend.*

Fliessendi: Flowing river; one of the three sacred streams that run within the *Lewesbaam* between *Mannheem* and the *Dunkelgegend.* See also *Gwellendi* and *Schprudlendi.*

Gwellendi: Bubbling brook; one of the three sacred streams that run within the *Lewesbaam* between *Mannheem* and the *Dunkelgegend.* See also *Fliessendi* and *Schprudlendi.*

es Hatzholz: The heartwood of the *Lewesbaam*. This is our physical universe.

es Heisli: Holle's cottage located in the *Dunkelgegend.*

der Hexenkopf: "Witch's head." Mountain pillar located in Northampton County, PA.

die Himmelgegend: Sky or heaven region, home of many of the *Elwe* and elevated ancestral spirits.

die Hohegegend: Highest region on the *Lewesbaam*. Home of both the *Wane* and the *Ase* deities.

es Lewesbaam: World tree, the multiverse upon which our known creation exists. It might be one world tree among many world trees, with possible connections in the *Dunkelgegend* to the roots of other trees.

es Mannheem: Earth and our accessible surroundings; the home of humans.

die Miehl: Holle's Mill in the *Dunkelgegend*. This is where a soul's journey comes to an end. When someone dies, *Urglaawer* say that person "went to the Mill."

die Naddbledder: Northern leaves of the *Lewesbaam*. This is the home of the *Reifries*, or the frost giants.

die Oschtbledder: Eastern leaves of the *Lewesbaam*. This is the home of *Weisskeppichi Fraa* and the origin of *Megge*, or life-force energy.

Schprudlendi: Brimming stream; one of the three sacred streams that run within the *Lewesbaam* between *Mannheem* and the *Dunkelgegend*. See also *Fliessendi* and *Gwellendi*.

der Seelbreecher: "Soul Breaker," the grindstone located within Holle's *Miehl* in the *Dunkelgegend*. Splits the souls of the deceased apart into separate components.

die Suddbledder: Southern leaves of the *Lewesbaam*. Home of the *Feierries*, or the fire giants.

die Unnergegend: Underworld of the *Lewesbaam* located on the lower trunk. Home of Berchta and the location of new soul constructs awaiting rebirth.

die Verbrennteskischt: Ashbin of the Incinerated. This is a place in the *Suddbledder* of the *Lewesbaam*, where the *Feierries* set the ashes of the beings or souls they have captured and burned; there is no recovery from this location.

der Verfroreskeller: Cellar of the Frozen. This is a location in the uppermost section of the *Naddbledder* of the *Lewesbaam*, where the *Reifries* store the frozen souls of the beings whom they have captured. Recovery from this area is possible.

es Weiwerfeld: Field of wives or field of women. This is a field located near Holle's home in the *Dunkelgegend*. This is where a legion of women who wear sickles on their feet and who were loyal to *Holle* in life continue in Holle's service in the afterlife.

die Weschtbledder: Western leaves of the *Lewesbaam*. This is the realm physically closest to the *Hatzholz* and is thus the easiest to journey to. It is the primary realm of activity and travel on the *Lewesbaam*, and the spirits of many beings may be contacted within this realm.

GLOSSARY

This glossary aims to provide you with enough information about the language so that you will be able to understand the *Deitsch* words in this book and use them, should you choose to do so, in your practice. Additional information on simple grammatical concepts is provided for those who wish to delve deeper into the use of the *Deitsch* language.

Grammatical Gender

Unlike in English, every noun in *Deitsch* bears an attribute of grammatical gender; this gender does not always correspond to physical sex. For example, the word for a witch in *Deitsch* is the grammatically feminine *Hex*. Anyone who takes on the identity of a witch would use the word *Hex*—and its grammatically feminine adjectival suffixes—regardless of the physical sex of the person in question.

In other cases, there are suffixes that can be added to words that will identify the physical sex or gender identity of the person in question, much like how English can add an *-ess* ending to specify female or feminine. In the appendices and glossaries, words that carry these suffixes will be spelled in that way so as to reflect the gender or gender identity of the singular number (masculine, feminine, nonbinary/neutral) and of the plural number, which covers all grammatical genders.

English speakers need not memorize the grammatical gender of a word or the corresponding article; those who would like to use the *Deitsch* language in *Urglaawe* rituals will need to have this information as a reference.

Definite Articles

There are four grammatical cases in the *Deitsch* language: nominative, accusative, dative, and genitive. All entries in the appendices and glossaries utilize the nominative case. The accusative and dative appear in the *Deitsch* versions of some rituals, and the genitive appears in some of the definitions in the appendices and in the glossary.

A definite article precedes most *Deitsch* nouns in the appendices and in the glossary. The definite article shows the noun's grammatical gender. When used as the subject of a sentence, the four definite articles are as listed below. All of these words are the equivalent of the English word "the," but, unlike in English, they refer to nouns with grammatical gender.

Singular

der: "the" when referring to a grammatically masculine object

die: "the" when referring to a grammatically feminine object

es: "the" when referring to a grammatically neutral object

Plural

die: "the" when referring to multiple objects regardless of gender

If a noun, especially a name, is not preceded by a definite article in the appendices or in the glossary, it is because the name itself contains the information about the grammatical gender.

For example, Weisskeppichi Fraa is the commonly used name for the White-Haired Woman. Her name may also be expressed as die Weisskeppich Fraa. The *-i* suffix on Weisskeppichi eliminates the need for the use of the definite article *die*. The same applies to Ewicher Yeeger, whose name may also be rendered as der Ewich Yeeger; the *-er* suffix on Ewicher eliminates the need for the use of the definite article der.

This glossary lists words out alphabetically by the main component, typically being preceded by the definite article (der, die, es), all of which mean "the" in English.

Glossary

der Aaruf: Invocation; invitation for the deities and other honored beings to join the ritual.

die Aarufing: Convocation or call to worship.

die Addning: Core value of discipline.

die Aernet: August.

die Alcis: (pl.): Brother gods of the *Ase* who protect brothers during wartime.

der Aldaar: Altar.

es Alleliewweziel: Sunset October 30–November 11; major observance of the final harvest, the culling of herds, and Holle's departure onto the Wild Hunt.

die Allemaengel: "All deficiencies." A region in Lynn Township, Lehigh County, and Albany Township, Berks County.

es Arrensch: Orange, adds extra strength.

der As (masc.), die Asin (fem.), die Ase (pl.): Tribe of deities known in Scandinavian lore as the Aesir.

die Ausdauer: Core value of perseverance.

die Ausdeeling: Distribution of energies collected in the libation bowl to the participants of the ritual.

die Ausschitting: Pouring of libations as an offering to the deities or land spirits.

der Auszuck: Recessional

der Barick: Barrow. A funerary item used to transport the body, or the representation of the body, between the altar area and a disposal area, such as a funeral pyre or a burial plot. The barrow must be burned in a pyre regardless of the method of disposition of the body, which may be buried or cremated.

die Baricke Mariche: Maria Jung, also known as "Mountain Mary": legendary figure from *Deitsch* folklore who is associated with *Braucherei.*

es Bedenk: Ethical value or moral philosophy.

der Befeschdicher: Child's name fastener.

die Begriessing: Welcoming.

der Belsnickel: Composite figure that bears many of Wudan's attributes. Appears in December prior to Santa Claus to address the behavior of naughty children.

die Berchta: Goddess of the *Wane,* sister of Holle. Strongly associated with order of the mind and the completion arc of cycles.

die Berchtaslaaf: Sunset December 31–sunrise January 1: recognition of the end of the year, of the limits of existence within time. Traditional meal consists of oysters and crackers or of herring and gruel.

es Blanzegschwetz: Literally means "plant conversation"; talking to plants. *Braucherei* modality of engaging with plant spirits.

die Blanzeheilkunscht: Herbalism.

es Blo: Blue, represents calmness and clarity.

der Blobarrick: Blue Mountain ridge.

die Blokgeil: Plague horses, associated with Ewicher Yeeger.

es Blutrot: Blood red, represents the blood.

die Bollwies: Flax meadow located by Holle's home in the *Dunkelgegend.*

es Brau: Brown, represents soil.

der Braucher (masculine), die Braucherin (feminine), es Braucheres (nonbinary, neutral genders): Practitioner of *Braucherei.*

die Braucherei: Heirloom folk healing modality widely used by the *Deitsche* for outward benefit of community and client.

die Brechthelft: The bright half (or light half) of the year.

die Broochet: June.

Buckliches Mannli: "the Buckled Man," a goblin spirit who takes over the empty *Butzemenner* if not burned at *Allelieweziel.*

der Butzemann (masc.), die Butzemenner (pl.): A spiritually activated scarecrow.

die Daaf: Baptism.

Deitsch (adj.): Of the culture and language of the Pennsylvania Dutch.

die Deitsche: The Pennsylvania Dutch people.

der Deitschedaag: Also known as Deitsch Day, Pennsylvania German Day, Pennsylvania Dutch Day. Celebrated October 6, the date the first settlers arrived from Krefeld.

die Deitscherei: Noncontiguous areas that make up Pennsylvania Dutch Country.

es Ding: The Thing. Held in June.

der Dingsege: Ritual that accompanies the gathering of a *Ding*; often to handle legal matters, paperwork, and deity blessings within the community.

Dinschdaag: Tuesday.

der Distelfink: Translates to "thistle finch." It was the European goldfinch (*Carduelis carduelis*) that the folk art originally referenced, but then became associated more with the American goldfinch (Spinus tristis).

es Drankopfer: Libation.

der Dreifuuss: Iron trivet used to hold the libation bowl on *Urglaawe* altars.

driebdaub (adj.): Reversed or upside-down presentation of a rune.

die Dunkelgegend: The realm located at the roots of the *Lewesbaam*. This is a world of destruction and transformation, and it is the domain of the goddess Holle.

die Dunkelheft: Dark half of the year.

der Dunner: God of the *Ase* associated with thunder, the working class, and courage.

der Dunnerschdaag: Thursday.

der Dunnereeche: *Dunner*'s oak felled by Boniface.

der Ebbelwald: A forest of apple trees located near Holle's home in the *Dunkelgegend*.

der Edelmut: Core value of generosity.

der Eedring: Oath ring.

die Ehr: Core value of honor.

die Elwe: Elves, several tribes of beings from different realms on the Lewesbaam.

die Entschtanning: February 2–14; the emergence from winter and the celebration of potential life.

die Eppeldraagerin: The Apple Carrier; while the sacredness of apples is visible throughout Germanic lore, the name of the goddess associated with apples was unknown to *Deitsch* lore. *Urglaawe* has adopted the name *Idunn* from other Heathen traditions.

die Erda: *Wane* goddess of the earth and soil.

es Erntfescht: "Harvest Home"; the high harvest on the autumn equinox and celebration of the *Ase* deities.

Ewicher Yeeger: The Eternal Hunter; also known as der Holler. God of the *Wane* and consort to Holle and brother of Schlumm; associated with death, pestilence, and plague, yet also with second chances, transformations, and growth through strife.

Ewicher Yeeger Sege: Also known as *Hollersege*, November 11; end of Alleliewweziel.

die Farewe (noun): Colors, hues.

die Fasching: Also known as *Faschtnacht.* Shrove Tuesday.

die Faschtnacht: See *Fasching.*

Fastnachts or Faschtnachtskuche: See *Fettekuche.*

die Feierries: Fire giants; live in the *Suddbledder* realm on the *Lewesbaam.* Considered enemies of the deities.

die Fettekuche: Deep-fried yeast and potato doughnuts (also called *Faschnachts* or *Fastnachts*) consumed during *Entschtanning.*

Fliessendi: Flowing river; one of the three sacred streams that run within the *Lewesbaam* between *Mannheem* and the *Dunkelgegend.* See also *Gwellendi* and *Schprudlendi.*

der Folyer (masc.), die Folyerin (fem.) (sing.), die Folyer (pl.): Fetch, also called the *Guardian Spirit* or the *Journeyer.*

der Freibesitz: Fellowship or freehold. A group that gathers together to celebrate but does not take an oath to the group or to each other.

die Freid: *Ase* goddess of hearth, home, safety, security, motherhood; consort of to Wudan and sister of Voll and Volla.

der Freidaag: Friday.

die Freindschaft: A lineage or family of practitioners of Braucherei and Hexerei.

der Fro: *Wane* god of bounty, fertility, and fecundity; brother to Frouwa.

es Frofescht: Feast of Fro, January 1; traditional pork and sauerkraut feast of abundance.

die Frouwa: Wane goddess associated with bounty, wealth, sexuality, and business acumen; sister to Fro.

der Frouwasege: Frouwa's blessing day, March 17; end of the potato cycle, when the remnants of last year's potato crops are used to bake bread to honor Frouwa. Potatoes are planted to begin the planting season for hardy crops.

der Fruchsfriede: Peace, frith, customs, and etiquette within and between communities.

die Gedderdemmerung: Doom of the Gods. See also *die Ziewedemmerung*.

die Gedechtnisleicht: A memorial celebration of one's life.

die Gedechtniszettel: Making peace with a deceased person.

Gedreier Eckhart: Folk hero who runs ahead of the Wild Hunt to announce the coming fury; loyal servant to Holle.

es Gehl: Yellow, represents connection to divinity.

es Gehlbrau: Tan, represents connection to animals.

es Gehlgrie: Yellow-Green, represents fading or dying.

die Gehling: October.

der Geischderschtrutz: Parade of Spirits, mid December. This is a cultural parade through the streets of Philadelphia that echoes the parade of the *Deitsche* in earlier eras. This is the time of *Belsnickeling*, or *Deitsch* trick-or-treating.

der Geischt: Subset of the soul in ten parts (see also *es Gemiet, die Gewut, es Glick, der Hoch, die Megge, der Meind* or *der Sinn, der Ochdem, der Seelhaut, es Urleeg, der Wille*).

die Geischtlichkeet: Core value of spirituality.

es Gemiet: The complete self, including one's shadows and temperament.

Gemietlichkeet: A deep sense of belonging stemming from one's connection to and interaction with the community.

der Getz (sing.), die Getze (pl.): Representation of a deity that appears on *Urglaawe* altars during ritual. This representation is a place created for the deity to occupy when invited to participate in the event.

die Gewut: The center of one's desires, passions, and aspirations.

es Glick: This is where one collects and calls upon their own personal power and builds up their stores of luck.

es Gold: Gold, represents opulence and fortune.

es Grie: Green, represents fertility and bounty.

der Grieg Geeich die Reifries: The Battle Against the Frost Giants in May, when the army of *Butzemenner* rises to beat back the frost giants.

es Gro: Gray, represents uncertainty and liminality.

Grossmammi: Originator plant.

der Grumbieredaag: Potatoes Day, March 17. See *Frouwasege*.

der Grundsaudaag: Groundhog Day; time to make and activate *Butzemenner*, or scarecrows.

die Gschwisichabhenkichkeet: Core value of interdependence.

Gwellendi: Bubbling brook; one of the three sacred streams that run through the *Lewesbaam* between *Mannheem* and the *Dunkelgegend*. See also *Fliessendi* and *Schprudlendi*.

die Hadding: January.

der Hammer: Hammer, sacred tool of Dunner.

die Hanning: February.

es Hatzholz: The heartwood of the *Lewesbaam*. This is our physical universe.

die Heiliching: Hallowing of the site; making the ritual space sacred.

die Heinzelmenner: see *Kowwold.*

es Heisli: Holle's cottage located in the *Dunkelgegend.*

die Helling: One of the Oschdre sisters. Associated with the daytime sky, daylight, white, and bright colors.

die Hex: Practitioner of *Hexerei*; the feminine form used regardless of one's physical sex.

die Hexenacht: Witches' Night, sundown April 30; the beginning of *Wonnezeit.*

der Hexenkopf: "Witch's head." Mountain pillar located in Northampton County, PA.

die Hexerei: Witchcraft. Heirloom folk healing modality used by the *Deitsche* for inward growth and for the pursuits of deep mystical understandings.

es **Hexeschild:** Hex sign; artwork frequently found on *Deitsch* barns.

hexich (adj.): Our word for functions in our practice that are similar to shamanic practices of other cultures.

die Himmelgegend: Sky or heaven region, home of many of the *Elwe* and elevated ancestral spirits.

der Hoch: This part of the soul processes and analyzes the experiences of the entirety of the human being.

die Hohegegend: Highest region on the *Lewesbaam.* Home of both the *Wane* and the *Ase* deities.

die Hoiet: July.

es Hoietfescht: Haymaking festival; late July or early August at the first harvest. Celebration of the *Wane* deities.

Holle: *Wane* goddess and mother of Urglaawe, chiefess of the Urglaawe pantheon; oversees cycles of life, death, and rebirth. Consort to Ewicher Yeeger.

Holler: See Ewicher Yeeger.

der Hollersege: November 11. See *Ewicher Yeeger Sege.*

die Hollesichel: Sacred tool of *Holle*; also a sickle pendant commonly worn by *Urglaawer*.

der Holzhacker: The Woodchopper. Shapeshifting entity who tries to distract the souls of the departing from arriving at Holle's *Miehl.*

der Hottenstein: Giant council rock where the Thing was often held.

die Idis (sing.), die Idise (pl.): Female guides, advisors, and protectors of subsequent generations; origin of the concept of the fairy godmother.

der Immerraum: Literally "always-room"; Holle's sack of souls.

der Kannsege: Ceremony of the Corn to activate the *Butzemann* at *Entschtanning*.

es Karminrot: Crimson, represents death.

die Kowwold (pl.): Kobolds, a particular type of house elf also associated with the mining industry.

die Leich: Space in which the soul permeates the physical body.

die Leichtlaaf: Funeral procession.

die Lenzing: March.

der Letscht Sege: Last rite.

es Lewesbaam: World tree, the multiverse upon which our known creation exists. It might be one world tree among many world trees, with possible connections in the *Dunkelgegend* to the roots of other trees.

es Lewesraad: Cycle of life, death, and rebirth.

der Lutzelfraaslaaf: Progression of the Lantern Lady on the fifth night of Voryuul, December13.

der Luul: God of the *Wane*; doula to the yearly cycle of nature, particularly in protecting young spring greens from freezing.

der Macher: The Maker. An aspect of *Wurt* that set the process of creation into motion.

es Mannheem: Earth and our accessible surroundings; the home of humans.

die Mariyeschtann: Goddess of the *Wane* associated with the Morning Star (Venus); sister to Sunna.

die Megge: The energy that is in all life, what some might call *universal energy*. This energy is what is called upon for healing in *Braucherei*.

die Meggeheilkunscht: A modality of *Braucherei* that uses *Megge* to heal.

der Meind: The part of the soul where your memories are stored, both the ones you make during your own lifetime and your ancestral memories from generation to generation. See also *der Sinn*.

die Melkern: The Milkmaid. A shapeshifting being who tries to distract newly assembled souls from their route from the *Dunkelgegend* to the *Unnergegend*.

die Miehl: Holle's Mill in the *Dunkelgegend*. This is where a soul's journey comes to an end. When someone dies, *Urglaawer* say that person "went to the Mill."

es Mitleid: Core value of compassion.

der Mitleidzauber: The modality of sympathetic magic used in both *Braucherei* and *Hexerei*.

der Mittwoch: Wednesday.

der Mut: Core value of courage.

der Muun: God of the *Wane* associated with the moon, with tides, and with eclipses; star-crossed lover of Sunna.

der Muundaag: Monday.

es Muunraad: The *Deitsch* zodiac of lunar signs that guides when planting, harvesting, and even healing happen.

die Nacht: One of the Oschdre sisters. Goddess of the *Wane* associated with night, darkness, dark colors, the night sky, and space.

die Naddbledder: Northern leaves of the *Lewesbaam*. This is the home of *die Reifries*, or the frost giants.

die Nehalennia: Goddess of the *Wane* associated with safe passage over water.

die Neigierheit: Core value of curiosity.

Neine Heiliche Gegreider: Nine sacred herbs of *Braucherei* and *Urglaawe*.

die Neine Winde (pl.): Nine Winds, children of Holle: Gibbel (north), Bodde (south), Schteig (east), Setz (west), Schnall (northeast),

Warrem (southeast), Kalt (northwest), Riffel (southwest), Wärwel (whirlwind).

die Newweling: November.

der Noochyuul: "After-Yule," which runs from sunset on January 1 until *Grundsaudaag*, February 2.

Observance of the Desecrated Shrines: Day of remembrance, June 5, to honor the deities whose sacred shrines were destroyed through the acts of religious terrorism.

der Ochdem: The literal breath of life given to humanity by Wudan at the time of our creation.

es Opfer: Offerings given to the deities, land spirits, or ancestors.

die Oschdra: One of the Oschdre sisters. Goddess of the *Wane* who transforms grays into colors; associated with the dawn, the east, and new beginnings.

die Oschdre (pl.): Three sister goddesses of the Wane (see Helling, Nacht, and Oschdra), who introduced color, cardinal directions, bird migrations, and the rotation of earth to the Hatzholz.

die Oschdresege: Spring equinox celebration of the birth and rebirth.

die Oschdret: April.

die Oschtbledder: Eastern leaves of the *Lewesbaam*. This is the home of *Weisskeppichi Fraa* and the origin of *Megge*, or life-force energy.

rechtdaub (adj.): Upright presentation of a rune.

die Reifries (pl.): Frost giants, whose realm is in the *Naddbledder* of the *Lewesbaam*. Their power grows by weakening the order of the other realms.

die Reiniching: Cleansing with decocted birch leaves and twigs.

die Richtschnier: Rules of action, including morals, rules, protocols, and both the written laws and the unwritten morals of the community or greater society.

der Ries (masc.), die Riesin (fem.), die Ries (pl.): Giants from several related races of beings who are perceived as much larger than humans and who possess ancient knowledge and fierce power, and who are generally considered antipathetic toward humans.

die Roon (sing.), die Raane (pl.): Rune.

es Rot: Red, represents passion, the body, and justice.

die Saaga: Goddess of the *Ase*; keeper of stories; maintainer of language; inspiration behind ideas, concepts, and great works.

es Sammel: Gathering.

der Samschdaag: Saturday.

der Schadde: Deitsch trickster figure of unknown family origin.

die Schaffichheit: Core value of industriousness.

die Scheiding: September.

es Schifferich: Slate, represents connection to the mineral world.

der Schlumm: God of the *Wane* associated with sleep, dreams, altered states, visions; brother of Ewicher Yeeger.

der Schmaus: Feast.

Schprudlendi: Brimming stream; one of the three sacred streams that run within the *Lewesbaam* between *Mannheem* and the *Dunkelgegend.* See also *Fliessendi* and *Gwellendi.*

die Schuld: Indebtedness, restitution, payment.

es Schwatz: Black, represents protection.

der Seelbreecher: Soul Breaker is the grindstone located within Holle's *Miehl* in the *Dunkelgegend.* It splits the souls of the deceased apart into separate components.

die Seele: Soul.

der Seelhaut: The part most often recognized as "ghost." This is the soul skin, which is an ethereal mold of the physical body.

der Sege: Spoken blessing ritual.

die Segezweig: Blessing twig used to draw runes on ritual participants' foreheads.

der Seidel: Stein used for blessed drink during ritual.

der Selbschtreiguck: Core value of introspection.

die Selbschtverbessering: Core value of self-improvement.

die Sichel: Sickle. Sacred tool of Holle.

der Sinn: The part of the soul where your memories are stored, both from this lifetime and past ancestral memories. See also *der Meind.*

die Sippschaft: A kindred where the members are oathbound to one another.

die Siwwa: Goddess of the Ase; strongly associated with grains and grain harvests.

die Suddbledder: Southern leaves of the *Lewesbaam*. Home of *die Feierries*, or the fire giants.

der Summeraafang: The summer solstice, longest day of the year, representing more active participation in community events.

die Sunna: Goddess of the *Wane* associated with enlightenment; personification of the sun; star-crossed lover of Muun and sister of Mariyschtann.

der Sunndaag: Sunday.

die Treie: Core value of troth/loyalty.

der Tuisko: *Wane* god, son of Zisa and Ziu.

die Uffwaarting: Core value of hospitality.

es Umdenk: The mindshift.

die Unnergegend: Underworld of the *Lewesbaam* located on the lower trunk. Home of Berchta and the location of new soul constructs awaiting rebirth.

Unser Zweck: "Our Purpose." A section of *Urglaawe* ritual that states the ritual's purpose.

der Urglaawe: *Deitsch* Heathen spirituality and religion.

der Urglaawer (masc.), die Urglaawerin (fem.), es Urglaawers (neut.), die Urglaawer (pl.): Practitioner of *Urglaawe.*

Urglaawischi Drauersupp: *Urglaawe* grief soup.

es Urleeg: The most primal layer of the soul. This is where our actions from our lifetime are recorded, the reverberations of which will follow us into our next incarnation.

die Uudaaf: "Unbaptism" held to release one from obligations to prior religious identities.

es Veilich: purple, violet, represents cosmic energy and nobility.

der Verbot: A forbidden activity.

die Verbrennte: The Incinerated.

die Verbrennteskischt: Ashbin of the Incinerated. This is a place in the *Suddbledder* of the *Lewesbaam* where *die Feirries* set the ashes of the beings or souls they have captured and burned; there is no recovery from this location.

die Verfrore: The frozen souls captured by the *Reifries*.

der Verfroreskeller: Cellar of the Frozen. This is a location in the uppermost section of the *Naddbledder* of the *Lewesbaam*, where *die Reifries* store the frozen souls of the beings whom they have captured. Recovery from this area is possible.

die Verschimpfing Geeich der Reifkeenich: Railing Against King Frost; spellwork from *Hexerei* held in November to disavow any hold that *der Reifkeenich*, or King Frost, and winter will have over one's well-being.

die Verwalting: Core value of stewardship.

die Verwandschaft: Core value of kinship.

der Voll: *Ase* god of abundance; twin of *Volla*, brother of *Freid.*

die Volla: *Ase* goddess of abundance; twin of *Voll*, sister of *Freid.*

der Voryuul: The twelve nights before the winter solstice, a time for introspection of one's own motivations and of the integration of the shadow size.

die Waahra: Goddess of the *Ase* who oversees the taking and maintaining of oaths.

die Waahrheit: Core value of truth.

die Waerrickgawwel: Distaff, spindle.

der Wan (masc.), die Wanin (fem.) (sing.), die Wane (pl.): Tribe of deities known to the Scandinavians as the Vanir.

der Wasserdaafiwwergangsgebrauch: Water consecration rite for the blessing of a child.

die Weisheit: Core value of wisdom.

es Weiss: White, represents illumination, brilliance, inspiration, and knowledge.

Weisskeppichi Fraa: The White-Haired Lady or White-Haired Woman; goddess of the *Wane*; strongly associated with *Braucherei* and *Megge* (life-force energy).

es Weiwerfeld: Field of wives or field of women. This is a field located near Holle's home in the *Dunkelgegend.* This is where a legion of women who wear sickles on their feet and who were loyal to Holle in life continue in Holle's service in the afterlife.

die Weschtbledder: Western leaves of the *Lewesbaam.* This is the realm physically closest to the *Hatzholz* and is thus the easiest to journey to. It is the primary realm of activity and travel on the *Lewesbaam*, and the spirits of many beings may be contacted within this realm.

der Wille: Literally translates to "our will." The capacity to make things happen.

die Wonnenacht: see *Hexenacht.*

die Wonnet: May.

die Wonnezeit: Time of Joy, observance that begins at sunset on April 30 (01. Wonnet on the *Urglaawe* calendar) and runs for twelve nights and twelve days. This is the time of honoring trees that are significant to the economies of the local area and of recognizing the reawakening of the dormant plants.

der Wudan: *Ase* god associated with fury, pursuits of higher consciousness, the collection of knowledge, warfare, and "thinking outside the box" solutions; consort to Freid.

der Wurt: The Maker of creation and the ensuing threads that weave all of creation together.

die Wurthexe: Goddesses who weave and manage everyone's *Wurt*; believed by many *Urglaawer* to be manifestations of *Wurt* itself; there are an unknown number of these goddesses, but *Deitsch* oral tradition holds that there is at least one for every verb tense and mood.

es Yaahrsraad: Wheel of the Year.

der Yuul: Winter solstice, representing both a new sun for the upcoming year and the new soul construct being assembled.

die Yuuling: December.

der Yuulsege: Winter solstice ritual, typically involving the burning of a large log or the lighting of a burning sunwheel.

die Yuulzeit: Yule time sundown December 20–December 31, represents the time between lives prior to the soul's next conception. Observance features meditations on *Urglaawe*'s core values.

die Zammede: Pancakes of flour and water eaten at *Berchtaslaaf.*

der Zauber: Spell, spoken charm, or an incantation.

der Zauberzettel: "Charm ticket." A spell that is written onto a piece of paper.

der Ziegdaag: April 1, Moving Day. Honors the shadowy, shady, and trickster figures in our lore.

die Ziewe: Neologism to serve as a nonbinary term for "deities."

die Ziewedemmerung: Doom of the Gods. See also *die Gedderdemmerung.*

der Ziewer (masc.), die Ziewerin (fem.), or es Ziewermensch (nonbinary) (sing.), die Ziewer (pl.): Godspeople.

die Zisa: *Ase* goddess associated with doing or undoing "knots" or placing or removing obstacles in order to guide one's right action. Associated with the South Star (Vega).

der Zisasege: Feast of Zisa, September 28. Originally a harvest festival celebrated by the ancient Suevi tribe, this observance is part of the *Erntfescht* celebrations.

der Ziu: *Ase* sky god associated with justice and right action. Overseer of the *Ding.* Associated with the North Star (Polaris).

zum Schluss: Closing.

die Zusaagpflicht: An unwritten agreement of stewardship among the human, animal, mineral, and plant kingdoms.

die Zwarich: Dwarves, whose home realm on the *Lewesbaam* is in the Unnergegend. Created by the deities before humans.

der Zweck: Purpose.

Zwelfder Daag: Twelfth Day of Yuul, running from sunrise to sunset on January 1; date of *es Frofescht* and the end of *die Yuulzeit.*

ACKNOWLEDGMENTS

As with all things in *Urglaawe*, this book was a community effort. Whether through the direct efforts of those cited or the indirect interactions through the years at various gatherings, meetups, and interviews, the knowledge gained and exchanged forged the content here. And to those we have met through the years who asked for advice and direction on this path, those requests motivated us through the process.

First and foremost, we thank the gods and goddesses and specifically Fraa Holle. Without their inspiration, guidance, and, at times, not-so-subtle nudges, none of this would have been possible.

We would be remiss to not thank our community elders, both on this path and off. *Urglaawe* was a concept developed in the hearts and minds of its cofounders, Robert L. Schreiwer and Patricia Niedrich. Our community would like to thank Patricia for her guidance during the early years of the movement. This includes many *Braucher/ins/es* and *Hexe* who shared, sometimes begrudgingly, their knowledge attained through many years of training and practice.

Many thanks to Kate Cullifer for her work on developing the *Urglaawe* logo and to Athena Dugan for her beautiful illustrations. To Ralph Young for their ongoing work with their podcast, *Holle's Haven: The Urglaawisch Podcast*, which continues to be an invaluable source of information for *Urglaawer* near and far, new and seasoned. To Staci Baisch, Ralph Young, Larry Goble Jr., Beck Spille, and Arden Taylor for all of their contributions and time dedicated to the book and the community at large. To Brian Weiss for help in the early formation of our rituals.

To all those strangers in the *Deitscherei* who have shared their stories and the lore they know. Sometimes, the most unexpected revelations have come from chance encounters.

And, finally, to our forebears who planted, nurtured, and guarded this seed from before they stepped foot on the lands of southeastern Pennsylvania from the Palatinate and its environs. We hope that we make you proud as we reap what you have sown. We will do our best to further propagate your hard work.

BIBLIOGRAPHY

Adams, Charles J., III. *Ghost Stories of Berks County*. Book 2. Exeter House Books, 2002.

Adams, Charles J., III. *Haunted Berks County*. Exeter House Books, 2005.

Ashliman, D. L., trans. "Merseburg Incantations." Updated April 23, 2021. https://sites.pitt.edu/~dash/merseburg.html.

Aurand, A. Monroe, Jr. *Popular Home Remedies and Superstitions of the Pennsylvania Germans*. Published by the author, c. 1941.

Barrick, Mac E., ed. *German-American Folklore*. American Folklore Series. August House, 1987.

Beam, C. Richard, ed. *The Thomas R. Brendle Collection of Pennsylvania German Folklore*. Vol. 1. Center for Pennsylvania German Studies, 1995.

Behringer, Wolfgang. *Shaman of Oberstdorf: Chonrad Stoeckhlin and the Phantoms of the Night*. Translated by H. C. Erik Midelfort. University of Virginia Press, 1998.

Boyer, Dennis. *Once Upon a Hex: A Spiritual Ecology of the Pennsylvania Germans*. Badger Books, 2004.

Boyer, Dennis. "Soul Work on Halloween." *Hollerbeier Haven: Newsletter for the Herbal and Healing Arts* 1, no. 3 (2007): 2–3.

Breininger, Lester. "Beekeeping and Bee Lore in Pennsylvania." *Pennsylvania Folklife* 16 no. 1, (1966): 34–39.

Brendle, Thomas R., and Claude W. Unger. *Folk Medicine of the Pennsylvania Germans: The Non-Occult Cures*. Proceedings of the Pennsylvania German Society. Vol. 45. Pennsylvania German Society, 1935, 223–303.

Brendle, Thomas R., and Claude Unger. "Witchcraft in Cow and Horse." *The Pennsylvania Dutchman* 8 no. 1 (1956): 28–31.

Brown, Frank. "New Light on 'Mountain Mary.'" *Pennsylvania Folklife* 15, no. 3 (1966): 10–15.

Burger, Simone. "Pennsylvania German and the Public Schools." *Der Reggeboge* 29, no. 1 (1995): 21–28.

Byock, Jesse L., trans. *The Prose Edda: Norse Mythology*. Penguin, 2005.

Chisholm, James. *Grove and Gallows: Greek and Latin Sources for Germanic Heathenism*. Runa-Raven Press, 2002.

Clubb, Orva Gaile. "Frau Holda's Tale." *Hollerbeier Haven 10: Newsletter for the Herbal and Healing Arts* 3, no. 2 (2009): 3–4, 10–13.

Coulter, James Hjuka. *Germanic Heathenry: A Practical Guide*. 1stBooks Publishing, 2003.

Davidson, H. R. *Gods and Myths of Northern Europe*. Penguin Books, 1965.

Devlin, Ron. "Early Pike Township Folk Healer Remembered." *Reading Eagle*, November 9, 2009. Accessed March 11, 2012. http://readingeagle.com/article.aspx?id=165072. (Page discontinued.)

Dickerson, Cody. "Weißt Du Zu Ritzen?" *Hex Magazine* 1 (2007): 36–40.

Donmoyer, Patrick. "Blumme-Schterne: Flower Stars." *Hollerbeier Haven: Newsletter for the Herbal and Healing Arts* 2, no. 2 (2008): 17.

Donmoyer, Patrick. "Hagal—The Holy Hail." *Hollerbeier Haven: Newsletter for the Herbal and Healing Arts* 4, no. 1 (2010): 9–10.

Dieffenbach, Victor C. "Diaper Lore." *The Pennsylvania Dutchman* 8, no. 1 (1956): 23.

Drachman, Albert I. "Tracking the Elusive Distelfink." With Marian Winston. *The Dutchman* 6, no. 5 (1955): 28–35.

Fogel, Edwin Miller. *Beliefs and Superstitions of the Pennsylvania Germans*. Center for Pennsylvania German Studies, 1995.

Fogel, Edwin Miller. *Proverbs of the Pennsylvania Germans*. Center for Pennsylvania German Studies, 1995.

Frey, J. William, ed. "The Dutch in Word and Song." *The Pennsylvania Dutchman*, vol. 1, no. 22, January 1950, 8.

Friesen, John W. "The Myth of the Ideal Folk Society versus the Reality of Amish Life." *Pennsylvania Folklife* 43, no. 3 (1994): 140–45.

Friesen, Steve. "Home Is Where the Hearth Is." *Pennsylvania Folklife* 40, no. 3 (1991): 98–118.

Gehman, Henry Snyder. "Ghost Stories and Old Superstitions of Lancaster County." *Pennsylvania Folklife* 19, no. 4 (1970): 48–53.

Gibbons, Phebe Earle. *Pennsylvania Dutch & Other Essays*. Stackpole Books, 2001.

Graeff, Arthur D., and George M. Meiser, IX. *Echoes of Scholla—Illustrated: Choice Bits of Berks County History and Lore*. Berksiana Foundation, 1976.

Graeff, Marie K. "Folk Songs." *Pennsylvania Folklife* 31 no. 1 (1981): 20–25.

Grimm, Jacob, *Teutonic Mythology*. 4 vols. Translated by James Steven Stallybrass. Dover Publications, 1966.

Guerber, H. A. *Hammer of Thor: Norse Mythology and Legends*. Edited by Shawn Conners. El Paso Norte Press, 2010.

Gundarsson, Kveldúlfr. *Things, Signs and Their Meanings: A Dictionary of Heathen Symbols*. Edited by Ben Waggoner. The Troth, 2010.

Haag, Earl C. *Die Pennsylaanisch Deitsche*. Pennsylvania German Society, 2010.

Heindel, Ned D. *Hexenkopf: History, Healing & Hexerei*. Northampton County Historical and Genealogical Society, 2005.

Herr, Karl. *Hex and Spellwork: The Magical Practices of the Pennsylvania Dutch*. Weiser Books, 2002.

Hertzog, Phares H. "Snakelore in Pennsylvania German Folk Medicine." *Pennsylvania Folklife* 17 no. 2 (1967–1968): 24–26.

Hess, Susan. "Homestead Herbalism" (course). Pottstown, PA: Farm at Coventry, 2010.

Hess, Susan. "Mugwort." *Hollerbeier Haven: Newsletter for the Herbal and Healing Arts* 1, no. 3 (2007): 11.

Hess, Susan. "Nine Sacred Herbs." *Hollerbeier Haven: Newsletter for the Herbal and Healing Arts* 2, no. 1 (2008): 10.

Hohman, John George. *Pow-Wows or, Long Lost Friend: A Collection of Mysterious and Invaluable Arts and Remedies for Man as well as Animals*. NuVision Publications, 2007.

Hohman, Johann Georg. *Der Lang Verborgene Freund.* N.p., 1820.

Hope, Anne Fulton. *Sequel to the Conversion of the Teutonic Race: S. Boniface and the Conversion of Germany.* R. Washbourne, 1872.

Howells, William. *The Heathens: Primitive Man and His Religions.* Doubleday Anchor Books, 1962.

Hyatt, E. Max. *Hávámal: Sayings of the High One.* Wodanesdag Press, n.d.

Jones, Prudence, and Nigel Pennick. *A History of Pagan Europe.* Routledge, 1995.

Jordan, Mildred. *The Distelfink Country of the Pennsylvania Dutch.* Crown Publishers, Inc., 1978.

Kriebel, David W. *Powwowing Among the Pennsylvania Dutch.* Penn State University Press, 2007.

Lafayllve, Patricia M. *Freyja, Lady, Vanadis.* Outskirts Press, 2006.

Larrington, Carolyne, trans. *The Poetic Edda.* Oxford University Press, 1996.

Leh, R. R. "Eilaschpiggel…Eisahannes." *The Pennsylvania Dutchman* (newspaper) 1, no. 7, June 16, 1949, 7.

Lick, David E., and Thomas R. Brendle. "Plant Names and Plant Lore Among the Pennsylvania Germans." In *The Pennsylvania-German Society: Proceedings and Addresses at Reading, PA, October 6, 1922.* Vol. 33. Pennsylvania German Society, 1923.

List, Edgar A. "Frau Holda as the Personification of Reason." *Philological Quarterly* 32 (1953): 446–48.

Long, Amos, Jr. "Dutch Country Scarecrows." *Pennsylvania Folklife* 12, no. 3 (1961): 54–59.

Lusch, Robert. "Living Land." *Hollerbeier Haven: Journal of Traditional Deitsch Wisdom* (2009): 16.

Luther, Martin. *The Table Talk, or Familiar Discourse of Martin Luther.* Translated by William Hazlitt. David Bogue, Fleet Street: 1848.

Marks, David S. "Fretted Dulcimers." *Kutztown Folk Festival, Pennsylvania Folklife.* 37, no. 4 (1988): 14–17.

Milspaw, Yvonne J. "Witchcraft Belief in a Pennsylvania German Family." *Pennsylvania Folklife* 27, no. 4 (1978): 14–24.

Milnes, Gerald C. *Signs, Cures, & Witchery.* University of Tennessee Press, 2007.

Montgomery, Jack. *American Shamans: Journeys with Traditional Healers.* Busca, 2009.

Montgomery, Jack. "Traditional Germanic Healing Arts in America: Pow-wowing." *Hex Magazine* 2 (2007): 47–50.

Mutzbauer, Monica. "Leaving the Old World for the New: Rules Governing Emigration from Landau in the Palatinate." *Pennsylvania Folklife* 44, no. 3 (1995), 137–144.

Müller-Ebeling, Claudia, Christian Rätsch, and Wolf-Dieter Storl. *Witchcraft Medicine: Healing Arts, Shamanic Practices, and Forbidden Plants.* AT Verlag, 1998.

Nolt, Steven M. *Foreigners in Their Own Land: Pennsylvania Germans in the Early Republic.* Pennsylvania State University Press, 2002.

Oppenheimer, Paul, trans. *Till Eulenspiegel: His Adventures.* Oxford University Press, 1995.

Parsons, William T. *The Pennsylvania Dutch: A Persistent Minority.* The Immigrant Heritage of America Series. Twayne, 1976.

Paxson, Diana L. *Essential Ásatrú: Walking the Path of Norse Paganism.* Citadel Press, 2006.

Paxson, Diana L. *Taking Up the Runes: A Complete Guide to Using Runes in Spells, Rituals, Divination, and Magic.* Weiser Books, 2005.

Pennick, Nigel. "The Goddess Zisa." In *Tyr: Myth, Culture, Tradition.* Vol. 1. Edited by Joshua Buckley, Collin Cleary, and Michael Moynihan. Ultra, 2002.

Polley, Jane, ed. *American Folklore and Legend.* Reader's Digest, 1978.

RavenWolf, Silver. *HexCraft: Dutch Country Pow-Wow Magick.* Llewellyn Publications, 1995.

Russell, James C. *The Germanization of Early Medieval Christianity: A Sociohistorical Approach to Religious Transformation.* Oxford University Press, 1994.

Rüttner-Cova, Sonja. *Frau Holle, die Gestürtzte Göttin: Märchen, Mythen, Matriarchat.* Sphinx-Verlag, 1993.

Schreiwer, Robert L. *A Brief Introduction to Urglaawe.* Published by the author, 2009.

Schreiwer, Robert L. *The First Book of Urglaawe Myths.* Published by the author, 2014.

Schreiwer, Robert L. "Urglaawe | Baptism Renunciation | Heathen Traditions." The Troth. June 26, 2023. https://thetroth.org/resource/uglaawe-baptism-renunciation-heathen-traditions/.

Schreiwer, Robert L., and Ammerili Eckhart. *A Dictionary of Urglaawe Terminology*. Published by the authors, 2012.

Shaner, Richard H. *Hexerei: A Practice of Witchcraft Among the Pennsylvania Dutch*. A. G. Halldin, 1973.

Schantz, F. J. F. *The Domestic Life and Characteristics of the Pennsylvania-German Pioneer*. Part 4. Pennsylvania: The German Influence in Its Settlement and Development: A Narrative and Critical History. The Pennsylvania German Society, 1900.

Sheffield, Ann Gróa. *Frey: God of the World*. Published by the author, 2007.

Sheil, Thor, and Audrey Sheil. *Hedenskap: The Folk Religion of Ancient Scandinavia*. Trollwise Press, 1992.

Sheil, Thor, and Audrey Sheil. *Old Norse Charms, Spoken Spells and Rhymes*. Trollwise Press, 1992.

Sheil, Thor, and Audrey Sheil. *Old Norse Runecraft and Spellcraft*. Trollwise Press, 2007.

Shoemaker, Alfred L. *Eastertide in Pennsylvania: A Folk-Cultural Study*. Stackpole Books, 2000.

Shoemaker, Alfred L. "Belsnickel Lore." *The Dutchman* 6 no. 3 (1954–1955): 34–38.

Shoemaker, Alfred L. "Water Witching." *Pennsylvania Folklife* 12 no. 3 (1961): 25–27.

Shoemaker, Alfred L. *Christmas in Pennsylvania: A Folk-Cultural Study*. With Don Yoder. Stackpole Books, 1999.

Sicher, Lauren. "The Tree of Life: Der Lewwebaam." *Hollerbeier Haven* 2, no. 2 (2008): 6, 16.

Simek, Rudolph. *Dictionary of Northern Mythology*. Translated by Angela Hall. Boydell & Brewer, Ltd., 2007.

Smith, Norman A. "Der Alt Hexa Zehner." *The Pennsylvania Dutchman* 1, no. 17 (August 25, 1949), 2.

Stead, Lewis, *The Raven Kindred Ritual Book*. The Raven Kindreds, 1993. Accessed May 29, 2025. https://www.sacred-texts.com/bos/bos623.htm.

Stine, Eugene S., ed. *Pennsylvania German Dictionary*. Pennsylvania German Society, 1996.

Stoudt, John Baer. *The Folklore of the Pennsylvania Germans*. Pennsylvania German Society, 1916.

Tacitus, Cornelius. *Agricola, Germany, and Dialogue on Orators*. Revised ed. Translated by Herbert W. Benario. Hackett Publishing Company, Inc., 2006.

Tatar, Maria, ed. *The Annotated Brothers Grimm*. W. W. Norton, 2004.

Tobin, Jesse. *Der Braucherei Weg*. The Three Sisters Center for the Healing Arts, 2008. CD, 12-month course.

Tobin, Jesse. "Es Pennsilfaanisch Muunraad." *Hollerbeier Haven: Newsletter for the Herbal and Healing Arts* 2, no. 1 (2008): 4, 8–9.

Tobin, Jesse. "Powwow Birds." *Hollerbeier Haven: Journal of Traditional Deitsch Wisdom* 1, no. 3 (2007): 7.

Tobin, Jesse. "Elder Berry Cordial." *Hollerbeier Haven: Journal of Traditional Deitsch Wisdom* 1, no. 1 (2007): 2.

Tobin, Jesse. "May Day!" *Hollerbeier Haven: Journal of Traditional Deitsch Wisdom* 2, no. 1 (2008): 3.

Tobin, Jesse. "The Praiseworthy Virtues of the North." *Hollerbeier Haven: Newsletter for Herbal and Healing Arts* 1, no. 2 (2007): 15.

Tobin, Jesse. "The Sacred Promise at Erntedankfescht." *Hollerbeier Haven: Newsletter for Herbal and Healing Arts* 1, no. 2 (2007): 14, 16.

Tobin, Jesse. "The Wild Hunt Begins." *Hollerbeier Haven: Journal of Traditional Deitsch Wisdom* 1, no. 3 (2007): 4, 9, 10, 13.

Tobin, Jesse. "Walpurgis Nacht." *Hollerbeier Haven: Newsletter for Herbal and Healing Arts* 1, no. 1 (2007): 6.

Turville-Petre, Gabriel. *Myth and Religion of the North: The Religion of Ancient Scandinavia*. Weidenfeld and Nicolson, 1964.

Von Padberg, Lutz E. *Bonifatius: Missionar und Reformer*. C. H. Beck, 2003.

Von Schönwerth, Franz Xaver, and Erika Eichenseer, ed. *Sagen und Märchen aus der Oberpfalz*. E.ON Bayern, 2010.

Weaver, William Woys. *Sauer's Herbal Cures: America's First Book of Botanic Healing*. Routledge, 2001.

Wentz, Richard E. *Pennsylvania Dutch: Folk Spirituality*. Paulist Press, 1993.

"What Distinguishes Urglaawe From Other Heathen Paths?" *Urglaawe. BlogSpot*, July 19, 2013. https://urglaawe.blogspot.com/2013/07/what-distinguishes-urglaawe.html.

White, Thomas. *Forgotten Tales of Pennsylvania*. Charleston: The History Press, 2009.

Wieand, Paul R. *Folk Medicine Plants Used in the Pennsylvania Dutch Country*. Remembrance Press, The Rosemary House, Inc., 1992.

Winey, Fay McAfee. "Belsnickeling in Paxtonville." *Pennsylvania Folklife* 19, no. 2 (1970): 10–13.

Winkler, Louis. *Pennsylvania German Astrology and Astronomy*. Pennsylvania Folklife Society, 1982.

Winkler, Louis. "Pennsylvania German Astronomy and Astrology V: Religion and Astronomy." *Pennsylvania Folklife* 22, no. 3 (1973): 37–40.

Wood, Francis Asbury, trans. *The Hildebrandslied: Translated from the Old High German into English Alliterative Verse*. University of Chicago Press, 1914.

Yoder, Don, ed. "A Legend of Alle-Maengel." *The Pennsylvania Dutchman*, vol. 1, no. 12 (July 21, 1949): 5.

Yoder, Don. "Folk Medicine." In *Folklore and Folklife: An Introduction*, edited by Richard M. Dorson. University of Chicago Press, 1972.

Yoder, Don. *Groundhog Day*. Stackpole Books, 2003.

Yoder, Don. "Harvest Home." *Pennsylvania Folklife* 9, no. 4 (1958): 2–11.

Yoder, Don. "Hex Signs and Magical Protection of House and Barn: Folk-Cultural Questionnaire No. 35." *Pennsylvania Folklife 23, Folk Festival Supplement* (1974): inside cover.

Yoder, Don. "Trance-Preaching in the United States." *Pennsylvania Folklife* 18 no. 2 (1968–1969): 12–18.

Yoder, Don. "Twenty Questions on Powwowing." *Pennsylvania Folklife* 15, no. 4 (1966): 38–40.

Yoder, Don. "The Strouse Dance." *Pennsylvania Folklife* 9, no. 1 (1957–1958): 13–17.

Yoder, Don, and Thomas E. Graves. *Hex Signs: Pennsylvania Dutch Barn Symbols & Their Meaning*. Stackpole Books, 2000.

To Write to the Authors

If you wish to contact the authors or would like more information about this book, please write to the authors in care of Llewellyn Worldwide Ltd. and we will forward your request. Both the authors and the publisher appreciate hearing from you and learning of your enjoyment of this book and how it has helped you. Llewellyn Worldwide Ltd. cannot guarantee that every letter written to the authors can be answered, but all will be forwarded. Please write to:

Robert L. Schreiwer
Michelle A. Jones
Stacey Lynne Stewart
℅ Llewellyn Worldwide
2143 Wooddale Drive
Woodbury, MN 55125-2989

Please enclose a self-addressed stamped envelope for reply, or $1.00 to cover costs. If outside the U.S.A., enclose an international postal reply coupon.

Many of Llewellyn's authors have websites with additional information and resources. For more information, please visit our website at http://www.llewellyn.com.